D0680531

THE MISFORTUNATE MARGRAVINE

THE MISFORTUNATE MARGRAVINE

THE EARLY MEMOIRS OF
WILHELMINA

Margravine of Bayreuth
Sister of Frederick the Great

EDITED WITH AN INTRODUCTION BY
NORMAN ROSENTHAL

AND A FOREWORD BY
PAMELA HANSFORD JOHNSON

MACMILLAN
ST MARTIN'S PRESS

Introduction © Norman Rosenthal 1970

First published 1970 by
MACMILLAN AND CO LTD
London and Basingstoke
Associated companies in New York Toronto
Dublin Melbourne Johannesburg and Madras

SBN boards: 333 10047 6
Library of Congress catalog card no. 72-133448

Printed in Great Britain by
ROBERT CUNNINGHAM AND SONS LTD
Alva, Scotland

CONTENTS

LIST OF ILLUSTRATIONS

7

FOREWORD

The most fascinating thing about these Memoirs is the personality
of the memorialist. It is hard to feel that the truth is wholly in
her, or, perhaps, to acquit her of a degree of gross exaggeration.
It seems to me that she likes to make a bad story worse : though
heaven knows, her story is bad enough. But it is her attitude to
herself which snags the attention. She goes about her self-
analysis, warts and all, with a devotion bordering upon the
scholarly : beside her, Saint-Simon is an almost entirely disinterested figure. Nevertheless, this girl thrown on the inter-
national marriage market and living in a brutal court, had
enough to bear. Maltreated by a savage governess, even worse by
a savage, half-mad father, and maltreated psychologically by a
cruelly cold and ambitious mother, she still kept her zest, her
hopes, her spirits, almost preposterously high. Wilhelmina was
not an easy girl to get down, even when the efforts of all about
her seemed to be tending solely towards that end.

She has quite a degree of literary skill. True, she knows
nothing of " constructing " a story : but she enlivens her string
of incidents, nearly all of them disagreeable, by means of mental
vigour and a piercingly sharp eye. Her account of the visit of the
rough Russian Court, which, when it withdrew, sacked Mon
Bijou, is full of energy and a great deal of pure fun. Indeed, her
sense of fun is always striving to come to the surface : whether
or not her life in the Prussian Court was as terrible as she claims,
this must have been her saving grace. In the teeth of all the
evidence, Wilhelmina persistently believed in the better time
coming. Had she married the Prince of Wales (England's
" Poor Fred ") she would have been among the most remarkable
of our queens.

She lived in a rough age : but in circumstances rougher than
the royal norm. One shudders to think of all the things she does
not specifically describe : the dirt, the drunkenness, the per-
sistent hurly-burly. It does not seem as though she was a difficult
daughter. Indeed, not so difficult as her brother, who was to
become Frederick the Great. She was usually willing to do what

she was told, except in the case of the impossible marriages proposed to her : one feels on the whole, that she was lucky to step down from hopes of glory on the grand scale, to glory on a far lesser one, when she married the amiable Margrave of Bayreuth. By this time, all she longed for was to get away from her parents' house, and it is a comfort to the somewhat shattered reader to know that she was leaving in relatively gentle company.

Our mind boggles at the parental lack of interest in the life that could be led under a violent, cruel and spying governess. I was reminded of Lord Curzon's detestable governess, whose ingenious punishments were carried out almost daily without, it appears, either the knowledge of his father and mother, or any indication of care on their part for the wretched children.

" Miss Letti," Wilhelmina writes, " wished to revenge herself for the denial given to her by the queen ; and as she was firmly resolved to quit me, so wished to leave some marks upon me that should make me remember her. I think that if she could have broken either an arm or leg of mine, she would have done so : but the fear of detection prevented her. She therefore did all she could to spoil my face : she frequently hit my nose with such a violence that I bled like an ox."

All very well : though one is obliged to ask why a spoiled face could not be detected as easily as a broken arm. Perhaps the king and queen merely thought that she had " asked for it." They were a strange and horrid pair and it was a misfortune to be born to them.

Some of the most brutal scenes border, just slightly, on the farcical. Was this instinct to force Wilhelmina's method of self-protection or was it purely a literary tendency, a strangely emollient form of literary trick ? For, ferocious though her memoirs are, they are of the sort one can read " eating an apple." They shouldn't be, but they are : and the reason for this almost certainly lies in Wilhelmina's instinct to heighten out of all reason.

Where we can believe her utterly is in her description of the fashion in which young Frederick was compelled to watch the execution of his friend Katte. This is related with a sobriety uncommon to her. Yet who can really tell whether she was truthful in other things as well ? It is not possible to charge her with exaggeration without feeling the cold breath of fear and guilt which must strike us when we consider that she may not have been exaggerating at all, and that all things at the Prussian court were *as dreadful as she said they were.*

But there is a total truth in this book, which is the truth of a whole age, and a whole ambience. Yes, one feels, it must have been like that. There is something in the atmosphere of this court not unlike the coarse atmosphere in the court of *Jew Süss* : perhaps Feuchtwanger would have felt less dubiety about Wilhelmina's revelations than I do. Yes, the truth of an age, the smell of an age, is here in this remarkable book written by an altogether remarkable person.

If the king is too awful to be true, the queen less unlike a mother than the wicked stepmother in Snow White, we nevertheless feel that the world they inhabit has pebbles and boulders, fields and skies and oceans, slums, palaces, corn and fallow land. This is to Wilhelmina's credit : however deplorable life was, she was at all times profoundly aware of it.

She even managed to enjoy herself when the slightest occasion arose for enjoyment. As she looks back down the years, she never forgets that she was a young and spirited girl, with such a girl's resilience. We feel that this is an account which could have been written by somebody in a Grimms' fairy-tale—which makes tolerable (because the happy ending is on the way) what might have been intolerable if told by an ordinary person. And Wilhelmina is not ordinary at all. Somehow, it would have seemed quite plausible if the king and queen, at the end, in the manner of the Brothers Grimm, were put into barrels filled with nails and rolled down a hill.

PAMELA HANSFORD JOHNSON

INTRODUCTION

Frederica Sophia Wilhelmina, Crown Princess of Prussia and later Margravine of Bayreuth, was born on 3 July 1709 and died on 14 October 1758. She was one of the more delightful characters of her time. That she was little known even in her own country, and hardly at all outside it, was largely because Bayreuth, to which she was consigned after her marriage in 1732, was an obscure south German court. No one would remember it now, were it not that Richard Wagner happened later to make his home there. Wilhelmina deserved better and was indeed confidently brought up to expect it, since it was originally intended that she should become Princess of Wales, and thus perhaps Queen of England. The principal theme of this first volume of her *Memoirs* is of how these expectations were thwarted.

This apart, it would be quite wrong to think of her as just another ambitious German princess who failed. She was also the elder sister by some two and a half years of Frederick the Great and held a very special place in his affections. Indeed, Wilhelmina was probably the only woman for whom he ever had any respect and love. Nobody today needs to be reminded of Frederick, whose position as King of Prussia, combined with his unique personal and intellectual gifts, made him as fascinating to his contemporaries as to posterity. Endowed with every bit as much intelligence as her brother, Wilhelmina undoubtedly influenced the development of his extremely sophisticated tastes, which contributed in no small measure to his image of " greatness " and which later caused Voltaire to proclaim him the " Philosopher King ".

As the two eldest surviving children of Frederick William I, the soldier-king of Prussia, and of Sophia Dorothea, daughter of George I of England, Wilhelmina and Frederick were from the beginning meant to develop parallel lives. Certainly this was true of their early years. The tragedy of the youth of Frederick the Great is a familiar story. As a historical " set piece " it fires the imagination as an episode in German history in a way that perhaps only the story of his and Wilhelmina's direct ancestor, Mary

Queen of Scots does in British history. The tragedy of Mary lay in the confrontation of two half-sisters. The tragedy of Frederick lay in the confrontation of father and son. It was a conflict of personality as well as of the generations, but it took as its mainspring the problem of marriage, and Wilhelmina was inextricably involved in this political marriage market.

Marriage at all levels of society in the eighteenth century, and indeed throughout most of history, was conceived of as an institution for cementing relationships of family, land, business and thus, at the highest level, those of politics. Candidates for royal marriage were treated as diplomatic pawns. However, Frederick and Wilhelmina were unfortunate in that their father, for all his considerable virtues, was markedly unskilful in playing the diplomatic game, even if he was well endowed with pawns. Ten of his fourteen children survived childhood. His own grandfather, Frederick William (1640–88), known as the Great Elector, had through his diplomatic and administrative astuteness contrived to turn little Brandenburg-Prussia from an insignificant border state of the Empire into a European power, if not of the first rank, then certainly one to be taken into account by the European statesmen and diplomats of his day. After him respect for Prussia never entirely vanished— her army, the fourth largest in Europe, was too powerful for that —and she always remained the most significant state within Germany apart from the Austrian Empire itself. Yet under Frederick William I Prussia did to a large extent allow herself to become the plaything of the larger European powers, especially Great Britain and Austria.

As regards Great Britain, the crucial factor was the relationship with Hanover. The link between Hohenzollern and Welf, between Berlin and Hanover, was virtually traditional. Both Frederick William and his father Frederick I married Hanoverian princesses, and only four months after Wilhelmina was born her mother, Sophia Dorothea, who for obvious reasons wished to continue this tradition, was writing of a proposed alliance with " Le Petit Fritz ", meaning Frederick, later Prince of Wales and known in English historical mythology as " Poor Fred ", but for the moment just the grandson of the Elector of Hanover. His sister, the Princess Amelia, was similarly proposed for Frederick of Prussia.

However, in 1714 a new dimension was added to the special relationship, which ultimately was to ruin all chance of the proposed alignment. This was when Hanover, which had in fact only achieved Electoral status within the Empire in 1692, assumed its important new role across the English Channel. Henceforth strain caused by jealousy between the two houses was virtually continuous, even when relations were officially classed as good. When George II became king in 1727 things went from bad to worse. Between George II and Frederick William there existed a special mutual antipathy. Frederick the Great was later to write that " though brothers-in-law, they could never abide each other even when children . . . the King of England used to style the King of Prussia *my brother the sergeant,* and the King of Prussia, the King of England *my brother the player.*"[1] Thus both Georges, but especially the latter, in their newly exalted position, were content to allow the double marriage to dangle in front of Frederick William like some carrot.

The marriages were in fact provided for in the Treaty of Charlottenburg in 1723, the high point of Anglo-Prussian relations in this period. However, the relevant clause was never to be ratified. Indeed the marriages constitute little more than a footnote in the history of British foreign policy. At this time Great Britain's aim in Europe, as viewed by Walpole, was the maintenance of peace as far as this was consistent with the security of her trade. For instance, she was far more concerned with the threat of Austria as manifest in the expansion of the Ostend Trading Company and with the growing strength of Russia in the Baltic. Prussia was important only in so far as she might ally with either Russia or Austria, or as her relations with Hanover might complicate any issue.

On the other hand, for the Emperor Charles VI and the great Prince Eugene in Vienna, Prussia was of the greatest possible importance, if only for reasons of stability within the Empire and Eastern Europe. It was therefore much more important for Austria to try to detach Prussia from any English alliance than it was for England to maintain any existing alliance with Prussia, with or without marriages. Thus Seckendorff, the Austrian

[1] Frederick the Great, *Memoirs of the House of Brandenburg* (London, 1763) 69.

resident in Berlin, was much more powerful and intelligent[1] than the English envoy, Sir Charles Hotham, a man of little consequence or real influence either in London or in Berlin. The latter arrived in Berlin in 1730, ostensibly to finalise the marriage arrangements, but in reality, as his instructions from George II show,[2] to try again to detach Prussia from her alliance with Austria. This was no easy task. If Charles VI would agree to almost anything in return for support of the Pragmatic Sanction (the guarantee that would secure Maria Theresa's undivided inheritance to the Empire), Frederick William's one concern was his succession in Jülich and Berg, two small Catholic states in the Rhineland. A mutual exchange of support served to keep Frederick William loyal to the Empire until the year before he died.

If the European diplomatic situation was one essential backcloth in front of which the drama of the youth of Frederick and Wilhelmina was played, another perhaps more interesting one was the domestic and family situation. The dominant impression that has come down to us of Frederick William is that of an irrationally tempered near-monster, concerned merely to spite his wife and children, who enjoyed hunting, drinking and above all maintaining his famous brigade of giant grenadiers; this was also the contemporary view of him. In February 1730 at the height of the marriage negotiations, Lord Egmont noted in his diary that

> Accounts from Prussia say that the King has exceedingly disobliged his army by the cruel example made upon his tall Grenadiers, who having conspired to desert and being discovered he punished by causing the ringleaders to be broken on the wheel, after pinching the flesh off with hot irons, a death far exceeding what desertion merited and what the French thought severe enough for the murder of King Henry the Fourth.[3]

[1] He was also provided with considerably more ample funds.

[2] Wilhelm Oncken, " Sir Charles Hotham und Friedrich Wilhelm I im Jahre 1730 ", in *Forschungen zur Brandenburgischen und Preussischen Geschichte* (Leipzig, 1894), VII (2) 83ff.

[3] John Percival, later Lord Egmont, " Diary ", *Historical Manuscripts Commission* (London, 1920) I 50.

Yet Wilhelmina's own pen-portrait early in the *Memoirs* credits Frederick William with all the characteristics which make him admired by modern historians ; his genuine religious piety, his extreme personal frugality and, above all, his administrative genius. Berlin was in reality transformed from the Athens to the Sparta of the North, as contemporaries noted—not usually with much pleasure. Frederick the Great in later life acknowledged the debt he owed his father.

He left behind him an army of fifty-six thousand men, whom his great economy enabled him to maintain ; his finances increased ; the public treasure full ; and the most surprising order in all his affairs. If one may truly say that it is to the acorn from which it sprung we are indebted to the shade of the oak, the whole world must allow, that it is in the labour and wisdom of this prince, we must look for the sources of prosperity which the royal house has enjoyed since his death.[1]

Though the merits of Frederick William have in this century become generally acknowledged, it is difficult to think of any European monarch whose youth and apprenticeship to kingship have been the subject of so much speculation and writing as Frederick the Great himself. Carlyle in his massive biography takes three long volumes to reach his accession in 1740 ; popular and scholarly books continue to appear on the subject.[2] Attempts have been made to explain the many paradoxes within his reign in the story of his early years. He was the poet-philosopher who was also the conquering hero ; the patent Machiavellian who could compose a reasoned refutation of *Il Principe*. He was the king who while discoursing with Voltaire or amusing himself with his friends, Chazot, Keyserling or perhaps Algarotti, was at the same time preparing for the most blatant of military adventures. The former, as Wilhelmina commented sardonically, " were merely recreations for him ; the object which occupied his mind was the conquest of Silesia ".[3]

---

[1] Frederick the Great (op. cit., 110).

[2] Recent popular books are : Edith Simon, *The Making of Frederick the Great* (London, 1963), and Constance Wright, *A Royal Affinity* (London, 1967). The latter book deals specifically with the relationship between Frederick and Wilhelmina.

[3] *Memoirs* (London, 1812) II 347.

Stories of a Crown Prince's opposition to his father are as old as written history, and in the eighteenth century they were the rule rather than the exception. Wilhelmina in these pages herself refers to Don Carlos and Alexei, both " murdered " by their fathers Philip II of Spain and Peter the Great, although in both these cases the victims were mentally subnormal and thus to a real degree unworthy of their station. In England too, throughout the eighteenth century and beyond, the figure of the Prince of Wales invariably gathered around his person a more or less influential centre of opposition. Indeed the great hatred between George II and " Poor Fred ", and the king's reluctance to allow his son to marry at all, also contributed to the failure of Wilhelmina's English marriage. Nevertheless the extremes which the Prussian episode reached, the great clash of conflicting and in their ways equally impressive characters, give it a quite special fascination. It does indeed epitomize this kind of conflict. For Frederick William it has been claimed that he was the only Hohenzollern absolutist who never placed himself in direct conflict with his father.[1] This was despite the fact that he was fundamentally far more in opposition to his own father's extravagant rule than Frederick was ever opposed to his. For Frederick William had a straightforward and simple belief in the doctrine of legitimate authority. At the outset of his reign, in addition to all the political and economic changes that he made, he announced that he would never tolerate the *Kabalen* that had characterised the reign of Frederick I ; hence his furious distaste of the Queen's " Hanoverian party ". As we have seen, the worst crime he could conceive of was desertion from the army. This was what both Frederick and his friend Katte were formally charged with. At one point he stated that if he lived to be a hundred years old he would still expect total obedience from his son. After the great crises of 1730, given a year or so for both parties to come to their senses, Frederick began to co-operate splendidly with his father. He was given villas at Ruppin and later at Rheinsberg, both near Berlin, where he could enjoy " *ein Französchen, ein bons mots, ein Musiquechen und Komödiantchen* ", as his father referred to his *effeminierten* and frenchified tastes. It should be pointed out that, for his time, Frederick William was almost uniquely a *German* prince, when most

[1] Carl Hinrichs, *Der Kronprinzenprozess* (Berlin, 1936) 33ff.

German courts were doing their best to imitate French court life. This too may help to explain his preference for marrying his children within rather than outside German lands. On his deathbed Frederick William confirmed that he had total confidence in his son's ability to succeed him, and the fact that Frederick was later able to declare " I am the first servant of the state " was less a statement of his belief in the virtues of so-called " enlightened despotism " than an acknowledgement of the debt he owed to his father, and that in all essential respects he was following in his path.

Frederick's was a path to prominence and greatness. In the long run it mattered little to him that in 1733 he was finally bullied by his father into marrying Elizabeth Christina of Braunschweig-Wolfenbüttel, whom he totally disregarded after his wedding. But for Wilhelmina, who in May 1731 was given the invidious choice by her father of three minor German princes, Frederick the hereditary Prince of Bayreuth, Count Johann Adolf of Sachsen Weissenfels, or the Margrave Frederick William of Schwedt, it was a path to near obscurity. As she tells us in the *Memoirs*, she chose Bayreuth, as she knew least about him. Perhaps too his station was slightly superior to that of his rivals. In fact by contemporary standards it was not an entirely unsuccessful marriage, and Wilhelmina, in describing the primitive Bayreuth court, tells us that she loved him passionately and that he was " the only alleviation that I could find of my misery ".[1] Soon after her marriage she bore him her only child, Elizabeth Frederica Sophia, later Duchess of Württemberg (1732–80). Though the flowering of Bayreuth culture took as its mainspring the enthusiasms of Wilhelmina, she was fully supported in all her ventures by Prince Frederick, especially after he became Margrave in 1735. He was well educated, having studied for some eight years in Geneva, and among his accomplishments was playing the flute, which must have endeared him to his brother-in-law. But he was also unfaithful, taking as his mistress Wilhelmina's own companion, Dorothea von der Marwitz, whose activities as an Austrian agent were the cause of the one major row between Wilhelmina and her brother. Wilhelmina's unhappiness in Bayreuth too was greatly aggravated by illness ; she suffered terribly from gout, the hereditary complaint of the

[1] *Memoirs*, II 19.

19

Hohenzollerns, increased doubtless by the ill-treatment, physical and psychological, which was meted out to her in her early days in Berlin and which she describes so graphically in these pages.

She did, however, contrive to make her life in Bayreuth acceptable by maintaining her friendship with her brother, largely through an extensive correspondence and through her largely successful attempt to create for herself a *milieu* which she could consider compatible with civilised living. It was in Bayreuth that she tried to kindle something of the spirit of that island of Cythera which she and so many like-minded people of her time sought and referred to in their writings. That island of pleasure she found in her villa, the Hermitage, which lay outside Bayreuth and which was given to her by her husband for her birthday in 1735. Formerly just a folly in the form of a hermitage, complete with little cells, it was transformed into a small rococo summer palace, not unlike Frederick's own Sans Souci, surrounded by fountains, grottos, pavilions and walks as well as an open-air theatre, and set in an idyllic landscaped forest.

There, on occasions, she could reciprocate her brother's hospitality and entertain those like Voltaire with whom she felt a spiritual affinity. In the town of Bayreuth she built one of the most perfect eighteenth-century opera-houses in Europe, designed by the renowned theatre architects Giuseppe Galli Bibiena and his son Carlo. The opera-house was opened in 1740 with a performance of *Argenore*, a complete opera composed by Wilhelmina herself in which she acted. She took up painting and drawing, composed verses and libretti. All branches of the decorative arts flourished, and Bayreuth became a veritable little Dresden. An Academy of Art was founded, as was the University of Erlangen. " Bayreuth ", wrote Voltaire in 1743, one year after his only visit there, though he met Wilhelmina on many other occasions, " is a delicious retreat, where one can enjoy all the advantages of a court without being inconvenienced by its grandeur."[1] In 1755 Wilhelmina went to Italy, getting as far south as Naples and Herculaneum, and wrote back enthusiastically to Frederick about the pleasure she took in " crawling about on all fours " amongst the ruins, whilst he in reply poured scorn

[1] George Horn, *The Margravine of Bayreuth and Voltaire* (London, 1888) 23.

on Italy as a "courtesan past her prime ".[1] Wilhelmina returned from Italy just three months before Winckelmann's arrival in Rome. She was indeed in the vanguard of modern taste. Thanks to her, Bayreuth, that small and sleepy Franconian town, somehow manages to epitomize the dichotomy that has always appeared to exist in German cultural life. Significantly situated at the top of a hill, the Wagnerian *Festspielhaus* looks down over the Margrave's recently restored opera-house, which asserts the influence of French culture on Germany in the eighteenth century that was later largely to be rejected.

It was between 1741 and 1745 that Wilhelmina composed her memoirs. Clearly they were written when she was lying under the shadow of a dark emotional cloud—when her relationship with her brother was temporarily under strain, and when she was beginning to discover her husband's unfaithfulness. At one or two points in the narrative she gives 1744 as the date of composition, though the composition extended over a long period, and internal textual evidence shows it to have undergone revision as late as 1747.[2] The second volume of the *Memoirs* as they stand take the reader until 1742, but at this point Wilhelmina seems to have got bored with the venture and they appear to break off in the middle of a paragraph.

They may be seen as an attempt to rationalize and sort out the cause of her unhappy life as she saw it. In keeping with the spirit of her age she claimed to have " liberated myself from many prejudices and pride myself on being something of a philosopher ". She maintained that she wrote for

> my own amusement and not with the slightest idea that these memoirs will ever be printed ; perhaps I may even one day make a sacrifice of them to Vulcan ; perhaps I shall give them to my daughter ; on this subject I am quite undecided. I repeat once more, I write for my own amusement and take pleasure in concealing nothing of what has happened to me, not even my most secret thoughts.[3]

[1] Quoted in *Markgräfin Wilhelmine von Bayreuth und ihre Welt* (Exhibition Catalogue, Bayreuth, 1959) 55.

[2] G. B. Volz, " Die Markgräfin von Bayreuth und ihre Denkwurdigkeiten ", in *Forschungen zur Brandenburgischen und Preussischen Geschichte* (Leipzig, 1924) XXXVI 164.

[3] *Memoirs*, II 296.

Wilhelmina's own rather subjective brand of honesty causes her opinions and judgements to alter during the narrative as is appropriate to each event. Thus her mother, who appears to have taken a long time to recover from the failure of her English marriage plans, becomes less, her father more reasonable and sympathetic in the second volume. Even Grumbkow and Seckendorff, Wilhelmina's arch-enemies in Berlin, become less horrific as they are seen—as was in fact the case—to have assisted Frederick's reconciliation with his father after the traumatic experiences of 1730.

Bearing all this in mind, what can we say of the accuracy and historical relevance of the *Memoirs*? Ranke, Pertz and Droysen, the three high priests of German history in the nineteenth century, all tend to dismiss them as being hardly worthy of attention, and Carlyle found them " full of mistakes indeed ; and exaggerates dreadfully in its shrill female way : deduct the subtrahend—say perhaps twenty-five percent, or in extreme cases as high as seventy-five—and you will get some image of human actuality from Wilhelmina ".[1] Nevertheless all these writers had no scruples about quoting her. Carlyle did so particularly extensively, though he often disguised her words in paraphrase.

Close comparison, for instance, with the extensive source material published by the German historian, Carl Hinrichs, concerning the arrest and trial of Frederick and Katte, shows that Wilhelmina must have " researched " in order to have achieved the accuracy that she clearly does, and though she may simplify her story a little, her narrative conveys an immediacy quite equal to the grim succession of documents. Furthermore, whatever we might suspect, Wilhelmina in no way exaggerates her story in the telling, though it must be admitted that even as Crown Princess she was never at the centre of events in Berlin. For instance in a correspondence of nearly a thousand letters to his friend, the Prince of Anhalt-Dessau, which contain much Berlin gossip, Frederick William mentions his daughter but once, and that in relation to an illness in 1732 after she had married.[2] Marriages and misdemeanours of ministers, officers, even of ordinary soldiers, clearly interested him more than his daughter's activi-

---

[1] Thomas Carlyle, *Frederick II of Prussia* (London 1858) I 384.

[2] O. Krauske, *Die Briefe Friedrich Wilhelm I an den Fürsten Leopold zu Anhalt Dessau* (Berlin, 1905).

ties. Nor, despite her evident precociousness, is Wilhelmina
likely to have remembered the events of her early childhood in
such detail. To compose her narrative she must have acquired
much information indirectly, partly no doubt through stories
told to her earlier by her mother and by her governess and
friend Dorothea Sonsfeld, whom she took with her to Bayreuth,
but also through direct inquiry. For these reasons the first
volume of the *Memoirs*, with their strong themes of the negotiations for the marriages, the trial and ill-treatment of Frederick
and Katte, interspersed with such colourful incidents as the visit
to Berlin with their exotic retinues of Peter the Great and later of
Augustus the Strong, is more interesting, concise and perhaps less
biased than the latter narrative. In the second volume Wilhelmina, being closer to the events she describes, which are in themselves less interesting, becomes more exclusively concerned with
herself, especially her state of health, descriptions of which are
interspersed with malicious accounts of life at the small court of
Bayreuth.

The *Memoirs* were written in French, and in a French so
idiomatic and stylish that Sainte Beuve proclaimed, " *C'est donc
un écrivain français de plus que nous avons en elle, et un écrivain
peintre tout à fait digne d'attention* ", and maintained that she
could hold her own without embarrassment beside Grammont,
Sévigné, Saint Simon and a host of other French writers whom he
names.[1] Certainly Wilhelmina's perception, her rare ability to
see through the gross pretentiousness which was such a feature of
eighteenth-century court life, and her surprisingly sharp sense of
humour make her worthy of such comparisons. To accuse
Wilhelmina of historical bias and inaccuracy is to forget that her
Memoirs do not aspire to the sort of modern scientific history as
Ranke, for example, is supposed to have understood it. Saint
Simon does not alone constitute the history of Regency France,
even if his attitudes have fundamentally coloured our impression
of his times. Similarly the *Memoirs* of Wilhelmina have undoubtedly coloured our view of the reign of the Soldier King.
First published in 1811, at that moment when Prussia had been
reduced to her lowest point in her ignominious defeat by Napoleon,
they served in their small way to help divert attention from the

[1] C.-A. Sainte Beuve, " Le Margrave de Bareith ", in *Causeries du
Lundi* (Paris, 1857) XII 397–8.

supposed glories of Frederick the Great's reign to the darker aspects of Prussianism, which even now constitute its image. An early review of the first English edition put it like this :

> The display of Court cruelty in these pages must inspire horror for the instigators of such cruel policy . . . were it not for the artless simplicity with which the events are detailed we should gladly hope that it might be an exaggerated account and that such intolerant conduct had not been manifested in a civilized court during the eighteenth century.[1]

Sainte Beuve concluded that Wilhelmina always remained " *une sœur de roi* ",[2] and it is as such that she claims our attention in the first instance. But her own qualities also make her worthy of recognition, and this fact was acknowledged by Frederick himself. Her death, which came on the very day that he suffered one of his worst defeats in the Seven Years War at the hands of the Austrians at Hochkirch, was a great blow to him. In his *History of the Seven Years War*, published in 1768, he wrote of her : " She was a princess of rare talents. She was possessed of a refined spirit, great knowledge . . . an outstanding artistic temperament," and privately he wrote to his brother, the great general Prince Henry : " Consider that I was born and brought up with my sister of Bayreuth, the ties that existed between us were unbreakable, and no difference could serve to breach our deep love ; we were separate in body, but have one soul ".[3] The " Temple of Friendship ", inspired by an ode to Wilhelmina written by Voltaire, that he had built in her memory in his gardens at Sans Souci, was a unique tribute from one, indeed two great men of her time. The English reader, after putting down her *Memoirs*, can be excused a little momentary speculation on what this gifted princess might have achieved had she indeed become Princess of Wales.

NORMAN ROSENTHAL

[1] *Gentleman's Magazine*, LXXXXII (December 1812) 554.
[2] Op. cit., 431.
[3] Bayreuth Catalogue (op. cit., 30).

A NOTE ON THE TEXT

George Gooch, writing in 1944 in his volume *Courts and Cabinets*, was the last important English historian to draw his reader's attention to the delightful memoirs of Wilhelmina, Margravine of Bayreuth, the first volume of which we are publishing here. In his essay he suggested that there was a need for a proper critical edition. This is not our purpose here ; it would be more suitable for a French or German edition.[1] However, by providing a brief historical introduction and elucidating some of Wilhelmina's obscurer points and characters we hope we can increase the reader's enjoyment of the narrative.

The facts about the evolution of the manuscript itself are extremely complicated—at least seven versions would appear to have existed, some in Wilhelmina's hand, most not, which show considerable variation and revision. The present edition follows the text of the first English translation of 1812 exactly, except that Wilhelmina's erratic spelling of proper names has been corrected. Despite a few minor inaccuracies, and the fact that it was based on the Paris edition of 1812 rather than the first edition which appeared in Brunswick in 1811, it has very great charm and probably captures the flavour of the original far better than any modern translation could do. During the nineteenth century there were many editions in French and German, based on various manuscripts and of varying degrees of accuracy. The English edition was reprinted in a series of autobiographies in 1828, but since then there have only been a prim translation arranged by Princess Christian of Schleswig-Holstein, daughter of Queen Victoria, in 1887, and in 1877 a bowdlerised American translation " prepared especially for family reading ", with the best passages omitted.

The original was in the form of a continuous narrative but for the convenience of the reader we have divided the book into chapters.

[1] The most recent edition in French was published in 1967 by Mercure de France, Paris, with a few notes by Gérard Doscot and an introduction by Pierre Gaxotte.

In the preparation of this edition, I should like to thank Mr Cedric Glover, Dr Heinrich Thiel of Bayreuth, and especially Diana and Fred Uhlman for their great help in choosing the splendid illustrations.   N. R.

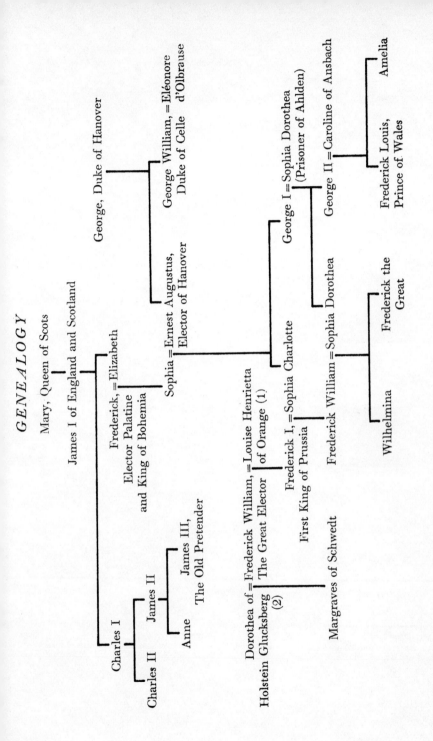

GENEALOGY

Mary, Queen of Scots

James I of England and Scotland

Charles I

Charles II

James II

Anne

James III,
The Old Pretender

Frederick, = Elizabeth
Elector Palatine
and King of Bohemia

Sophia = Ernest Augustus,
Elector of Hanover

George, Duke of Hanover

George William, = Eléonore
Duke of Celle   d'Olbrause

George I = Sophia Dorothea
(Prisoner of Ahlden)

George II = Caroline of Ansbach

Frederick Louis,
Prince of Wales

Amelia

Sophia Dorothea

Dorothea of = Frederick William, = Louise Henrietta
Holstein Glucksberg   The Great Elector   of Orange (1)
(2)

Frederick I, = Sophia Charlotte
First King of Prussia

Margraves of Schwedt

Frederick William = Sophia Dorothea

Wilhelmina

Frederick the
Great

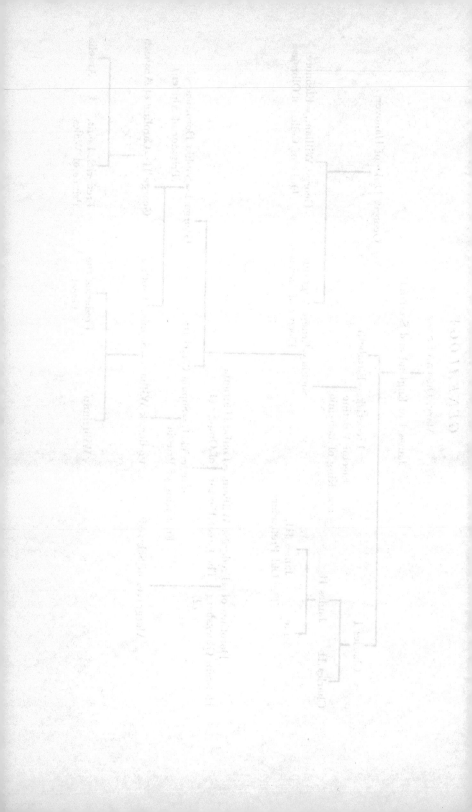

THE MEMOIRS

I

I introduce the principal characters at Court — The unfortunate condition of my birth — The death of one King and accession of another — A spectre walks and the consequences — A royal will — Plots and counterplots — A planned assassination — The Court of Barbarians.

FREDERICK WILLIAM, King of Prussia, at that time Prince Royal, was married in the year 1706, to Sophia Dorothea, Princess of Hanover. Frederick the first, King of Prussia, his father, had allowed him to select for a consort one of the three following Princesses ; viz : a Princess of Sweden, sister to Charles XII ; a Princess of Saxe-Zeitz ; or a Princess of Orange, niece to the Prince of Anhalt. The latter, to whom the Prince Royal had always been uncommonly attached, had flattered himself with the hope that the Prince's choice would fall upon his niece : but the heart of the Prince Royal having been captivated by the charms of the Princess of Hanover, he declined the proposals of his royal father, and by his intreaties and intrigues prevailed with his Majesty to consent to his union with the Hanoverian Princess.[1]

It is proper that I should convey some idea of the character of the principal persons of whom the court of Berlin was composed, and particularly of that of the Prince Royal. This Prince, whose education had been entrusted to Count Dohna,[2] possesses all the qualities which constitute a great man ; his genius is elevated and capable of the greatest

[1] Frederick William I (1688–1740). He became king in 1713. Marriages between the Prussian and Hanoverian royal houses were traditional. Frederick William's father, Frederick I, the first king of Prussia, was married to a Hanoverian princess, Sophie Charlotte.

[2] Christoph, Burggraf und Graf zu Dohna (1665–1733).

actions ; to an uncommon facility of conception he adds much judgment and application ; his disposition is naturally good. From his early youth he always manifested a decided predilection for the military ; it was his ruling passion, and he has justified it by the excellent order into which he has put his army. His temper is lively and hot ; it frequently betrayed him into excesses of which he has since bitterly repented. He mostly preferred justice to clemency. His excessive love of money has made him pass for an avaricious man. It is however only in his personal and family concerns that he can be reproached with that vice ; for he liberally lavished wealth upon his favourites and those who were zealously attached to his service.

The charitable foundations which he established and the churches he built are proofs of his piety. His devotion degenerated into bigotry ; he hated pomp and luxury. He was suspicious, jealous, and frequently guilty of dissimulation. His governor had sedulously inspired him with contempt for the female sex. His opinion of women was so bad, that his prejudices caused many vexations to the Princess, of whom he was jealous to an excess.

The Prince of Anhalt may be ranked among the greatest generals of the age. With a consummate experience in war he combines a particular genius for public affairs. His brutal mien inspires fear, and his physiognomy does not belie his disposition. His unbounded ambition incites him to commit any crime to obtain his ends. He is a steady friend, but an irreconcileable enemy, and vindictive to excess towards those who have had the misfortune of giving him offence. He is addicted to cruelty and dissimulation. His mind is cultivated, and his conversation entertaining when he chuses.[1]

[1] Leopold, Prince of Anhalt-Dessau (1676–1747), was known in Germany as *der Alte Dessauer*. His father had allowed the regiment of his small German principality to come under Prussian control. In 1709 Frederick William met Leopold while campaigning in Brabant, and their mutual enthusiasm for military affairs made them close friends. Although Leopold was a supporter of the pro-Austrian party at the

M. de Grumbkow may pass for one of the ablest ministers that have appeared for a great length of time. He is uncommonly polite, his conversation is both easy and witty. Though possessed of a cultivated, pliant and insinuating mind, he chiefly pleases by that talent for satire which is so prevalent in our times. He knows how to blend the serious with the agreeable ; but this brilliant exterior conceals a depraved, selfish, and perfidious heart. Nothing equals the licentiousness of his conduct ; his character is a compound of vices which render him abhorrent to the virtuous.[1]

Such were the two favourites of the Prince Royal. It may easily be supposed, that being intimately connected and proceeding hand in hand, they had no difficulty in corrupting the heart of a young prince and overturning a whole state. They beheld their project of reigning frustrated by the marriage of the Prince Royal. The Prince of Anhalt could not forgive the Princess Royal her having been preferred to his niece ; he feared lest she might obtain possession of the heart of her consort. To prevent this, he attempted to sow the seeds of discord between them ; and availing himself of the Prince's disposition to jealousy, they endeavoured to render him jealous of his spouse. This unfortunate Princess was doomed to endure the most cruel torments from the

Prussian court, and thus a great enemy of the queen, he later gave Frederick the Great valuable support and military advice in his wars to seize Silesia from the Austrians.

[1] Friedrich Wilhelm von Grumbkow (1678–1739). Before Frederick William's accession Grumbkow had had a distinguished military and diplomatic career. After 1713 he quickly rose to become director of the *Generalkriegskommissariat* and in 1723 became minister and vice-president of the *Generaldirektorium*, the new ministry which united the administration of general and military finance. Like Anhalt-Dessau he was pro-Austrian, and in order to keep his large family, as well as one of the grandest houses in Berlin, he accepted large bribes from the Austrian Ambassador, von Seckendorff. However, although the *Memoirs* at this stage gives the impression that the two were close friends, they were in reality rivals, continually attempting to oust each other from the king's confidence. (See below, pp. 96 ff.)

violence of the Prince Royal ; and notwithstanding the proofs which she gave him of her virtue, nothing but patience could cure him of the prejudices with which he had been inspired against her.

The Princess in the meantime gave the Prince a son in 1707.[1] But the joy which this event occasioned was soon converted into grief by the death of the young Prince twelve months after his birth. The Princess found herself a second time in a state which revived the hopes of the country. On the 3d of July 1709, the Princess Royal presented her royal husband with a daughter, who was very unfavourably received, because the ardent wishes of all had been for a prince. I was the child who met with that ungracious reception. I came into the world at a time when the monarchs of Denmark and Poland happened to be both at Potsdam to sign a treaty of alliance against Charles XII, King of Sweden, for the purpose of appeasing the troubles of Poland.[2] These two sovereigns and the King my grandfather, were my sponsors and present at my being christened, which ceremony was performed with great pomp and magnificence. I was christened Frederica Sophia Wilhelmina.[3]

The King, my grandfather, soon grew uncommonly fond of me. At eighteen months of age I was much more forward than other children. I articulated pretty distinctly, and at two years of age I walked by myself. The childish tricks which I played amused this good Prince, whom I sometimes diverted for whole days.

The following year the Princess had again a son who did

[1] Friedrich Ludwig (22 November 1707–5 May 1708).

[2] Charles XII, since the outbreak of the Great Northern War in 1701, had been the cause of the greatest possible havoc in Poland. He succeeded in 1706 in deposing the Elector of Saxony, Augustus the Strong, as king and replaced him with the French candidate, Stanislas Leczinski. But the defeat of Charles XII by Peter the Great at Poltava in 1709 radically altered the situation, and Frederick William and Frederick IV of Denmark were able to put Augustus back on to his Polish throne.

[3] Wilhelmina died on 14 October 1758.

not live. But on the 24th of January 1712, the Princess Royal presented her consort with a third Prince, who was christened Frederick.[1] My brother and myself were both entrusted to the care of the Countess de Kamecke, lady of the grand master of the wardrobe to the King and his great favourite. But the Princess Royal having been shortly after on a visit to the Elector, her father, at Hanover, Madam Kielmansegge,[2] known afterwards by the name of Lady Darlington, recommended to the Princess a young person who was with her as a companion, to preside over my education. Her name was Letti. She was the daughter of an Italian monk who had escaped from his convent to settle in Holland, where he had abjured his Catholic faith. He lived by his pen. He is the author of a history of Brandenburg, which has been very much criticised, and of the lives of Charles V and Philip II.[3]

His daughter had earned a living by correcting the proofs of newspapers. A true Italian in heart and mind, she was as remarkable for vivacity, pliancy, and depravity, as for selfishness, haughtiness, and violence. Her morals were in unison with her origin. Her coquetry gained her a crowd of admirers, whom she did not suffer to pine in long expectation. Her manners were Dutch, that is to say

[1] Afterwards known by the surname of the *Great*. (Author's note. He died on 18 August 1786.)

[2] Sophie Charlotte Kielmansegge (1675–1725), later Countess of Darlington. She was the mistress of George I, and was described by Horace Walpole as having " two fierce black eyes, large and rolling . . . two acres of cheek spread with crimson, an ocean of neck that overflowed ".

[3] Gregorio Leti (*sic*), an extremely prolific Italian historian and poet. The book noted here is called *Rittrati historice politici chronologici e genealogici della Casa Elettorale di Brandenburgo*, 1687. Leti was the author of books on every conceivable subject, including biographies of Elizabeth I and Cromwell. One of his books, which was translated into English, shows where this ex-monk's sympathies lay, and also perhaps why Miss Letti could recommend herself to the Berlin court. It was called *Il Purinismo di Roma, or the History of the whores and whoredom of the Popes of Rome. Discouvered by a conclave of ladies convened for the election of a new pope. Written in Italian by the author of Cardinalismo and Nepotismo and now made English.*

excessively rude : but she knew how to conceal these faults under so fine an exterior, that she delighted all who beheld her. The Princess Royal, who was dazzled with her, like others, determined to appoint her my governess, with the prerogative that she should accompany me every where, and be admitted at my table.

The Prince Royal had attended the Princess to Hanover. The Electoral Princess had been delivered of a son in 1707.[1] As our ages agreed, our parents resolved still more to strengthen the ties of their friendship by destining us for each other. My little admirer began even at that time to send me presents, and no post day passed without these princesses corresponding about the future union of their children.

The King my grandfather had been unwell for some time. Hopes had been entertained that his health would be re-established : but his weak constitution could not long resist the attacks of a hectic complaint. He died in the month of February 1713. When he was informed of his impending fate, he submitted with firmness and resignation to the decrees of Providence. As he felt the approaches of death, he took an affectionate leave of the Prince and Princess Royal, and recommended to them the prosperity of the country and the welfare of his subjects. He afterwards sent for both my brother and me, and gave us his blessing at eight o'clock in the evening. His death followed close upon this mournful ceremony. He expired on the 25th, universally regretted throughout the kingdom.

On the very day of his death, King Frederick William, his son, inquired into the establishment of his court, and completely reformed it, on condition that no one should retire before the funeral of the late King. I shall not describe the magnificence of his solemn obsequies ; they

[1] Friedrich Ludwig of Hanover (1707–51), later Duke of Gloucester and Prince of Wales. Within two months of the birth of Wilhelmina her mother Sophia Dorothea was writing optimistically " *Le petit Fritz me demands toujours les nouvelles de sa Braut* ". (See introduction, p. 14).

were not celebrated till some months after. The face of every thing was altered at Berlin. Those who wished to insure the favour of the new king assumed the helmet and cuirass ; every thing became military ; not a vestige remained of the ancient court. M. de Grumbkow was placed at the head of affairs, and the Prince of Anhalt had the direction of the army. These two individuals possessed themselves of the confidence of the young monarch, and helped him to bear the burthen of government. The whole year passed in settling the administration and introducing order in the finances, which the immense profusions of the late king had somewhat deranged.

The death of Queen Anne, of Great Britain, which happened the following year, proved a very interesting event to the King and Queen. The Elector of Hanover having become her heir, by the exclusion of the Pretender, or rather of the son of James II., went over to England to ascend the British throne ;[1] the Electoral Prince his son accompanied him, and took the title of Prince of Wales. The latter left the Prince his son, who was nominated Duke of Gloucester, at Hanover, being unwilling to expose him to the risks of the sea at so tender an age. The Queen my mother was, about the same time, delivered of a Princess, who was named Frederica Louisa.[2]

Meanwhile my brother was of a very weak constitution ; his silent disposition and his want of vivacity caused well-grounded alarms for his life : his frequent maladies began to revive the hopes of the Prince of Anhalt. In order to strengthen and increase his credit, he persuaded the King to give me in marriage to his nephew. That Prince was first cousin to the King. The Elector, Frederick William, their grandfather, had been twice married. By the Princess of Orange, his first consort, he had Frederick the first, and

---

[1] Frederick William was the first European monarch to recognise the Hanoverian succession.
[2] Frederica Louise (1714–84), later, in 1729, to be unhappily married to Karl Wilhelm Friedrich, Margrave of Brandenburg-Ansbach.

two princes who died shortly after their birth. His second consort, a Princess of Holstein-Glücksburg, widow of the Duke Charles Louis of Luneburgh, brought him five princes and three princesses, *viz.* Charles, who was poisoned in Italy by order of the King his brother ; Prince Casimir, who was also poisoned by a Princess of Holstein, whom he had refused to marry ; and the Princes Philip, Albert, and Louis.[1] The first of these three princes married a Princess of Anhalt, sister to him whose portrait I have drawn ; by her he had two sons and one daughter. After the death of the Margrave Philip, his eldest son the Margrave of Schwedt became first prince of the blood and presumptive heir of the crown, on failure of the royal line.[2] In that case all the allodial demesnes and estates would have devolved to me. The Prince of Anhalt, supported by Grumbkow, persuaded the King, that while he had but one son, policy required of him to marry me to his cousin, the Margrave of Schwedt. They represented that my brother's delicate state of health would not allow much reliance to be placed on his life ; that the Queen began to grow so corpulent that it was to be feared she would have no more children ;[3] that the King ought to provide before hand for the preservation of his dominions, which would be dismembered if I contracted any other union ; and lastly, that if he had the misfortune to lose my brother, his son-in-law and successor would supply the place of his son.

For some time the King contented himself with giving them vague answers : but they found an opportunity of

---

[1] In fact Frederick William, the Great Elector, had only four sons by his second marriage to Dorothea von Holstein-Glücksburg. Friedrich Casimir von Kurland was his son-in-law. Philipp-Wilhelm (1669–1711) was his father's favourite son and became Margrave of Schwedt in 1692. A distinguished soldier, he is reputed to have given Frederick William his passion for the giant grenadiers.

[2] Heinrich Friedrich, Margrave of Schwedt (1700–88), a nephew of Leopold of Anhalt-Dessau. His line died out with his death.

[3] In fact Sophia Dorothea bore fourteen children all told between 1707 and 1730, seven boys and seven girls, ten of whom survived infancy.

seducing him into some debaucheries ; when heated with wine they obtained whatever they wished. It was even resolved that the Margrave of Schwedt should from that time be at liberty to visit me, and that all means should be attempted to produce a mutual inclination between us. Miss Letti, gained over by Anhalt's party, incessantly talked to me of the Margrave of Schwedt, and sounded his praises, adding continually that he would become a great king, and that it would be very fortunate for me if I should marry him.

This Prince, who was born in 1700, was very tall for his years. His face is handsome, but his countenance is not prepossessing. Though he was but fifteen, his wicked disposition already betrayed itself : he was brutal and cruel ; his manners were rude, and his propensities mean. I had a natural antipathy to him, and I endeavoured to play him tricks and frighten him, for he was a coward. Miss Letti would not permit these jokes, and punished me severely for them. The Queen, who was ignorant of the object of the Prince's visits, allowed them with so much the more facility, as I received those of the other princes of the blood, and as they could not be of any consequence at my tender age. In spite of all their efforts the two favourites had hitherto been unable to sow any dissensions between the King and Queen : but, although the King was passionately fond of his royal spouse, yet he could not help using her ill, and allowed her no share whatever in public affairs. He apologised for his conduct by saying, that *it was necessary to keep women under proper subjection, else they would rule their husbands.*

However, it was not long before the Queen was acquainted with the plan of my marriage ; it was entrusted to her by the King. It was a thunder-stroke to the Queen. But I must first sketch her temper and person. The Queen never was handsome. Her features are strongly marked, and none of them fine. Her complexion is pale ; her hair a dark brown ; her shape has been one of the handsomest in the world : her noble and majestic gait inspires all who behold her with respect ; a perfect acquaintance with the world, and a brilliant understanding, seem to promise more solidity than she is possessed of. Her heart is benevolent, generous, and kind ; she cherishes the arts and sciences, without having ever devoted much time to the study of them. No one is without faults ; the Queen has hers. All the pride and haughtiness of the House of Hanover are concentrated in her person. Her ambition is unbounded ; she is excessively jealous, of a suspicious and vindictive temper, and never forgives those by whom she fancies she has been offended.[1]

The alliance which she had projected with England through the marriage of her children, was the most ardent wish of her heart ; and she flattered herself she should gradually succeed in governing the King. Her second object was to secure a strong protection against the persecutions of the Prince of Anhalt, and lastly, to obtain the guardianship of my brother in case of the King's decease. The King was subject to frequent diseases, and the Queen had been told that he could not live long.

It was nearly about this time that the King declared war against the Swedes. The Prussian troops began to march in the month of May into Pomerania, where they joined those of Denmark and Saxony. The campaign opened with the taking of the strong town of Wismar. The whole army, amounting to thirty-six thousand men, afterwards marched to lay siege to Stralsund. The Queen my mother, though again pregnant, followed the King in this expedition. I shall not enter into a detail of the campaign ; it ended gloriously for the King my father, who took possession of a great part of Swedish Pomerania.[2] During the absence of the Queen I was left entirely to the care of Miss Letti ; and Madam

---

[1] Sophia Dorothea (1687–1757). She was the daughter of George Louis, Elector of Hanover, later George I of England.

[2] After Poltava, Charles XII had fled to Turkey. The siege of Stralsund, a port in Swedish Pomerania, by an army of Prussians and Danes

de Roucoule, who had educated the King, was entrusted
with my brother's education. Miss Letti took infinite
pains to cultivate my understanding ; she taught me the
principal elements of history and geography, and endeavoured, at the same time, to polish my manners. The
great number of persons by whom I was visited, contributed
to render me acquainted with the usages of society. I
was extremely lively, and every one took pleasure in
conversing with me.

The Queen, on her return, was charmed with my little
figure. The endearments which she lavished upon me
caused me so lively a joy, that all my blood being thrown
into agitation, I had an hemorrhage which nearly sent me
to the other world. It was a sort of miracle that I escaped
from this disease, which kept me several weeks confined to
my bed. No sooner was I restored to health, than the
Queen wished to avail herself of my prodigious facility in
learning. She gave me several masters, among others the
famous La Croze,[1] who has been celebrated for his historical
knowledge and his profound acquaintance with the languages of the East, and with sacred and profane antiquities.
My whole day was taken up with teachers who succeeded
each other, and left me very little time for my recreations.

The Court of Berlin, although most of the men of which
it was composed were military, was nevertheless very
numerous, on account of the influx of strangers that re-

36,000 strong, marked the beginning of Charles's return campaign,
which lasted until his death in 1718. Stralsund was taken after three
months on 19 October 1715.

[1] Veyssière de La Croze (1661–1740) was the outstanding teacher of
Wilhelmina. A close friend of the two leading figures of the early
enlightenment, Pierre Bayle and Leibniz, La Croze obtained his position
indirectly through Leibniz. Considering that he was with Wilhelmina
from 1717 to 1724, he is passed over too lightly in these pages, for it was
he above all who was responsible for instilling into her the highly
cultivated tastes she later took with her to Bayreuth. La Croze had
previously taught the Margrave of Schwedt as well as Colonel Duhan,
tutor of Frederick the Great. (See M. Jordan, *Histoire de la vie . . . de
M. La Croze* (Amsterdam, 1741), 149 ; H. Thiel, *Wilhelmina von
Bayreuth* (Munich, 1967) 37 ff.)

sorted to it. The Queen held a drawing-room every evening during the absence of the King, who was generally at Potsdam, a small town at the distance of four German miles from Berlin. There he lived more as a private gentleman than as a king : his table was served with frugality ; it never exceeded necessaries. His principal occupation was to drill a regiment, which he had began to form in the life time of Frederick the First, and which was composed of colossal men six feet in height. All the monarchs of Europe eagerly sent recruits for it. This regiment might justly be styled *the channel of royal favour*,[1] for to give or to procure tall men for the King, was sufficient to obtain any thing of him. He used to go a shooting or hunting after dinner, and in the evening he frequented a smoking club[2] with his general officers.

There were at that time several Swedish officers at Berlin, who had been taken prisoners at the siege of Stralsund. One of these officers, of the name of Cron, had acquired some notoriety for his knowledge in judicial astrology ; the Queen had the curiosity to send for him. He foretold her that she would be delivered of a princess : to my brother he said, that he would become one of the greatest princes that ever reigned, that he would make considerable acquisitions and die an emperor. My hand did

---

[1] According to Ranke (" Über die Glaubwürdigkeit der Memoiren der Markgräfin von Bayreuth ", in *Abhandlung und Versuche*, Erste Sammlung (Leipzig, 1872) 59), this remark, the most oft-quoted in the book, only occurs in the margin of the manuscript, apparently as an afterthought. However, there can be little doubt of the truth of the matter. Anhalt-Dessau, as his printed correspondence shows, was continually supplying the king with tall soldiers. F. Förster, the early nineteenth-century historian of Prussia, relates that on his accession Frederick William abolished all newspapers, considering they contained nothing but foreign dispatches. Everyone consequently took to reading Dutch newspapers. When Frederick William's attention was drawn to a report in one, that a piper of the Grenadiers had died and that his dissection had revealed him to have two stomachs but no heart, newspapers in Berlin were permitted again. After his father's death Frederick the Great disbanded the regiment.

[2] The so-called *Tabergei*.

not prove so lucky as that of my brother ; the astrologer examined it a long time, and shaking his head, said : *that my life would be a tissue of fatalities, that I should be asked in marriage by four crowned heads, namely, the monarchs of Sweden, of England, of Russia, and of Poland ; that, however, I should marry none of those sovereigns.* This prediction was fulfilled, as we shall see hereafter.

I cannot forbear relating here an adventure which will acquaint the reader with the character of Grumbkow, and though unconnected with the memoirs of my life, it may nevertheless be thought entertaining. The Queen had among her maids of honour a Madam Wagnitz, who at that time was her favourite. The mother of this young person was lady of the household to the Margravine Albert,[1] the King's aunt. Madam Wagnitz concealed under the mask of devotion the most scandalous conduct. Her intriguing disposition led her to prostitute herself and her daughters to the favourites of the King, and those who were concerned in administration ; by these means she was informed of the secrets of the state, which she immediately sold to the Count de Rottembourg,[2] the French ambassador.

In order to attain her ends, Madam Wagnitz procured the assistance of M. Creutz, a favourite of the King.[3] This man was a son of a farmer. From the situation of paymaster of a regiment, he had ascended to the rank of director of finances and minister of state. His mind was as

[1] Presumably the wife of Albert Frederick, the youngest son of the Great Elector by his second marriage.

[2] Count Alexander Conrad de Rottembourg was the French Ambassador in Berlin from 1714 to 1728.

[3] Ehrenreich Boguslaus von Creutz (*c.* 1670–1733), the son of a domain bailiff in Brandenburg, and a typical example of a civil servant of Frederick William's. He studied law in Frankfurt, and impressed Frederick William, who was then still crown prince while he was serving as an auditor in his regiment. After 1713 he was made a privy councillor and general controller of the heads of all the royal treasuries. Frederick William had complete faith in Creutz's financial integrity, but as an upstart he could not fail to arouse disdain at the court, not least from Wilhelmina herself.

low as his birth ; it was a compound of all vices. Although
his disposition was so much like that of Grumbkow, yet they
were sworn enemies, being reciprocally jealous of the King's
favour. Creutz had gained the good will of the King, by the
pains which he had taken to increase the royal treasure and
to augment the King's revenues, at the expence of his poor
subjects. He was delighted with Madam Wagnitz's
projects ; they were comformable to his views. By giving a
mistress to the King, he created a support for himself, and
thought he might succeed in destroying Grumbkow's
favour and obtaining the sole possession of the King's ear,
and of public affairs. He undertook to instruct the future
sultana in the steps she was to take to accomplish her
purpose. But several interviews which he had with her,
inspired him with a strong passion for the young lady. He
was immensely rich. Her cruelty was soon disarmed by his
magnificent presents ; she gave herself up to him, but
without losing sight of the first plan. Creutz had secret
emissaries about the King's person ; these wretches
endeavoured, by various observations seasonably introduced,
to inspire him with aversion for the Queen. They even
praised the beauty of Madam Wagnitz, and neglected no
opportunity of extolling the felicity of possessing such a
charming person. Grumbkow, who had spies every where,
was soon acquainted with these proceedings. He had no
objection to the King's having mistresses, but he wished
him to have them of his choosing. He therefore determined
to defeat this intrigue, and to employ the same weapons
which Creutz intended to use for his destruction. Madam
Wagnitz was an angelic beauty, but of a weak understanding. She had been badly educated ; her heart was as
depraved as that of her mother, and to this depravity she
added an insupportable haughtiness ; her slandering
tongue knew no mercy against those who had the misfortune of displeasing her.

Hence it may easily be supposed, that she had scarcely
any friends. Having caused her to be narrowly watched,

Grumbkow was informed, that she had long conferences with Creutz, and that it appeared, they did not always turn on state affairs. To obtain complete information, he employed a scullion whom he found artful enough for the part he was to perform. He fixed the time when the King and Queen were at Stralsund to execute his plan. One night when all were buried in sleep, a terrible noise was heard in the palace. Every one awoke, thinking the building was on fire : but how great was the surprise to hear that it was a ghost which caused all that noise. The centinels placed before the apartments of my brother and my own, were half dead with fear, and declared they had seen the spectre pass by and entering a gallery which led to the apartments of the maids of honour to the Queen. The officer on duty immediately placed double guards before our apartments, and then searched the whole palace himself without discovering any thing. However, the ghost re-appeared as soon as the officer had retired, and he frightened the centinels so much that they were found deprived of sensation. They said *it was the great fiend sent by the Swedish sorcerers, to kill the Prince Royal.*

The next day the alarm spread all over the town. People were afraid it might be some plot of the Swedes, who, with the assistance of this spectre, might set fire to the palace and attempt to carry off my brother and me. Every necessary precaution was taken for our safety, and for the purpose of catching the ghost. It was only on the third night that this pretended fiend was caught. Grumbkow, through his credit, found means to have him examined by his own creatures. He treated the whole as a joke, and made the King change the severe punishment, which he wanted to inflict on the wretch, into that of being carried about three successive days on a wooden ass with all his ghostly attire. In the mean time Grumbkow was informed by this spectre of what he wanted to know, viz. the nocturnal interviews of Creutz and Miss Wagnitz. Moreover the waiting woman of the latter, whom he found means to bribe with large sums, informed him that her mistress had already miscarried once, and that she then actually was in a state of pregnancy. He waited for the return of the King to Berlin, to make him acquainted with this scandalous story.

The King was highly irritated against Miss Wagnitz ; he wished to have her immediately banished from court : but the Queen, by her earnest intreaties, obtained that she should be suffered to remain a little longer, till some pretence could be found for dismissing her with a good grace. It was with great difficulty that the King granted this respite ; he required however of the Queen, that her dismission should be notified to her that very day. He related all her intrigues and the pains she had taken to become his mistress. The Queen, who felt for that creature a predilection which she could not overcome, sent for her, and spoke to her in the presence of Madam de Roucoule, who would not leave her in her then state of pregnancy. The Queen acquainted her with the orders of the King and repeated what the monarch had said : *You must submit to the will of the sovereign,* added the Queen. *I expect to be brought to bed in three months' time. If I give birth to a son, the first thing I shall do will be to solicit your pardon.* But far from acknowledging the kindness of the Queen, Miss Wagnitz would scarcely listen to her Majesty to the end of her speech, and declared bluntly that she had powerful patrons, by whom she was sure to be protected.

The Queen was going to reply : but Miss Wagnitz fell into so violent a passion, that she vented a thousand imprecations against her Majesty and the infant in her womb. Her rage threw her into convulsions. Madam de Roucoule led away the Queen who was terrified. But as her Majesty still hoped to soften the King, she did not wish to make his Majesty acquainted with this conversation. Miss Wagnitz herself however destroyed these kind intentions. She posted the next day a violent libel against the King and Queen, and was soon discovered as the author. Unwilling to carry his lenity any farther, the King banished her ignominiously from Court. Her mother soon followed her into banishment. Grumbkow informed the King of the intrigues of that lady with the French Ambassador. She was fortunate in undergoing no greater punishment than exile, instead of being confined in a fortress for the remainder of her life. Creutz maintained himself in the good graces of the Monarch, in spite of the pains taken by his antagonist to work his ruin. The Queen was soon consoled for the loss of Miss Wagnitz ; whose situation as favorite was given to Madam de Blaspil. The Queen was delivered of a son some time after this pretty adventure. His birth diffused universal joy. He was christened William.[1] This prince died of a dysentery in 1719. The sister of the Margrave of Schwedt was in the same year (1715) married to the hereditary Prince of Württemberg. The caprices of that Princess caused the Duchy of Württemberg to fall into the hands of the Catholics.

I shall close this year with relating the accomplishment of one of the prophecies of the Swedish officer. Count Poniatowski arrived at that time *incognito* at Berlin, whither he had been sent by Charles XII. King of Sweden. As the Count had been intimately acquainted with the Grand Marshal de Printzen,[2] when they were both Ambassadors in Russia, he applied to him to obtain a secret audience from the King. His Majesty went towards night to M. de Printzen, who lodged in the palace at that time. Count Poniatowski made some very advantageous proposals from the court of Sweden to the King, and concluded with his Majesty a treaty which has always been kept so carefully secret, that I never could learn more than two articles of it : the first, that the King of Sweden would cede for ever Swedish Pomerania to the Prussian Monarch, and that the latter should pay a very considerable sum by way of indem-

---

[1] Ludwig Karl Wilhelm (born in March 1717).
[2] Marquard Ludwig, Freiherr von Printzen (1675–1725) had been in Moscow in 1699 and 1701.

nity. The second article stipulated my marriage with the Swedish monarch ; it was determined, that at twelve years of age, I should be sent to Sweden, to be educated there.[1]

Hitherto I could only relate facts with which I was not personally concerned. I was but eight. My tender years would not allow me to take a share in what was passing. All my time was taken up with my masters, and my only recreation was to see my brother. Never was affection equal to ours. His understanding was good, but his disposition gloomy. He was long considering before he returned an answer : but then his answers were just. He had great difficulty in learning, and it was expected that in time he would be more remarkable for good sense than for wit. My vivacity on the contrary was very great. I was prompt at repartee and my memory was excellent. The King was passionately fond of me : he never paid so much attention to any of his children as to me. But my brother was odious to him, and never appeared before him but to be ill used ; this inspired the Prince Royal with an invincible fear of his father, which grew up with him even to the age of maturity.

The King and Queen took a second journey to Hanover. The Swedish and the Prussian monarchs, having both maturely weighed the alliance which was to unite their houses, had found our ages too disproportionate and agreed to break off the match. The King of Prussia resolved to renew the alliance, which had already been in agitation, with the Duke of Gloucester.[2]

King George I of England gladly assented to this plan :

[1] The Polish Count Stanislas Poniatowski (1677–1762) was a close adviser of Charles XII. His son Stanislas-August later becams the last King of Poland. J. G. Droysen (*Geschichte der Preussischen Politik*, IV, ii (Leipzig 1873) 36) states that this paragraph is fictitious and that Poniatowski was in Berlin merely to obtain a safe-conduct. However, though Prussia and Sweden were at war, secret peace efforts were being made (see, for instance, R. Wittram, *Peter I* (Göttingen, 1964), II 305ff), and suggestions of a marriage occur in letters printed in the *Hohenzollernjahrbuch 1917.*

[2] This paragraph is a figment of Wilhelmina's imagination. George I

but he wished that a double marriage might draw still closer the ties of their friendship, viz. the marriage of my brother with Princess Amelia, second sister of the Duke of Gloucester. This double alliance was resolved upon to the great satisfaction of the Queen, who had always so ardently wished for it. Her Majesty brought the bridal rings to my brother and me. I even opened a correspondence with my little admirer and received several presents of him. Prince Anhalt and Grumbkow were still continuing their intrigues. The birth of my second brother had only deranged their projects, without inducing them to lose sight of them : but the time for their execution was not yet arrived.

The new alliance, which the King had just entered into with England, did not appear a great obstacle to surmount. As the interests of the Houses of Brandenburg and Hanover had always been opposed, they fully expected that their union would not be of long duration. They were perfectly acquainted with the disposition of the King, who easily suffered himself to be irritated, and, in his first gust of passion, never kept within bounds and always deviated from true policy. They therefore resolved calmly to wait until they should meet with an incident conformable to their views. It was in this year that a secret conspiracy, formed by a certain *Clement*, was discovered. He was accused of high treason, of having counterfeited the sign manual of several great princes, and attempted to embroil several powers. This Clement was at the Hague, and had frequently written to the King. His bad conscience would not allow him to leave that asylum, and the King had been unable to draw him into his dominions. His Majesty at last employed a Calvinist clergyman, named Jablonski to get possession of that man. Jablonski, who had been

had returned to England in January 1717. At this time Anglo-Prussian relations were at a low ebb, on account of Frederick William's growing friendship with Russia. Droysen op. cit., 207, quotes Frederick William's note written in February 1717 : " *Gut mit dem Zaaren zusammen Frieden. England will ich mit dem grössten Plaisir, und auch wenn ich etwas Schaden dabei haben sollte, im Stich lassen.*"

his fellow student, went into Holland, and so completely persuaded him of the good reception and the honours which awaited him at the court of Prussia, that he at last prevailed with him to come to Berlin. As soon as Clement had set his foot in the county of Cleves, he was arrested. It has always been supposed that Clement was of distinguished extraction. Some pretended he was a natural son of the King of Denmark, and others of the Duke of Orleans, Regent of France. The great likeness he bore to the latter induced a belief that he was related to that prince. He was put upon his trial immediately after his arrival at Berlin. Report says that he unveiled Grumbkow's intrigues to the King, and offered to justify his accusation by the letters of that minister, which he was ready to deliver into the hands of the monarch. Grumbkow was on the brink of ruin : but Clement fortunately could not produce the letters he had promised ; his accusation was therefore treated as calumnious. The circumstances of his trial have constantly been kept so secret, that I never could learn more than the few details which I have related.

The trial lasted six months, at the end of which he was condemned to be pinched three times with red hot pincers, and then hanged. He heard his sentence with heroical firmness, and without any alteration in his countenance. *My life*, said he, *is in the King's hands. I have not deserved death. I have but done what the King's ministers are doing every day ; they endeavour to cheat and to deceive those of other powers, and are but honest spies at foreign courts. Had I had my credentials like them, I should perhaps now be at the pinnacle of glory, instead of being lodged at the top of the gallows.*

His fortitude did not fail him to the last. He may be ranked among men of great genius. His erudition was very extensive. He spoke several languages, and delighted his hearers with his eloquence, which he had an opportunity to display in addressing the people. As his speech has been printed I shall not state it. Leman, one of his accomplices, was torn in pieces by horses. They had for companion of their misfortune a third individual, who was punished for a different crime. His name was *Hildeskamm* ; he had been ennobled in the reign of Frederick I. He had said and written that " the king was not a legitimate child." He was sentenced to be publicly whipped by the executioner, declared infamous, and confined in the castle of Spandau for the remainder of his life. During Clement's imprisonment the king fell dangerously ill at Brandenburg. He had a nephritic cholic, attended with a violent fever. He immediately dispatched an express to Berlin, to inform the Queen of his situation, and to request her to join him.[1]

The Queen set out instantly, and travelled with such haste that she arrived at Brandenburg in the evening. She found the King extremely ill, and busy making his will, as he thought his death very near. Those to whom he dictated his last dispositions were persons of probity and of known fidelity. The Queen was appointed regent of the kingdom during the minority of my brother, and the Emperor and the King of England were named his guardians. No mention was made of either Grumbkow or the Prince of Anhalt : from what motive I do not know. The King had however sent them an express a few hours before the arrival of the Queen, and ordered them to come to him. I do not know what incident delayed their departure. The King had not signed his will : it is probable that he sent for them to acquaint them with its contents, and perhaps to insert some clause in their behalf. He was so offended at

[1] Wilhelmina does not really explain what the " Clement " plot really was. Probably relying on biased information from her mother, she separates Clement from the plot described below to assassinate the king, when in fact both are the same as well as being bound up with the king's illness and depression. Frederick William believed, apparently correctly, that Clement, in reality a Hungarian nobleman, Freiherr von Rosenau, was sent by Count Flemming, chief minister of Augustus the Strong, Elector of Saxony, to create trouble between the king and the emperor which might lead to a war in which Prussia might be the loser and from which Saxony hoped to gain territorial benefits. All these events may be dated to the summer and autumn of 1718.

their delay, and his illness increased to such a degree, that he no longer deferred signing his will. A copy of it was handed to the Queen, and the original deposited in the archives of Berlin.[1] No sooner was the deed finished that the King grew calmer. Holtzendorff, the surgeon of his regiment of foot guards, employed very seasonably a remedy very fashionable at that time, *viz*. Ipecacuanha :[2] this drug saved the King's life. The fever, and the pains which he suffered, abated considerably towards morning, and great hopes were entertained of his recovery. This was the beginning of the fortune and favor of Holtzendorff, of whom I shall have occasion to speak hereafter.

In the mean time the Prince of Anhalt, and his companion of iniquity, arrived towards morning. Their presence embarrassed the King very much, as he expected from them the most cruel reproaches, for being omitted in his will. To get over this embarrassment the King made the Queen, the witnesses and those who had written the will, promise upon their oath to bury its contents in eternal silence.

But, in spite of these precautions, the two parties concerned were soon informed of what had happened. The mystery observed towards them created suspicions of the truth of the fact ; particularly as they heard that a copy of the deed had been delivered to the Queen. This was to

---

[1] This will has not been traced in the Berlin archives. Letters from the King show him to have been ill and depressed, but not seriously so. He wrote to Anhalt-Dessau in September 1718 in his peculiar German " *meine afferen in der grossten Krise sein, und in der weldt alles seht confus aussiehet* ". But as there is no mention of any will, even in the reports of the Hanoverian ambassador, whom Sophia Dorothea would have informed, it is unlikely to have existed. The Queen, the Austrian ambassador Seckendorff reported to Vienna, had no influence over the King, who never consulted her. At the beginning of his reign one solitary instruction of 27 June 1714 indicated that if during a crisis the King should be indisposed, the Queen should be consulted. This is what Sophia Dorothea and through her Wilhelmina probably interpreted as a " regency ".

[2] A common eighteenth-century drug derived from a South American root plant, which caused excessive vomiting.

them a fatal blow. The King was better, but not yet completely out of danger ; they durst not mention any thing about it, as the least emotion might have endangered his life. But their uneasiness was soon removed : his illness abated so rapidly that he was perfectly recovered in a week. As soon as he was able to walk out he returned to Berlin ; thence he went to Wusterhausen, whither he was followed by the Queen. The King grew every day more suspicious and distrustful. Ever since Clement's intrigues had been discovered, all the letters that left and entered Berlin were examined ; he never laid down without having near his bed his sword and a pair of loaded pistols. The sleep of the Prince of Anhalt and Grumbkow was equally disturbed ; the business of the royal will distressed them, and they had not given up their former plans. The King and my brother were both in rather a weak state of health, and my second brother was yet in the cradle. The arts they employed enabled them to learn the contents of that interesting deed, and, perhaps, to get it out of the hands of the Queen ; they had no doubt that, provided they could succeed in effecting this, they should be able to cause the will to be annulled, to set the King at variance with the Queen, and to accomplish their designs. They proceeded in this manner. I have already mentioned Madam de Blaspil, as a favourite with the Queen ; this lady might pass for a beauty : the charms of her person were enhanced by the solidity and cheerfulness of her understanding. Her heart was noble and upright : but two essential faults, which are unfortunately inherent in most females, eclipsed these brilliant qualities : she was fond of intrigue, and coquetish. A gouty and disagreeable husband of sixty was not very captivating to a young person.[1] Many even pretend that she lived with him as the Empress Pulcheria with the Emperor Marcianus. Count Manteuffel, the Saxon ambassador at the Court of

---

[1] Madame de Blaspil's husband, Johann Moritz von Blaspil, had been General War Commissar, until he was replaced by Grumbkow in 1717. This would explain her fruitless vendetta against Grumbkow.

Prussia, had moved her heart. Their amorous intercourse had been conducted with so much secrecy, that there had never been the least suspicion raised against the virtue of the lady. To console himself for the absence of her he loved, he wrote to her by every mail, and as regularly received her answers. This fatal correspondence caused Madam de Blaspil's misfortune ; her letters, and those of her lover, fell into the hands of the King.

This distrustful prince supposed them concerned in state intrigues, and to clear up his suspicions he showed the letters to Grumbkow. The latter, better versed in the language of love than the King, immediately guessed the truth. Without seeming to take any notice of it, he considered this incident as the most fortunate he could have met with. He was an intimate friend of Count Manteuffel, and in great favour with the King of Poland. This monarch[1] was particularly anxious to keep on good terms with the Court of Berlin. Charles XII. of Sweden was yet alive ; this circumstance made him continually apprehensive of fresh revolutions in Poland, against which he might be protected by the support of my royal father. Grumbkow promised him his assistance, and engaged to maintain the good harmony between the two courts, if the Polish monarch would enter into his views, and give proper instructions on that head to Count Manteuffel. The King of Poland consented without hesitation, and sent that minister back to Berlin. Grumbkow acquainted him with the whole affair of the King's will ; and let him know, at the same time, that he was informed of his love intrigue with Madam de Blaspil, and that the service which he requested of him consisted in prevailing with that lady to get the King's will out of the hands of the Queen. It was a delicate business. Manteuffel knew Madam de Blaspil's attachment to the Queen ; however he ventured to break the matter to her. It was with great difficulty that Madam de Blaspil complied with his request ; but love made her at

[1] i.e. Augustus the Strong.

length forget what she owed to herself and to her mistress.
Dazzled by the attachment which Manteuffel professed to
the Queen, Madam de Blaspil thought the matter not of
very great consequence, and availing herself of the absolute
empire which she had over that princess, she assumed so
many different parts, till at last she succeeded in persuading
her to trust her with that fatal deed, on condition, however,
to return it after perusal.

. . . .

. . . .

which followed was not less fruitful in events. As soon as
Count Manteuffel saw himself in possession of the King's
will, he took a copy of it, and sent it to Grumbkow. But the
object of the latter was only half-attained : he wished to
get the original will. By proceeding with address, he did
not despair of obtaining it in time. The Queen was beginning to gain an ascendancy over the King's mind : she
procured him recruits for his regiment, and the King of
England shewed him great attention. The coolness with
which the King had replied to the solicitations of the Prince
of Anhalt and Grumbkow, to marry me to the Margrave of
Schwedt, had made them sensible that they were declining
in favour. Several circumstances concurred to confirm
them in this idea. The King latterly had seldom appeared
in public ; he was afflicted with a kind of hypochondria : he
saw no one but the Queen and his children, and dined
privately with us. To prevent their disgrace, they attempted to diminish the credit of the Queen.

From the portrait which I have drawn of the King, it may
be observed that he was easily irritated, and that one of his
principal faults was an excessive love of money. Grumbkow
wished to avail himself of these weaknesses. He imparted
his design to Mr. de Kamecke, minister of state. But this
honest man informed the Queen of the attempt. This
princess was fond of play, and had lost considerable sums,
which had forced her to borrow secretly a capital of 30,000

dollars (£5,000 sterling). The King had recently presented her with a pair of broached diamond earrings, of very great value. She wore them but rarely, because she had often dropped them. Grumbkow, who had spies everywhere, was soon acquainted with the bad situation of her affairs ; and supposing that the Queen had pawned these ear-rings to procure the money I have mentioned, he resolved to communicate the matter to the King, whom he knew sufficiently well to be certain before-hand, that he would be highly incensed. The Queen did not fail to forewarn her royal consort of the circumstance, and to complain of the accusations that were meditated against her. Exasperated at Grumbkow's base attempt, she intreated the King to allow her to chastise him for it. But upon the King's observing that no one ought to be punished without sufficient proofs, she had the imprudence to confess that it was from Mr. de Kamecke that she had received her information. The King sent for him instantly. The gracious manner in which he was received, encouraged him to persist in what he had imparted to the Queen. He even added several circumstances very prejudicial to Grumbkow. But having been acquainted with his projects merely by conversations which he had had with him, without any witnesses, the denial of Grumbkow prevailed, and Kamecke was sent to Spandau.—This fortress, which is only at the distance of two German miles from Berlin, was shortly after filled with illustrious prisoners.

A Silesian nobleman of the name of Trosqui had just been arrested. He had acted as a spy in the Swedish camp during the attack of Stralsund. Though his services had been useful to the King, yet the King entertained no esteem for him, and secretly distrusted him. He was accused of having performed at Berlin the same part which he had acted in the Swedish camp : and his papers, which were seized, corroborated the accusation in some degree. Trosqui was a man of great genius, and wrote with much spirit : these two talents supplied the want of personal beauty.

His desk contained all the love-anecdotes of the court, of which he had made a severe satirical description, and a great number of letters written to him by several Berlin ladies, in which the monarch was not spared. Those of Madam de Blaspil were especially violent against the King, whom she styled a tyrant and *a horrible scriblifax*.[1] Grumbkow, who was appointed to examine these papers, availed himself of this opportunity to ruin this lady. He had entrusted her with part of his projects, in hopes of bringing her over to his party, and obtaining the King's will. Madam de Blaspil, who had seen through his designs, had amused him with false promises, in order to wrest from him his secrets. As she had not sufficient evidence against him, and Kamecke's misfortune being still recent, she dared not to venture upon a discovery to the King until she was provided with convincing proofs. Grumbkow having put into the King's hands the letters which she had written to Trosqui, and prepossessed him very much against her ; his Majesty sent for her, and after having addressed her in very harsh terms, he showed her these fatal letters. Madam de Blaspil, not dismayed on seeing her own hand-writing, and knowing the contents to be true, took that opportunity to reproach the King with his faults ; adding that, notwithstanding what she had written against him, she was more attached to his Majesty than any one else was ; being the only one who had the boldness to speak to him with frankness and sincerity. Her energetic and ingenuous speech made a strong impression upon the King. After some consideration he replied : " I forgive you, and I thank you for your manner of behaving. You have convinced me that you are my real friend, by speaking the truth to me. Let us both forget the past, and be friends." Whereupon he took her by the hand, and leading her to the Queen, he

[1] The English translation reads equally mysteriously " *cribli-fax* ". But despite ingenious suggestions that this derives from *criblé* (pock-marked) and means " one who propagates the pox ", it seems more likely that scriblifax, as in the original French, was the name of some character in a satire.

said : " This is an honest woman, for whom I feel much esteem."

Madam de Blaspil, notwithstanding, was by no means at ease : she was acquainted with all the circumstances of the wicked design, which Grumbkow and the Prince of Anhalt were plotting against the sovereign and my brother ; she saw it on the point of being carried into effect, and knew not what to resolve, as there was evidently equal danger in speaking or continuing silent.—But it is time to unveil this horrible mystery : the views of the two companions of iniquity were directed to place the Margrave of Schwedt on the throne, and to usurp the government.

Both the King and the Prince-Royal were daily improving in health ; and this circumstance dissipated all the flattering hopes which Anhalt and Grumbkow had conceived of their approaching demise. They resolved to remove this bar to their measures : the business was delicate ; nothing less than the royal lives were at stake ; and the conspirators only waited for a favourable opportunity to execute their infamous design : and such an opportunity soon presented itself, agreeably to their wishes. There had been for some time a company of rope-dancers at Berlin, who performed German plays on a pretty stage erected in the New market ; the King was highly entertained with them, and never omitted to attend their performances.—This spot was selected by the conspirators, for the scene of their detestable tragedy. They wished my brother to be also present, that they might at once immolate the two victims to their abominable ambition. The palace and the stage were to be set on fire at the same moment, to avert all suspicion from them ; and the King and my brother were to be strangled during the confusion which the conflagration would inevitably cause, as it was only a wooden barrack, with very narrow entrances, and always excessively crowded, which must have facilitated the attempt. Their party was so strong, that they were sure to usurp the regency during the absence of the Margrave of Schwedt, who was still in Italy ;

particularly as the army was subservient to the Prince of
Anhalt, by whom it was commanded, and who possessed the
affections of the soldiers. It is probable that Manteuffel,
abhorring this dreadful conspiracy, discovered it to Madam
de Blaspil, and mentioned to her the day on which it was to
take place. I remember perfectly well . . . .
Grumbkow urged the King to take my brother to the play,
under the pretence that he ought to dissipate his gloom, and
enliven him by cheerful diversions. This was on a Wednes-
day : the Friday following was fixed upon for the execution
of their plan. The King having nothing to oppose to such
arguments, assented. Madame de Blaspil, who was present,
and knew their design, shuddered with horror. Unable to
remain any longer silent, she intimidated the Queen, without acquainting her with what was in agitation, and advised
her to prevent, at any rate, my brother's attending the
King. The Queen, knowing my brother's timid disposition,
inspired him with such a dread of the theatre, that he cried
whenever it was mentioned. Friday at length arrived ;
and the Queen, after having lavished many endearments
upon me, ordered me to amuse the King, so as to make him
forget the play ; adding, that if I could not otherwise
succeed, and that the King still persisted in wishing to take
my brother with him, I was to bemoan, weep, and use every
effort to detain him. To impress it more strongly upon my
mind, she told me that my life and my brother's were at
stake.—I acted my part so well, that it was half past six
before the King was aware of it ; when, rising all at once,
and walking towards the door, leading his son by the hand,
the latter began to struggle, and utter piercing cries. The
King, surprized, attempted to comfort him by gentle means ;
but seeing that his efforts were unavailing, and that the
poor boy would not follow him, he was going to strike him.
The Queen opposed it : but the King, taking the boy in his
arms, strove to carry him away by main force. I then
threw myself at his feet, which I embraced and bedewed
with my tears. The Queen placed herself against the door,

intreating the King to stay that day in the palace. The Monarch, astonished at this strange behaviour, demanded an explanation.

The Queen knew not what to reply : but the King, naturally suspicious, conjectured that there was some conspiracy against him. Trosqui's trial was not yet over : he supposed the apprehensions of the Queen to proceed from that quarter. Having earnestly entreated her to inform him of the ground of her fears, she contented herself with replying, that his life and my brother's were at stake : without naming Madam de Blaspil. This lady being with the Queen in the evening, thought that, after the scene which had taken place, she could no longer remain silent. She therefore discovered the whole plot to Her Majesty, and conjured her to procure her the next day a secret audience from the King. This the Queen easily obtained.

Madam de Blaspil having informed the Monarch of all the particulars with which she was acquainted, the King asked whether she would, in the presence of Grumbkow, substantiate what she had asserted : and as her answer was in the affirmative, the minister was immediately sent for. He had taken his precautions before hand, and had no cause to be afraid. The attorney-general Katsch,[1] a man of obscure origin, was indebted to him for his fortune. Full worthy of Grumbkow's protection, and the lively image of the " unjust judge " of the gospel, he was feared and abhorred by all honest people. Grumbkow, besides, had a great number of his creatures in the courts of justice and offices of administration. He therefore appeared boldly before the King ; who communicated to him the evidence of Madam de Blaspil. Grumbkow protested that he was innocent ; exclaiming that it was impossible to be a faithful minister, without being exposed to persecutions ; and that it was sufficiently apparent, from Madam de Blaspil's letters to Trosqui, that this lady only sought to carry on an intrigue, and to set the Court at variance. He cast himself at the feet

---

[1] Christoph von Katsch (1665–1729), Minister of Criminal Justice.

of the Monarch, entreated him to have the matter rigorously and impartially inquired into, and offered authentic proofs of the falsehood of the accusations.

The King then sent for Katsch, as Grumbkow had foreseen. In spite of his intrigues, he was tottering on the brink of ruin : but Katsch saved him. He had an astonishing talent for perplexing the culprits who had the misfortune to have him for their judge : they were disconcerted by his captious and artful interrogatories. Madam de Blaspil fell a victim to his artifices : she could not bring any proofs of her accusations, which were accordingly treated as calumnies. Katsch seeing the King in a violent passion, proposed to put her to the rack. A vestige of regard for her sex and rank spared her this ignominy : the King contented himself with sending her that very evening to Spandau, whither Trosqui was conducted some days after. Madam de Blaspil supported her change of fortune with heroical firmness. She was at first treated with severity and harshness : she continued three days shut up in a damp room with a grated window, without either bed or furniture ; receiving only what was absolutely necessary for the support of life.

Although the Queen was pregnant, the King did not spare her ; and communicated to her in a very harsh manner, the misfortune of her favourite. Her Majesty was so grieved at it, that fears were entertained of a miscarriage. Independently of her friendship for Madam de Blaspil, she felt greatly alarmed at the recollection that the King's will was yet in the hands of that lady. Her uneasiness was relieved by a fortunate incident. Field-Marshal de Natzmer, a man of great merit and acknowledged probity, was ordered to put his seal upon Madam de Blaspil's papers. The Queen employed Boshart her chaplain to acquaint the Marshal with her uneasiness, and to intreat him to let her have the King's will. The chaplain forcibly represented the danger to which the Queen would be exposed, if that deed were found, and acquitted himself so well of his commission, that he prevailed with her Marshal to comply with the request of Her Majesty : which compliance frustrated Grumbkow's designs. Nothing suspicious was discovered among Madam de Blaspil's papers, and all farther proceedings were stopped.

I have been informed of the details which I have just written, by the Queen my mother : they were known to very few persons : the Queen had carefully kept them secret ; and my brother, since his accession to the throne, caused all the writings relating to the trial to be committed to the flames. Madam de Blaspil was set at liberty at the end of twelve months, and her confinement changed into banishment to the Duchy of Cleves. The King, who saw her some years after, behaved with great kindness to her, and forgave her for the past : and after the death of my father, the King my brother, with a view to gratify the Queen my mother, appointed her governess to my two younger sisters ; and she holds that situation at present. (1744.)

The patience of the Monarch was at length exhausted by this rapid succession of intrigues at Berlin. His under-standing was too acute not to discern that Prince Anhalt and Grumbkow could not be perfectly innocent. He there-fore sought to put an end at once to all their petty intrigues, and resolved to dispose of the Margrave of Schwedt in marriage. The close alliance which he had contracted with Russia made him turn his eyes to that quarter. M. de Martenfeld, his Envoy at Petersburg, was ordered to demand the Duchess of Courland (afterwards Empress)[1] in marriage for that Prince. The Czar showed himself very willing to accede to the wishes of the Prussian Monarch. The Margrave of Schwedt was therefore recalled from Italy, where he happened to be at that time. As soon as he was arrived at Berlin, the King proposed this alliance to him : he represented how advantageous it would be, and how well calculated to satisfy his ambition. But this Prince, who still hoped to marry me, peremptorily refused to comply with

[1] Anna Ivanova (1693–1740) the daughter of Ivan, brother of Peter the Great. She became_Empress in 1730.

the King's wishes. As he was eighteen years old and of age, the Monarch could not force him to obey ; and the business was dropped.

I forgot to mention, in the preceding year, the arrival of the Czar Peter the Great at Berlin. The anecdote is curious enough to deserve a place in these memoirs. The Czar, who was uncommonly fond of travelling, was coming from Holland. He had been obliged to stop in the Duchy of Cleves, where the Czarina had miscarried. As he disliked magnificence and society, he requested the King to lodge him in a summer-house which the Queen had in one of the suburbs of Berlin. Her Majesty was extremely sorry for this : she had erected a very pretty building, which she had decorated in a style of great splendour. The porcelain-gallery was superb, and all the rooms were adorned with beautiful glasses. As this charming retreat was really a jewel, it was called *Mon-Bijou*. A very pretty garden on the banks of the river heightened its beauty.

In order to prevent the mischief which the Russian gentlemen had done in other places where they had lodged, the Queen ordered the principal furniture, and whatever was most brittle, to be removed. The Czar, his spouse, and their court, arrived some days after by water at Mon-Bijou. The King and the Queen received them on their landing ; and the King handed the Czarina from the boat. The Czar was no sooner landed, than he held out his hand to the King, and said : *I am glad to see you, brother Frederick.* He afterwards approached the Queen with the intention to salute her ; but she pushed him back. The Czarina first kissed the Queen's hands several times ; and afterwards introduced to her the Duke and Duchess of Mecklenburg, who had accompanied them, and four hundred pretended ladies of their suite. These were mostly German servant-girls, who officiated as maids of honour, waiting-maids, cooks, and washer-women. Almost every one of these creatures carried in her arms a richly dressed infant : and when they were asked, whether these children were their own ? they answered, prostrating themselves in the Russian fashion : *the Czar has done me the honour to make me the mother of this child.* The Queen would not speak to these creatures ; and the Czarina, to be revenged, treated the Princesses of the blood with much haughtiness ; and it was with very great difficulty that the King prevailed with the Queen to notice the Russian ladies. I saw the whole of this Court, the next day, when the Czar and Czarina came to visit the Queen. Her Majesty received them in the state-rooms of the palace, and went to meet them in the hall of the guards. The Queen gave her hand to the Czarina placing her at her right and conducted her into the audience hall.

The King and the Czar followed. As soon as the latter saw me, he knew me again, having seen me five years before. He took me up in his arms, and rubbed the very skin off my face with his rude kisses. I boxed his ears, and struggled as much as I could, saying that I would not allow any such familiarities ; and that he was dishonouring me. He laughed very much at this idea, and amused himself a long time at my expence. I had previously been instructed what to say : and I spoke to him of his fleet and his con-quests ; which delighted him so much, that he several times told the Czarina, that if he could have a child like me, he would willingly give up one of his provinces. The Czarina also tenderly caressed me. She and the Queen placed themselves under the canopy, each in an arm-chair : I was by the side of the Queen, and the Princesses of the blood opposite to Her Majesty.

The Czarina was short and stout, very tawny, and her figure was altogether destitute of gracefulness. Its appearance sufficiently betrayed her low origin. To have judged by her attire, one would have taken her for a German stage actress. Her robe had been purchased at an old-clothes broker : it was made in the antique fashion, and heavily laden with silver and grease. The front of her stays was adorned with jewels, singularly placed : they represented a double eagle, badly set, the wings of which were of small stones. She wore a dozen orders and as many portraits of saints and relics, fastened to the facing of her gown : so that when she walked, the jumbling of all these orders and portraits one against the other, made a tinkling noise like a mule in harness.

The Czar, on the contrary, was very tall and pretty well made : his face was handsome, but his countenance had something savage about it, which inspired fear. He was dressed as a navy-officer, and wore a plain coat. The Czarina, who spoke very bad German, and did not well understand what was spoken to her by the Queen, beckoned to her fool, and conversed with her in Russian. This poor creature was a Princess Galitzin, who had been necessitated to fulfil that office in order to save her life : having been implicated in a conspiracy against the Czar, she had twice undergone the punishment of the *knout*. I do not know what she said to the Czarina, but the latter every now and then laughed aloud.

At length we sat down to table ; where the Czar placed himself near the Queen. It is well known, that this Prince had been poisoned in his youth : a very subtile venom had attacked his nerves, whence he was frequently subject to certain involuntary convulsions. He was seized with a fit whilst at table : he made many contortions ; and as he was violently gesticulating with a knife in his hand near the Queen, the latter was afraid, and wanted several times to rise from her seat. The Czar begged her to be easy, protesting that he should not do her any harm ; and at the same time seized her hand, which he squeezed so violently that the Queen screamed for mercy, which made him laugh heartily ; and he observed that the bones of her Majesty were more delicate than those of his Catharine. Every thing was prepared for a ball after supper : but he ran away as soon as he rose from table, and went back alone and on foot to Mon-Bijou.

The next day every thing worth seeing at Berlin was

shewn to him ; and among the rest, the cabinet of medals and antique statues. There was among the latter, as I have been told, one that represented a Heathen divinity in a very indecent attitude : it was with the ancient Romans an ornament of their nuptial chambers. It was considered as a very great rarity, and passed for one of the finest that was ever found. The Czar admired it much, and ordered the Czarina to kiss it. She wished to excuse herself : but he grew angry, and said to her, in broken German, *kopf ab* ; which signifies : " I shall have your head cut off, if you do not obey." The Czarina was so alarmed at this, that she submitted to whatever he required. He, without ceremony, asked for this statue and several others, which the king could not refuse. He did the same with a cabinet lined with amber : it was unique in its kind, and had cost immense sums to Frederick I : and this too had the misfortune to be taken to Petersburg and to the great regret of every one.

Two days afterwards this court of barbarians at length set out on their journey back. The Queen immediately hastened to Mon-Bijou : and what desolation was there visible. I never beheld any thing like it : indeed, I think Jerusalem, after its siege and capture, could not have presented such another scene. This elegant palace was left by them in so ruinous a state, that the Queen was absolutely obliged to rebuild nearly the whole of it.[1]

---

[1] This meeting, which took place in September 1717, was the seventh between the two monarchs, and also Peter's last visit to a Western European court. It confirmed an alliance struck the previous year at Havelberg, but the death of Charles XII soon afterwards led to a decline in the friendship of Prussia with Russia, as that with England began to rise. Wilhelmina's description of the visit is not exaggerated. Other contemporary accounts quoted by Wittram (op. cit., 585), tell of similar stories of the drunken behaviour of the Czar's entourage, and it compares favourably with John Evelyn's description of how he was allowed £150 by the crown to repair his house in Deptford after the Tsar had stayed there in 1698.

II

I am introduced to adversity — My education in the claws of a fury — At the point of death — A new governess — My figure is in doubt — Marriage plans — A visit from the King of England — I receive an English compliment.

BUT I must now return to my subject, from which I have but too long digressed.—My brother had entered his seventh year in the month of January ; and the King thought proper to take him out of the hands of Madam de Roucoule, and to place him under the tuition of proper governors. Cabals revived on this occasion. The Queen wished to chuse the governors ; and the two favourites were equally zealous to appoint their own creatures. Both were successful. The Queen prevailed with the Monarch to select General (afterwards Field-Marshal) Count Finkenstein,[1] a very honest man, universally esteemed for both his probity and his military talents, but whose confined genius rendered him rather incapable of imparting a good education to a young prince destined for the throne. He was one of those men who, imagining themselves to be possessed of a brilliant understanding, pretend to be great politicians, and, in short, indulge in high-sounding but inconclusive arguments. He had married the sister of Madam de Blaspil. His lady, fortunately, surpassed him in capacity, and completely governed him.

Prince Anhalt appointed the sub-governor. His name was de Kalkstein ;[2] and he was colonel of a regiment of foot.

[1] General Count Albrecht-Konrad Fink de Finkenstein. His son, Karl Wilhelm, born in 1714, was Prussian Minister of Foreign Affairs from 1749 until his death in 1800.

[2] Colonel Christoph-Wilhelm von Kalkstein.

The choice was worthy of its author. M. de Kalkstein is of an intriguing disposition. He had been educated in a convent of Jesuits, and profited by their lessons. He affects much devotion, and even bigotry : he always speaks of his probity, and has induced many to think him an honest man. His mind is subtle and insinuating : but, under all this fair outward appearance, he conceals the blackest soul. By his daily and sinister reports of the most innocent actions of his royal pupil, he soured the disposition of the King, and excited his displeasure against my brother.

I shall have occasion to introduce him more than once in these Memoirs. My brother would have been very badly educated in such hands, had not a tutor been added to these two mentors. He was a Frenchman of the name of Duhan of really great merit, possessed of an enlightened understanding and extensive knowledge. It is to him that my brother is indebted for his information and for the good principles, to which he adhered as long as his tutor was with him, and preserved any ascendancy over his mind.[1]

Thus closed the year 1718. I pass to the following when I was introduced into the world, and at the same time began to experience its adversities. The King staid almost the whole of the winter at Berlin : he passed his time in going every evening to the assemblies that were given in that city. The Queen was shut up the whole day in the room of the Monarch, by his order, without any other company than my brother and myself. We used to sup with her Majesty, and there was no one besides Madam de Kamecke, the lady of her household, and Madam de Roucoule. The Queen had brought the former with her from Hanover ;

---

[1] Duhan was born in Jandun in the Champagne in 1685, the year of the Revocation of the Edict of Nantes. His father, who had been secretary to Turenne, had like many Huguenots emigrated to Prussia, where he entered the administration of the Great Elector. The younger Duhan had distinguished himself at the siege of Stralsund, which no doubt commended him to Frederick William, but he had also been educated by La Croze, and Frederick wrote of him with great affection in later life.

and though she was of distinguished merit, she yet was not honoured with her Majesty's confidence. The Queen always was plunged in a dreadful melancholy, and fears were even entertained for her health, particularly as she was in a state of pregnancy. She was however safely delivered of a princess, who was named Sophia-Dorothea.[1] The sad life which she led occasioned her melancholy. Since the loss of her favourite, she found herself absolutely forsaken. She attempted to substitute another in her place : but though there were ladies of great merit at her court, she felt no inclination towards any of them ; and, contrary to all policy, she had recourse to me : but before she opened her heart, she wished to verify certain suspicions, which she harboured against Miss Letti, upon reports that had been made to her. One day when I was caressing her, the Queen began to jest, and asked, whether I wished to be married ? I answered, " that I did not think of it ; and that I was too young." " But if you were compelled to do so, (said the Queen ;) whom would you select ; the Margrave of Schwedt, or the Duke of Gloucester ? "

" Although Miss Letti is always telling me, (replied I) that I am to marry the Margrave of Schwedt, I cannot bear him, he delights in nothing but mischief : I should prefer the Duke of Gloucester."—" But of whom (said the Queen,) have you learnt that the Margrave is so wicked ? "—" Of my good nurse ; " was my answer. The Queen then asked me several questions concerning Miss Letti. She afterwards inquired, whether she did not oblige me to tell her every thing that happened in the King's apartments and in hers ? I hesitated, not knowing what answer to return : but she interrogated me in so many different ways, that I confessed it at last. The difficulty with which she had extorted this confession, gave her a good opinion of my discretion. She first made me some false confidences, to try whether I should divulge them ; and perceiving that I had kept her secret, she felt no longer any hesitation in

[1] Sophia Dorothea Maria born in 1719.

opening herself to me. Taking me one day aside, she said : " I am satisfied with you ; and as you seem now to be capable of judging for yourself, I wish to treat you as a grown-up person, and to have you always about me. But I insist upon your not making any more reports to Miss Letti : if she ask you any questions concerning what has passed, tell her you paid no attention to it. Do you understand me ? Will you promise to do so ? "—I answered in the affirmative.—" In that case (said she) I shall confide in you : but you must be discreet, and promise to attach yourself exclusively to me." This I most solemnly promised.

The Queen afterwards related to me all the intrigues of the Prince of Anhalt ; the disgrace of Madam de Blaspil ; in short, all that I have written on this subject ; adding, that she ardently wished me to be settled in England, and that I should be very happy if I married her nephew. When she told me that her favourite was confined at Spandau, I could not help shedding tears. I had been very fond of that lady, and I learned that she was at her country-seat. My sensibility wrought upon the Queen, and she spoke to me farther concerning Miss Letti, and asked, " whether she did not receive daily visits from Colonel *Forcade*, and a French refugee clergymen, named *Fourneret ?* "—I answered that it was true indeed.—" Do you know her motive ? " rejoined the Queen—" she has been bribed by Prince Anhalt, who employs these two individuals to intrigue with her." I attempted to take her part, but the Queen bade me silent. Young as I was, I meditated much upon what I had just learnt. Though I wished to exculpate Miss Letti, I judged from many circumstances, that the Queen's information was correct. I passed the evening under much embarrassment : I dreaded Miss Letti extremely ; for she frequently used to beat me, and treat me very harshly.

As soon as I reached my room, she inquired, as usual, for the news of the day. I was sitting with her in a window upon a platform of two steps. I returned the answer which the Queen had dictated to me. She was not satisfied with it, and asked me so many questions that she fairly perplexed me. She was too clever not to remark, that I had been instructed ; and in order to be certain of it, she lavished upon me every species of endearment. But when she saw that she obtained nothing by gentle means, she put herself into a horrible passion, gave me many blows on the arm, and threw me down the steps. My agility saved me from a broken arm or leg ; and I escaped with a few contusions.

This scene was repeated the next day, but with much more violence : she threw a candlestick at my head, which had well nigh killed me ; my face was all covered with blood. My cries attracted my good Meermann who snatched me from the claws of that fury : she chid her severely, and threatened to inform her Majesty of what had happened if she did not assume a different behaviour towards me. Miss Letti was now in her turn somewhat afraid : my face was all over scratches ; and she did not know how to extricate herself from the dilemma. Throughout the night she applied a quantity of cephalic water to my poor head ; and the next day I made the Queen believe I had met with a fall.

The whole winter was passed in the same way. I had no longer a day of rest ; and my poor back was a continual sufferer. But, on the other hand, I insinuated myself so well into the good graces of the Queen, that she withheld none of her secrets from me. She requested permission of the King to take me with her wherever she went. His Majesty gladly consented, and ordered likewise that my brother should follow him every where. We went out for the first time in the month of June, when their Majesties removed to Charlottenburg, a magnificent summer-palace near Berlin. Miss Letti was not of the party, and I was intrusted to Madam de Kamecke. I have already observed, that this lady was a person of infinite merit ; but though she had constantly lived in the great world, yet she had not imbided its manners : she might be called an excellent countrywoman, abounding in good sense, but destitute of wit. She was very devout, and made me say my prayers for two or three successive hours, which tried me very much : afterwards I repeated my catechism, and learned psalms by heart : but I was so absent, that I was scolded every day.

The King celebrated the anniversary of my birth ; he gave me some handsome presents, and there was a ball in the evening. I was entering my eleventh year : my understanding was rather beyond my age, and I began to indulge in reflections.

From Charlottenburg we want to Wusterhausen. On the evening of our arrival there, an express came from Berlin to inform the Queen than my second brother had a dysentery. This intelligence created much alarm. The King and Queen would have returned to Berlin, had they not been afraid of the contagion. The next day, a second express informed their Majesties, that my sister Frederica laboured under the same disease. It raged at Berlin like a plague : most people died of it on the thirteenth day.[1] They even barricaded the houses where the disease was, to prevent it being communicated. The Queen had not yet arrived at the end of her troubles : a few days after, the King likewise fell dangerously ill, being afflicted with the same cholic which he had some years before at Brandenburg.

I never suffered so much as I did during this malady. The heat was as great and oppressive as it can possibly be in Italy. The room in which the King was confined was kept close, and with a blazing fire, Young as I was, I was forced to stay in it all the day. My place was near the chimney. I was like a person in a violent fever, and my blood was in so great an agitation that my eyes were almost ready to start from their sockets. I was so overheated that I could not sleep. As the noise which I made at night awakened

[1] In a letter to Anhalt-Dessau of 12 September 1719 Frederick William wrote, " In the four regiments at Berlin, 700 are dying from the pox ; in my own regiment 200 are down. Thank God, the ones who are dying are the weaklings anyway. In Berlin itself 130–150 are dying each week, and in the country it is the same story."

Madam de Kamecke, she gave me psalms to learn to tranquillize me ; and when I attempted to represent to her that I was not sufficiently calm for it, she scolded me, and complained to the Queen that I had not the fear of God. Then I had a fresh chiding to encounter. At length I sunk under all these fatigues and vexations, and had the dysentery in my turn. My faithful Meermann immediately acquainted her Majesty with the circumstance. The Queen would not credit it ; and though I was already very ill, she forced me to go out, and would not listen to my nurse's representations, till I was at the point of death.

I was removed, dying, to Berlin. Miss Letti came to receive me at the top of the staircase. " Ah ! my Princess, (said she,) is it you ? Do you suffer much ? Are you very ill ? You must take good care of yourself ; your brother has just breathed his last this morning ; and I think your sister will not get through the day." This fine speech of her's grieved me very much : but I was so low, that I did not feel it so acutely as I should have done at any other time. I continued in the utmost danger for a whole week. Towards the end of the ninth day, my disease began to abate: but I recovered very slowly. The King and my sister were better before me. The bad treatment of Miss Letti delayed my convalescence ; she did nothing but use me ill in the day time, and at night she hindered me from sleeping, for she swore like a common trooper.

In the mean time, the Queen returned to Berlin ; and though I was still very weak, she ordered me to go out. Her Majesty gave me a very kind reception, but she scarcely looked upon Miss Letti. The latter, irritated at seeing herself despised, revenged herself upon me. Blows and kicks were my daily bread : language affords no invective that she did not employ against the Queen : she commonly called the Queen, *the great ass* ; and every person in her retinue had a nickname as well as her Majesty. Madam de Kamecke was *the big cow* ; Madam de

Sonsfeld *the foolish brute* ; and so on. Such was the excellent pattern which she set me. I was so angry and vexed, that the bile at last ran into my blood, and I was afflicted with the jaundice in eight days after my first going out. My malady lasted two months, and I only recovered from it, to fall into another much more dangerous disease. It began by a violent fever, which two days after turned into a purple one. I was continually delirious, and my illness increased so much on the fifth day, that it was expected I had only a few hours to live. The affection of the King and Queen for me prevailed over the care for their own preservation. They came to see me at midnight and found me senseless. I have been told since, that their grief was excessive : they gave me their blessing under a flood of tears ; and it was only by main force that they could be removed from my bed. I had fallen into a kind of lethargy. The pains that were taken to rouse me, and the goodness of my constitution, recalled me to life. My fever abated towards morning ; and two days after I was pronounced out of danger. Would to Heaven I had been permitted peaceably to have quitted this world ! I should have been much happier. But I was doomed to endure a train of misfortunes, such as the Swedish Prophet had foretold.

As soon as I was somewhat able to converse, the King paid me a visit. His Majesty was so delighted to see me out of danger, that he ordered me to ask a favour :—" I intend to gratify your wishes, (said he,) and I will grant you whatever you desire." I had a great share of ambition ; I was vexed to see myself treated as a child. I took my resolution instantly, and begged of his Majesty to be treated in future as a grown-up person, and to lay aside my frocks. The King laughed very much at my idea. " Well, (said he,) you shall be satisfied ; and I promise you shall no longer wear a frock."

I never felt greater joy : it was near bringing on a relapse ; and it was with extreme difficulty that my first emotion could be moderated.—How happy we are at that age ! The smallest trifle amuses and elates us ! The King however kept his word, and, notwithstanding the obstacles which the Queen opposed, he insisted upon my dress being changed.

I was not able to leave my room before the year 1720. I felt supremely happy at having left off frocks. I placed myself before a glass to view myself, and thought I looked uncommonly well in my new dress. I studied my gestures and my gait, that I might have the appearance of a grown-up person ; in short, I was superlatively satisfied with my little figure. I went down with a triumphant mien to the Queen, from whom I expected to have met with a highly gracious reception. I had gone there like a Caesar, and returned like a Pompey. As soon as the Queen perceived me at a distance she exclaimed : " Oh ! heavens ! how she looks ! a pretty figure indeed ! As like to a dwarf as one drop of water to another ! " I stood petrified with astonishment. My little vanity was highly disappointed ; and vexation brought tears into my eyes. To say the truth, the Queen would have been perfectly right if she had contended herself with the little mortification she had given me : but she scolded me severely for having applied to the King for any favour. She told me she would not allow any such thing ; reminded me that she had ordered me to attach myself to her exclusively ; and that if ever I applied to the King on any occasion, she would be excessively angry. I apologized as well as I could, and behaved so submissively, that I at last obtained her pardon.

Hitherto I have sufficiently pourtrayed the hasty temper of Miss Letti : but I must not omit relating an affair which, though childish in itself, was important in its consequences. —There was before the windows of my room an open wooden gallery, which formed the communication between the two wings of the palace. This gallery was always filled with dirt, which caused an abominable stench in my rooms. It proceeded from the neglect of Eversmann the keeper of the palace. This man was a favourite with the King, who had the misfortune to have none but rude fellows about him. Eversmann was a real imp of Satan. He delighted in nothing so much as doing harm, and was concerned in every cabal and intrigue.[1] Miss Letti had several times requested him to get the gallery cleaned ; he never took any notice of her request : her patience at length was exhausted : she sent for him one morning, and began to abuse him : he replied ; and they quarrelled to such a degree, that, had not Madame de Roucoule luckily arrived at the moment, and separated them, they would have proceeded to blows. Eversmann vowed to be revenged, and found an opportunity for it the very next day. He told the King, that Miss Letti paid no attention to my education ; that she was the mistress of Colonel Forcade and Mr. Fourneret, with whom she was closetted all the day ; that I no longer learned any thing of her ; and that, to convince himself of the truth of his assertion, his Majesty needed only to examine me.

Eversmann's report was true in every respect : but Miss Letti was innocent with regard to his last accusation. I had been ill for six months, which had thrown me considerably back ; and ever since my recovery, I had not been able to resume my studies, having constantly been with the Queen, to whose room I used to go at ten o'clock in the morning, and never leaving it before eleven at night.

The King, who wished to ascertain the truth, asked me one day several question concerning my religion. I stood the examination very well, and gave him satisfaction on every question he asked : but I was not perfect in the Ten Commandments, which he ordered me to recite. I confused myself, and never could repeat them : this put the King into such a passion, that he was very near beating me. My poor tutor became the sufferer. He was dismissed the next day ; neither was Miss Letti spared ; the King

---

[1] Rudolf Wilhelm Eversmann (1685–1745), Keeper of the Royal Palaces and head servant of Frederick William ; he was a member of the exclusive *Tabergei*.

ordered the Queen to give her a severe reprimand, and to
forbid her, under penalty of incurring his utmost displeasure, to admit the visits of any gentleman, or even
clergyman. The Queen obeyed with pleasure, and was glad
of a pretence to mortify her. Miss Letti apologized as well
as she could : she complained of me, saying that I had
neither respect nor regard for her ; that I did exactly the
reverse of what she ordered me ; and that, being hardly
ever with me, she could not be answerable for my conduct.
The Queen used me very ill, and employed expressions so
harsh, that they almost drove me to despair. Young as I
was, they made a strong impression upon me. " What !
(said I to myself) does a want of memory deserve so many
reproofs ? I disobeyed Miss Letti, it is true : I would not
make her any reports : she never could get from me the
secrets with which I had been entrusted by the Queen. I
have obeyed the commands of her Majesty in every point ;
and yet she now imputes it to me as a crime. I have
endured all possible vexations on her account. I have
submitted to blows ; and this is my reward ! "

A moment after I repented of my kindness towards Miss
Letti. I was at liberty to complain to the Queen of her bad
treatment, and I confess I hesitated for a short time whether
I should betray the Queen or my teacher. But the goodness
of my disposition overcame these vindictive thoughts, and I
determined to continue silent.

My way of life was now completely changed ; my lessons
commenced at eight o'clock in the morning, and lasted till
eight at night. I had no intervals but the hours of dinner
and supper ; and these, too, were passed in hearing reprimands from the Queen. When I returned to my room,
Miss Letti recommenced her reproaches. Her rage at not
being allowed to receive any visits vented itself upon me ;
few days passed without her exercising the strength of her
formidable fists upon my poor body. I spent my nights in
weeping ; I was in a continual despair ; I had not a moment
of recreation ; and I grew quite stupid : my vivacity

vanished ; and, in short, I was no longer the same either in body or mind.

This kind of life lasted six months ; at the end of which we went to Wusterhausen.

I was beginning to regain the Queen's good graces, and consequently to enjoy a little more repose. She even shewed me some confidence, and imparted to me all her thoughts. Before we returned to Berlin, she one day said, " I have informed you of all the sorrows I have hitherto endured, but I have only made you acquainted with a few of the persons who caused them : I will now name them all to you ; but I forbid you, on pain of death, ever to speak to, or to have any communication with, those persons. Drop them a courtesy ; that is all that is necessary." At the same time, she named three-fourths of the inhabitants of Berlin, whom she said were her enemies. " I would have you take care, also (added she), not to expose me. If you are asked why you do not speak to those persons, answer merely that you have your motives for not doing so."

I punctually obeyed the Queen's commands, and alienated every one from me. In the mean time, Miss Letti began to be tired of the constraint in which she lived. The King's prohibition had prevented her continuing her love and state intrigues. The credit of Prince Anhalt was considerably lowered since the adventure of Madam de Blaspil ; which deprived Miss Letti of the presents she had been used to receive from that prince. He no longer mentioned my marriage with the Margrave of Schwedt. All this induced her to request her patroness, Lady Darlington, to intercede in her behalf with the Queen ; and to obtain for her the title of governess, with the prerogative attached to that office ; intreating her, in case of a denial, to procure her the same situation with the Princess of England.

Lady Darlington wrote her a letter, which she might show to the Queen. It contained great promises of an establishment in England, together with an enumeration of the good qualities of Miss Letti. She pitied her that her merits were so badly acknowledged at Berlin ; advised her to ask distinctions and rewards for the pains she had bestowed upon my education ; and, in case of a refusal, to solicit her dismissal, and to come to a country where justice was more readily done to merit. All this was but a feint to induce the Queen to grant what she asked. Miss Letti sent Lady Darlington's letter to the Queen ; she annexed a very impertinent epistle of her own.—She wished, she said, to obtain what she demanded, or her dismissal. The Queen felt herself very much embarrassed, as she was obliged to keep upon good terms with Miss Letti, lest she should disoblige the individual who had recommended her, and who was all-powerful with the King of England. She therefore employed several persons to dissuade Miss Letti from her purpose, but in vain. She at last mentioned it likewise to me, and I was in the utmost surprise, as Miss Letti had kept secret the step she had taken. The Queen questioned me much concerning her behaviour to me. I praised her very much, and earnestly intreated her majesty not to shew her letter to the King, as she intended, before I had spoken to her. " If you can prevail upon her to alter her determination (said the Queen) within four and twenty hours, it is well ; but after that time it will be too late." As soon as I had returned to my own room, I spoke to Miss Letti. My tears, my intreaties, and my endearments moved her, or rather she was glad of a decent pretence to retract. She therefore wrote a second letter to the Queen, in which she petitioned her majesty not to show her first letter to the King.

Things were thus settled for this time. The friendship which I had manifested for her on this occasion, procured me a fortnight's calm : but the subsequent storm was the more violent for it. During six months I suffered the torments of purgatory. My good Meermann, who saw me beaten every day, wished to inform the Queen of my sufferings ; but I always prevented it. To complete her wickedness, the fury washed my face with a certain water, which she had purposely got from England, and which was so strong that it corroded the skin. In less than a week my face was covered with pimples, and my eyes were as red as blood. My nurse seeing the dreadful effect of this water, though I had used it but twice, threw the bottle out of the window ; else my eyes and my complexion would have been destroyed for ever.

The beginning of the year 1721 proved as unfortunate for me as the preceding : my torments continued still. Miss Letti wished to revenge herself for the denial given to her by the Queen ; and as she was firmly resolved to quit me, she wished to leave some marks upon me that should make me remember her. I think that if she could have broken either an arm or a leg of mine, she would have done so : but the fear of detection prevented her. She therefore did all she could to spoil my face : she frequently hit my nose with such a violence that I bled like an ox.

Meanwhile another answer arrived to a second letter which she had written to Lady Darlington. This lady encouraged her to come to England, where she offered her her patronage, and engaged to obtain her a pension. Miss Letti therefore applied a second time to the Queen for her dismission ; and the letter which she wrote to her majesty exceeded the former in insolence. " I clearly see (she stated) that your majesty is unwilling to grant me the prerogatives which I claim. My resolution is unshaken. I entreat your majesty to grant me my dismission. I shall leave a barbarous country, where I have found neither wit nor sense, to end my days in a happy climate, where merit is rewarded, and where the sovereign is not apt to distinguish scurvy officers, as is the fashion here, and to despise persons of talents." Madam de Roucoule was present when the Queen received this letter. Her majesty communicated it to her, and could scarcely moderate her anger. " For Heaven's sake ! (exclaimed Madam de Roucoule) let that creature go ; it is the best thing could befal the Princess. The poor child suffers martyrdom with her ; and I am afraid she will some day be brought to you with her ribs broken, for she is beaten like mortar, and runs the risk of being maimed every day. Her nurse will be best able to inform your majesty." The Queen, surprised, sent for my good nurse, who confirmed all that Madam de Roucoule had stated ; adding, that she durst not acquaint her majesty with the circumstance before, having been intimidated by the great credit which Miss Letti boasted of enjoying with the Queen, and by her menaces to cause her to be driven away. The Queen, therefore, did not hesitate any longer to shew her letter to the King. He was so incensed at it, that, in the first ebullition of his passion, he would have sent her to Spandau, had not the Queen prevented it. Her majesty was embarrassed about the choice of the person to whom I was to be entrusted : she proposed, however, two ladies to the King (I never learnt who they were), but his majesty refused them both, and appointed Madam de Sonsfeld to the situation. I cannot sufficiently acknowledge the kindness of my father.

Madam de Sonsfeld is of a very illustrious origin, connected with every great family in the empire ; her ancestors have distinguished themselves by their services, and by the high dignities with which they have been invested. A more able pen than mine would but feebly sketch her portrait. Her disposition will be manifested in the course of these memoirs. It is a very uncommon one ; a compound of virtues and sentiments ; a powerful understanding, great firmness, and much generosity, united with the most agreeable manners. Her noble politeness inspires respect and confidence. To all these advantages she adds a lovely figure, which she has preserved to a very advanced age. She had been maid of honour to Queen Charlotte,[1] my

---

[1] Sophia Charlotte (1668–1705), sister of George I, married Frederick I in 1684. Having spent some of her youth in Versailles, she was responsible for the extravagant French influence which characterized her husband's reign. Outstandingly clever and cultured, she was a particular friend of Leibniz. She also had built for herself the palace of Charlottenburg, often mentioned in the *Memoirs*. Her son described her as a "clever woman but a bad Christian".

81

grandmother, and held the same situation in the household of the Queen my mother. As she never would marry, she refused some very brilliant offers. She was forty years old when she was placed with me. I love and revere her like a mother ; she is still with me, and probably nothing but death will ever part us.[1]

The Queen could not endure her : she had a long contention with the King on the subject ; but as she could not advance any solid reasons against his choice, she was obliged to yield. I was informed of all this by my brother, who was present at the conversation : the Queen always kept it secret. She was much surprised, on returning to her room, to find me all in tears. " Oh ! oh ! " said she, " I see your brother has been chattering, and you know all about it. You are very silly to grieve, are you not yet tired of blows ? " I entreated her majesty to retain Miss Letti : but she replied, that I ought to acquiesce, and that it was no longer possible.

Madam de Sonsfeld, who had been sent for, entered at that moment. The Queen took her by the hand, and me by the other, and conducted us both to the King.

His majesty said many obliging things to Madam de Sonsfeld, and acquainted her with the situation for which she was intended. She respectfully intreated the King to excuse her accepting an office for which she felt herself incapable. The King used all manner of persuasions, and it was only by threatening her with his resentment that she at length accepted his offer. He gave her the proper rank at court, and promised her all sorts of advantages for herself and her family. She was introduced as my governess on the third Easterday. I felt very much for the misfortune of Miss Letti : she was dismissed in a very harsh manner. The King sent her word by the Queen, " that if he had followed his inclination, he would have sent her to Spandau ; that she was not to appear before him ; and that he granted her eight days to quit the court and the country." I did all

[1] Dorothea Luise von Wittenhorst-Sonsfeld (1681–1746).

I could to comfort her, and to show her my friendly regard.

I was not possessed of much at that time ; still I gave her, in precious stones, jewels, and plate, what might amount to the value of five thousand dollars, besides what she received from the Queen : and yet she had the wickedness to rob me of every thing. The day after her departure I had not a gown to put on ; she had carried off all my robes ; and the Queen was obliged to equip me anew from head to foot.

I soon got accustomed to my new governess. Madam de Sonsfeld began by studying my disposition. She observed that I was excessively timid. I trembled when she was grave : I had not the heart to say two words together without hesitating. She represented to the Queen, that it would be proper to divert me, and to treat me with much gentleness, to remove my fears ; that I was extremely docile ; and that, by exciting my ambition, she might do with me whatever she chose. The Queen left her complete mistress of my education. She every day reasoned with me about indifferent subjects, and endeavoured to inspire me with good sentiments on every occurrence. I applied myself to reading, which soon became my favourite occupation. The emulation which she excited in me, made me relish my other studies. I learned English, Italian, history, geography, philosophy, and music. My improvements were surprisingly rapid : I was so intent upon learning, that Madam de Sonsfeld was obliged to moderate my ardour. Two years elapsed in this manner ; and as I only relate facts deserving of notice, I pass to the year 1723.

This year opened with new vexations. But as henceforth the court of England will have a great share in these memoirs, it is proper to give an idea of it. The King of England was a prince who valued himself on his sentiments ; but, unfortunately, he had never applied to the enlightening of his mind. Many virtues, carried to an extreme, become vices. This was his case. He affected a firmness which degenerated into harshness, and a tranquillity which might be called indolence. His generosity extended only to his favourites and mistresses, by whom he suffered himself to be governed ; the rest of mankind were excluded. Since his accession to the crown, his haughtiness had become insupportable. Two qualities, however, his equity and justice, rendered him estimable. He was by no means an evil-disposed prince, but rather constant in his benevolence. His manners were cold ; he spoke little, and listened only to puerilities.

The Countess of Schulenburg (then Duchess of Kendal and Princess of Eberstein) was his mistress, or rather his wife by the left hand. She was of that class of beings who are so very good that they are, so to say, good for nothing. She had neither vices nor virtues : she only studied to keep in favour, and to guard against being supplanted.[1]

The Princess of Wales had a powerful understanding and great knowledge.[2] She had read much, and was possessed of a particular capacity for public affairs. On her arrival in England, she gained the hearts of all. Her manners were gracious ; she was affable, but she had not the good fortune to retain the affections of the people : means were found to ascertain her disposition, which did not correspond to her exterior. She was imperious, false, and ambitious. She has frequently been compared to Agrippina ; like that Empress, she might have exclaimed, *let all perish, so I do but rule.*

The Prince, her consort, had not more genius than his father : he was hot, passionate, haughty, and avaricious to an unpardonable extreme.

Lady Darlington, who held the second rank, was the natural daughter of the late Elector of Hanover and a Countess of Platen. It might truly be said of her that she

---

[1] Countess Ehrengarde Melusina von der Schulenburg, Duchess of Kendal, mistress of George I (1667–1743). In Hanover she had been no rival to the Countess Darlington (see p. 35 above, n.) but after George I arrived in England she began to establish her ascendancy. In contrast to Lady Darlington she was extremely thin and tall, and in London was nicknamed the " Maypole ". Her influence was extensive and she played a considerable role in securing the return of Walpole and Townshend to office in 1720.

[2] Later Queen Caroline (1683–1737), wife of George II.

possessed the disposition of a devil : for she was altogether inclined to work evil. She was vicious, intriguing, and as ambitious as the two ladies whose portraits I have just been sketching. These three females alternately governed the King, though they lived in great discord among themselves. On one point they all agreed, *viz.* that the young Duke of Gloucester should not marry a princess of a great house, and strenuously desired to have him united to a female of no very prominent talent, that they themselves might continue to govern.

Lady Darlington, who had her private views, dispatched Miss Pöllnitz[1] to Berlin. This person had been a maid of honour and favourite of Queen Charlotte my grandmother, after whose death she had retired to Hanover, where she lived on a pension settled upon her by the King of England. Her mind was as much inclined to evil as that of Lady Darlington. She was equally fond of intrigue ; her envenomed tongue spared no one ; she had only three *trifling* faults ; she loved men, gambling, and wine. The Queen my mother had known her for a great length of time. As she was informed that Miss Pöllnitz enjoyed great credit at the court of Hanover, she received her uncommonly well. When she presented her to me, she said, " This is one of my ancient friends, with whom you will be glad to be acquainted." I curtsied, and politely complimented her concerning what the Queen had just spoken. She surveyed me for some time from head to foot, and then turning to the Queen, she exclaimed : " Heavens ! how awkward the Princess looks ! What a shape ! what an appearance for a young person ! and how clumsy her attire ! " The Queen was a little disconcerted at this

---

[1] Baron Pöllnitz (1692–1775), her brother, was a courtier, adventurer and writer who spent some time at the court of Frederick the Great. He wrote extensive and amusing memoirs of many German courts, but his *Memoirs of the Court of Prussia*, published in 1791, bear a strong resemblance to Wilhelmina's, and Ranke and others have come to the conclusion that he must have known the manuscript before it was published.

address, which she was by no means prepared to expect. " It is true (said she) that she might look better : but her shape is strait, and will display itself when she has done growing. However, if you converse with her, you will find that she is not a mere automaton."

Miss Pöllnitz thereupon began to talk with me, but in an ironical manner, asking me questions which would have suited a child of four years. I was so vexed, that I did not deign to make any reply. My sullen behaviour gave her an opportunity to hint to the Queen, that I was capricious and haughty, and that I had scrutinized her from head to foot. This brought upon me severe reprimands, which continued all the time Miss Pöllnitz stayed at Berlin. She quarrelled with me about every thing.

One day the conversation turned upon the powers of memory. The Queen observed that I had an excellent memory. Miss Pöllnitz set up a malicious grin, as much as to say, that she disputed the fact. The Queen, nettled at this, offered to try me, and proposed a wager that I could learn one hundred and fifty verses by heart in an hour's time. " Well (said Miss Pöllnitz) I will try her *local* memory ; and I will bet she will not remember what I shall write down." The Queen was consequently very strenuous to maintain what she had asserted, and I was sent for. Having taken me aside, the Queen told me she would freely forgive me all that was past, if I proved successful, and so caused her to win her wager. I did not know what was meant by *local* memory, having never heard of it before. Miss Pöllnitz wrote what I was to learn. It was a series of one hundred and fifty fanciful names of her own invention, all numbered. She read them twice over to me, always mentioning the numbers ; after which I was obliged to repeat them in succession. I was very fortunate in the first trial : she desired a second, and asked the names out of order, mentioning merely the number. I again succeeded, to her great vexation. I had never made a greater effort of memory ; yet she could not prevail with herself so far as to bestow upon me the slightest commendation. The Queen could not account for her behaviour ; and was much offended, though she held her peace. Miss Pöllnitz at length freed us from her insupportable criticisms, and returned to Hanover.

Shortly after her departure, Miss Brunow, a sister to Madam de Kamecke, came also to Berlin. She had been maid of honour to the Electress Sophia of Hanover,[1] my great-grandmother, and she was still residing at that court, from which she received a pension. She was a good creature, but somewhat childish in her manners. She made many inquiries about me ; and as her sister was very much my friend, she praised me more than I deserved. Miss Brunow appeared astonished at what Madam de Kamecke told her. " To a sister (said she) you might speak more freely than you do, and not conceal things that are generally known : for we are very well informed at Hanover of whatever concerns the Princess : we know that she is de-formed, excessively plain, wicked, and haughty, in short, that she is a little monster, of whom it might be said, that it would have been better that she had never been born." Madam de Kamecke was angry, and had a violent dispute with her sister ; and to cure her of her prejudices, she took her with her to the Queen, with whom I then was. She could hardly be persuaded, when she saw me, that I was the same person : but to convince her that my shape was good, I was obliged to undress in her presence. Many women were sent at different times from Hanover to Berlin to examine me. I was obliged to submit to be viewed by them, and to show them my back to convince them that I was not crooked. All this vexed me ; and to heighten my misfortune, the Queen insisted upon making me more slender than I was. She ordered my stays to be laced so tight, that I became black, and was almost deprived of respiration. The attention of Madam de Sonsfeld had

---

[1] The Electress Sophia of Hanover (1630–1714), who, had she lived another two months, would have succeeded Queen Anne as queen of England.

restored my complexion : it was now tolerably fair, but the Queen spoiled it by keeping me so tight laced. The whole year passed in the same manner. As nothing interesting happened, I pass to the year 1724.[1]

The King of England arrived at Hanover in the Spring. The Duchess of Kendal and Lady Darlington were in his retinue ; and Miss Letti attended the latter of these ladies. She lived on her bounty, and on a pension which Lady Darlington had obtained for her from the King. My father, who at that time had no other object in view than my marriage with the Duke of Gloucester, went to Hanover soon after the arrival of the English monarch. He was received with all possible demonstrations of joy and affection, and returned to Berlin very much satisfied with his journey.

The Queen set out soon after his return, charged with secret instructions for the King her father to conclude an offensive and defensive alliance between the two monarchs, which was to be confirmed by my brother's marriage and mine.[2] Her Majesty did not meet with such favourable dispositions as she had flattered herself in expecting. The King of England agreed to every proposition except that of my marriage ; saying that he could not enter into any engagement without having consulted the inclination of his

[1] The first French edition of 1810 gives the year 1723 for the events that now follow, leading up to the treaty of Charlottenburg between England and Prussia, which is in fact correct. However, as Wilhelmina has already passed the year 1723, she would appear to have slipped in the dating of the narrative at this point.

[2] On p. 104, below, Wilhelmina gives a few more relevant factors which led to the Treaty of Charlottenburg. Frederick William was at this stage on bad terms with the Emperor Charles VI, who resented the aggrandisement, without his consent, of Stettin in her peace with Sweden. The suspicion of the revival of a Catholic League in Europe led the Prussian King to look to Hanover and England for support in his claim to succession in Jülich and Berg on the extinction of the Catholic Palatine House of Neuburg. This claim was one of the few constant concerns of Frederick William's foreign policy, and he was prepared to support anyone who gave him greatest encouragement in that direction. After 1726 it was to be Charles VI. Hence the ultimate failure of the English alliance and marriages.

grandson, and without knowing whether our inclinations corresponded. The Queen in despair, not knowing how to extricate herself, had recourse to the Duchess of Kendal. She bitterly complained to that lady of the King's answer, and wished her to interest herself in her behalf. By dint of caresses and intreaties, she at last obtained the intercession of the Duchess. The latter told the Queen, " that the aversion of the King of England to my marriage arose from certain malicious suggestions instilled into his mind concerning me : that Miss Letti had exhibited such a picture of me as was calculated to deter any man from marrying ; that she had described me as uncommonly plain and extremely deformed : that the *praises* she bestowed upon my disposition were in perfect harmony with those on my figure ; that she had represented me so wicked and passionate, that my rage threw me into fits several times a day. Your Majesty may judge (continued the Duchess) whether, after hearing such reports, which were confirmed by Miss Pöllnitz, the King your father could consent to this marriage." The Queen, who could not conceal her indignation, told her how Miss Letti had behaved to me, and what motives had induced her to dismiss her. She named to her every individual who had been sent from Hanover to Berlin, and referred to their testimony. At length, the untruth of all these rumours was so clearly demonstrated to the Duchess, that she was completely persuaded of the contrary.

The Duchess was the intimate friend of Lord Townshend, at that time first secretary of state. She resolved to accomplish this business herself, that the court of Berlin might be obliged to her alone. But perceiving how difficult it would be to eradicate from the mind of the King the prejudices which had been instilled into it against me, she advised the Queen of Prussia to persuade the King of England to take a journey to Berlin, that he might with his own eyes undeceive himself respecting the calumnies that had been vented against me. Assisted by the Duchess, the Queen managed it so well that her father complied with her wishes, and fixed on the month of October for his journey. The Queen returned in triumph to Berlin, and was uncommonly well received by the King my father. The promised visit of the King of England diffused incredible joy all over the country ; my father in particular was highly pleased. I was the only person who did not share in the general satisfaction ; for I was ill used from morning to night. Whatever I did, the Queen never failed to make her remarks : " These manners will not please my nephew ; you must from this moment conform to his humour, for he will not like your ways." Such reprimands, which I heard twenty times a day, were not very flattering to my childish vanity. It has ever been my misfortune to indulge in reflections : I say misfortune ; for indeed, when things are too deeply investigated, we often discover many that create no trifling vexations. Self-examination is very salutary : but we should be much happier, if we endeavoured to divest ourselves of all painful recollections. It is a physical evil, but a moral good : and although this moral good is sometimes very troublesome, I yet find it useful for the proper direction of my conduct. But while I am declaiming against the excess of reflections, I perceive I am making some which do not belong to the thread of my history. I return to those thoughts which were suggested to me by the behaviour of the Queen. " How hard it is (said I frequently to my governess) to be always reprimanded in so strange a manner by the Queen. I know that I have faults ; I am desirous to get the better of them ; but it is through the ambition of acquiring general esteem and approbation. Ought I to be encouraged by any other motives than honour ? Why am I always reminded of the Duke of Gloucester and of the pains I ought to take to please him some day ? I think I am full as good as he ; and who knows whether I shall like him, and live happy with him ? Why all these advances before my marriage ? I am the daughter of a king ; and it is not so very great an honour for me to marry that prince. I feel no inclination for him, and all that the Queen repeats to me daily, gives me more aversion than eagerness to marry him." Madam de Sonsfeld knew not what answer to return. My reasoning was too just to be condemned. I was naturally timid, and the perpetual caprices which I had to endure were not calculated to inspire me with confidence. Madam de Sonsfeld made some representations to the Queen ; but they were of no avail.

About that time, one of the gentlemen belonging to the Duke of Gloucester came to Berlin. The Queen held a drawing-room : he was presented to her and me. He delivered me a very handsome compliment from his master : I blushed, and replied only with a curtsey. The Queen, who was upon the listen, was vexed that I returned no answer to the Duke's compliment, and chid me severely, insisting upon my making amends the next day, on pain of her displeasure. I retired, weeping, to my room ; I was angry with the Queen and the Duke. I vowed I would never marry him : as my submission to his will was to begin even before marriage, I easily perceived that I should be more than his slave after the solemnity : the Queen was following her own ideas without consulting my heart ; and I was going to cast myself at her feet, and intreat her not to force me to marry a prince for whom I felt no inclination, and with whom, I clearly saw, I should be unhappy. My governess had much difficulty to calm me, and to prevent my taking this false step. The next day I was obliged to converse with the gentleman, and to talk to him of the Duke ; which I did with a very ill grace and great confusion.

In the mean time, the visit of the King of England drew near. On the sixth of October we went to Charlottenburg to receive him. My heart beat high ; and I felt violently agitated. The British monarch arrived on the 8th, at seven at night. The King, the Queen, and all the court, received him in the Palace-yard, because the apartments are on the ground-floor. After he had embraced the King and the Queen, I was presented to the English monarch. He embraced me, and, turning to the Queen, he observed : *your daughter is very tall for her age.* He gave his hand to the Queen, and conducted her to his apartment, where we all followed him. As soon as I entered the room, he took a wax light, and examined me from head to foot : while I all the time remained immoveable like a statue, and very much disconcerted. All this passed without his saying any thing. After having thus reviewed me, he turned to my brother, whom he caressed much, and with whom he entertained himself for a long time. I availed myself of that opportunity to withdraw. The Queen beckoned to me to follow her, and passed into an adjoining room, where the Englishmen and Germans of the King's retinue were presented to her. After having spoken with them for some time, she told the gentlemen that she left me to converse with them ; and addressing herself to the Englishmen : " address my daughter in English," said she, " you will perceive that she speaks it very well." I felt myself much less embarrassed when the Queen was gone ; and gaining a little confidence, I began to converse with those gentlemen. As I spoke their language as fluently as my native one, I got very well over it, and every one appeared delighted with me. They praised me very much to the Queen ; and told her that I had the air of an English lady, and that I was calculated to be one day their sovereign. This was saying a great deal ; for the English fancy themselves so much superior to other nations, that they think they pay a very great compliment when they say of a person, that he has the appearance of an Englishman. The manners of the King were those of a Spaniard ; he was uncommonly grave, and did not speak a word to any one. He received Madam de Sonsfeld very coolly, and asked whether I was always so grave, and of a melancholy disposition ? " Far from it, replied she ; but the respect which she has for your Majesty deprives her of her usual cheerfulness." He shook his head, but made no reply. The manner in which he had received me, and what I had just heard, inspired me with such fear, that I never could summon courage enough to speak to him.

At length we sat down to supper ; but the English monarch continued mute. I know not whether he was right, or wrong ; but I think he followed the proverb which says : "it is better to say nothing, than to talk nonsense." He felt himself indisposed towards the end of the repast. The Queen wished to persuade him to withdraw : many mutual compliments passed on the occasion ; at last the Queen threw her napkin on the table, and arose. The King of England began to totter, my father ran to support him : all rushed about him, but in vain : he fell upon his knees, his wig on one side, and his hat on the other. They gently laid him on the floor, where he remained senseless for a full hour. The care that was taken with him brought him at last gradually to his senses. Meanwhile the King and Queen were in the utmost consternation, and many people thought that this attack was the forerunner of an apoplexy. They earnestly intreated him to withdraw ; but he would not, and reconducted the Queen to her apartment. He was very ill all the night ; which we only learned by private means. But it did not prevent his re-appearing on the following day. The remainder of his stay was passed in pleasures and festivities. Secret conferences daily took place between the English and Prussian Ministers : the result of which was the ratification of the treaty of alliance, and the double marriage which had been broached at Hanover ; which were signed on the twelfth of the same month. The English monarch left us the next day ; and his parting with all his relations was as cold as their reception had been. The King and Queen of Prussia were to return him his visit at the Göhrde, a hunting-box near Hanover.

The Queen of Prussia had been ill for more than seven months ; the pains she suffered were so peculiar, that the physicians did not know what to say about them. Every morning her body was prodigiously swelled, and towards night the swelling disappeared. The faculty for some time supposed the Queen might be pregnant : but latterly, they had given it as their opinion that her indisposition proceeded from another cause, which is very troublesome but not at all dangerous.

The 8th of November was fixed upon for the King's journey to the Göhrde. He was to set out early in the morning ; and we all had taken leave of him : but an occurrence retarded his departure. In the night the Queen was attacked with a violent cholic : but she concealed her pains as much as she could, that she might not awaken the King. Knowing however by certain indications, that she was in labour, she called for assistance. But before either midwife or physician could arrive, she was safely delivered of a princess, without any other assistance than that of the King and of a single waiting-woman. There was neither linen nor cradle ready, and the confusion was general. The King sent for me at four o'clock in the morning. I never saw him in a better humour,[1] the recollection of the office he had performed to the Queen made him laugh heartily. The Duke of Gloucester, my brother, the Princess Amelia of England, and myself, were selected as sponsors to the infant. I stood godmother in the afternoon, when my sister was christened Anna Amalia.[2]

The King set off the next day. As he travelled very fast,

---

[1] Poyntz, an English diplomat at Göhrde, 15 November 1723, quoted by I. S. Leadam, *Political History of England* (1921) 311 : " The King of Prussia appears in the best humour imaginable and treats our king with an affection and respect which neither czar, nor perhaps the emperor, will be much pleased to hear of."

[2] Anna Amalia, born 9 November 1723. An amateur composer of some distinction, she wrote an oratorio called *Le Mort de Jésus*. Above all she was a great collector of musical manuscripts. The *Amalienbibliothek*, later deposited in Berlin, played a crucial role in the rediscovery of Bach in the mid-nineteenth century. She died in 1787. She is not to be confused with another aristocratic German composer, Anna Amalia, Duchess of Saxe-Weimar (1739–1807) a friend of Goethe, who set many of his works to music.

he arrived in the evening at the Göhrde, where the greatest uneasiness had prevailed about him ; the English monarch having expected him the day before. He was very much surprized on hearing the cause of his delay. Grumbkow was in my father's retinue. He had quarrelled some time before with the Prince of Anhalt, and was endeavouring to reconcile himself with the English monarch : but as he wished that all affairs should pass through his hands, and the Queen opposed his pretensions, he did not fail to sow fresh seeds of discord between the Queen and my father. I have already observed that the latter was excessively jealous. Grumbkow availed himself of this foible, and by some vague and artful discourses he instilled into his mind ideas very injurious to the virtue of his consort.

III

AFTER a fortnight, the King returned to Berlin in a great rage. He received his children very well, but he would not see the Queen. He went across her bed-room to the supper-room without saying a word. This behaviour filled the Queen and us with cruel anxieties. She at length spoke to him, and expressed in the most tender terms the sorrow she felt at this treatment. He answered her with reproaches, upbraiding her with her pretended infidelity ; and had not Madam de Kamecke prevailed with him to withdraw, his rage might have led him to a fatal violence. The following day he assembled the physicians, Holtzendorff the surgeon of his regiment, and Madam de Kamecke, to enquire into the conduct of the Queen. They all warmly espoused the part of her majesty. Madam de Kamecke even treated the King with great severity, and declared to him the injustice of his suspicions. Indeed the virtue of the Queen was superior to reproach, and the blackest calumny never could assert the contrary. The King gave way to reflection ; he implored the Queen's pardon with a flood of tears, which shewed the goodness of his heart, and peace was restored.

I have mentioned the enmity of the two favourites of the King. As it broke out in the year 1724, it is proper to give an account of it here. Ever since the disgrace of Madam de Blaspil, and the good harmony of the English and Prussian courts, the Prince of Anhalt had lost much of his favour.

He lived at Dessau, and came but seldom to Berlin. The King, however, had still a very great regard for him, and treated him with distinction on account of his military talents. Grumbkow, on the contrary, had retained his favour unimpaired. He was entrusted with both the home and foreign affairs.

The Prince of Anhalt had stood godfather to one of his daughters, and had promised her a portion of five thousand dollars. As this daughter was about to be married, her father wrote to the Prince to remind him of his promise. Dissatisfied with Grumbkow's conduct, who had no longer any regard for him, and possessed alone the King's favour, the Prince denied having made any such engagement. Grumbkow answered ; the Prince rejoined ; and at last they reproached each other with their villainies. The discourse became so abusive, that the Prince of Anhalt determined to settle their quarrel in a single combat. Grumbkow, with all his great merits, passed for an arrant coward : he had given proofs of his valour in the battle of Malplaquet, by remaining in a ditch all the time the action lasted : he had also distinguished himself at Stralsund, when he put one of his legs out of joint in the beginning of the campaign, which prevented his serving in the trenches : he had the same misfortune as a certain King of France, who could not see a naked sword without fainting : but still he was a brave general. The Prince sent him a challenge. Grumbkow, trembling with courage, and arming himself with the laws of religion and of the country, answered that he would not fight ; that duels were prohibited both by divine and human laws ; and that he was not inclined to transgress either. This is not all : he wished to merit a crown in Heaven by suffering insults with patience : he made every possible apology to his antagonist, by which he the more incurred his contempt. The Prince continued inexorable. The business at length got to the knowledge of the King, who used all his efforts to reconcile them, but in vain ; the Prince of Anhalt could not be appeased. It was therefore determined that they should settle their quarrel in the presence of two seconds. The Prince's second was a Colonel Korf, in the Hessian service ; and Grumbkow's, Count Seckendorff,[1] a general in the Austrian service, Grumbkow's intimate friend. The scandalous chronicle reported, that in their youth they had been partners at play, and had won considerable sums. Be this as it may, Seckendorff was the living picture of Grumbkow, except that he affected to be more religious, and was brave as his sword. Nothing was so laughable as the letters which Seckendorff wrote to Grumbkow, to inspire him with courage. The King, however, attempted once more to interfere.[2]

In the beginning of the year 1724, he assembled at Berlin a council of war, composed of all the generals and colonels commanding regiments of his army. Most of the generals were of the Queen's party. The fine promises given by Grumbkow, to remain firmly attached to her majesty, dazzled her ; she inclined the balance in his favour, or else he was in danger of being cashiered. He got off with an arrest of a few days, which was a kind of satisfaction the King gave to Prince Anhalt. As soon as he was released from his arrest, the King clandestinely advised him to fight. The field of battle was near Berlin : the two

[1] Friedrich Heinrich von Seckendorff (1673–1763) was one of the most important Central European diplomats of his time. Like many of his contemporaries he came to prominence as a result of having impressed Prince Eugene in the War of the Spanish Succession. From 1697 he was in the service of the Empire. From the point of view of the *Memoirs* he is important for the role he played in releasing Prussia from her alliance with France and England and affecting the treaties of Wusterhausen (1726) and Berlin (1728).

[2] The events leading up to the duel between Grumbkow and Anhalt-Dessau are exhaustively studied by O. Krauske in the preface of *Die Briefe König Friedrich Wilhelm I an . . . Anhalt-Dessau* (Berlin, 1905) 44–84. Counter-accusations of misappropriation of funds were answered by fervent pleas from the King to heal the breach. The two men met to fight on 14 May 1725 but never actually drew weapons. In spite of immense complications Krauske comes to the conclusion that " in general Wilhelmina gives an accurate picture of the relationship of the two men ".

combatants repaired to the spot, attended by their seconds. The Prince drew his sword, using some abusive language towards his adversary. Grumbkow cast himself at his feet, which he embraced, soliciting his pardon, and requesting to be restored to his favour. The Prince, instead of replying, turned his back upon him. Ever since they were sworn enemies, and their animosity ceased only with life. It caused a total change for the better in the Prince : most of whose bad actions have generally been attributed to the detestable counsels of Grumbkow. The same might be said of Prince Anhalt as was said of the Cardinal de Richelieu : " He has been guilty of too many bad actions to be well spoken of, and he has done too many good actions to be ill spoken of. "

The King of England crossed the sea this year, to visit his German dominions. The King my father did not neglect to go to him, in hopes of concluding my marriage. As the Queen had been so useful in this business, she was charged with the commission.[1] She went to Hanover, where she was received with open arms. With regard to the alliance of the two houses, she found her father in the same disposition in which he had been the preceding years : he even spoke affectionately of me ; but he observed, that two obstacles opposed his wishes ; the first that he could not marry us without having first proposed the matter to his parliament ; the second, that we were both very young : I was but sixteen, and the Duke only eighteen. To soften these difficulties, he assured the Queen he should settle

---

[1] George I went to Hanover in June 1725 and returned to England the following February. Sophia Dorothea went to Hanover on 17 August, but in spite of the new treaty signed on 3 September 1725 between France, England and Prussia, formed in answer to an alliance concluded earlier that year between Charles VI and the King of Spain, she still failed to obtain the ratification of the marriage clauses. However the idea was still alive, and on 10 August Townshend had written to the Prussian Foreign Minister, von Ilgen, who is, oddly, not mentioned in these pages, " *Je suis ravi avec V.E. à unir ces deux familles royales en toutes manières de plus en plus, et en même tems de fortifier la religion protestante et les Etats de l'Empire.*" (Droysen, op. cit., 381.) Sophia Dorothea returned home on 30 September.

things in such a manner, that our marriage might be solemnized the first time he should return to Germany. The Queen constantly flattered herself she should obtain more. She had never before been on such good terms with her father ; he even appeared to have a particular affection for her ; and it is certain that he paid her very great attentions. She asked leave of the King her consort to stay some time longer ; " engaging (she wrote) to succeed in her designs." The King my father granted her request, and allowed her to remain at Hanover as long as her affairs should require it.

In the mean time I was at Berlin, in great favour with the King. I passed every afternoon in conversation with him, and he used to sup in my room. He even shewed me some confidence, and often spoke of state affairs. To give me a still greater mark of distinction, he ordered me to hold a drawing-room like the Queen. The governesses of my sisters were placed under my command, and had orders not to stir a step without my knowledge. I did not abuse the King's favour. Young as I was, there was as much solidity in my conduct then, as there can be now ; and I might have superintended the education of my sisters : but I did myself justice, and clearly perceived that it did not become me ; neither would I hold a drawing-room. I contented myself with inviting a few ladies every day.

For six whole months I had been tormented with a dreadful head-ache ; it was so violent, that I frequently fainted : yet I dared not to keep my room, as the Queen opposed it. Her majesty, who was of a very strong constitution, did not know what it was to be sick. Her severity in this respect was excessive ; though dying, I must be cheerful, or else she would fall into a terrible passion against me. The day before her return, I had a kind of brain fever, accompanied with such aching pains in the head, that my cries were heard in the palace yard. Six persons were obliged to hold me, night and day, to prevent my killing myself. Madam de Sonsfeld immediately sent expresses to

the King and Queen to acquaint them with my situation.
The Queen arrived in the evening ; she was much alarmed
at seeing me so ill ; the physicians were despairing of my
life. An abscess in the head, which broke on the third day,
saved me : fortunately, the matter ran through the ear,
else I could not have recovered. The King came to Berlin
two days after, and immediately paid me a visit. He was
moved to tears at the miserable state in which he found me.
He did not go to the Queen, and caused all the communica-
tions of his apartments with hers to be barricadoed, so
great was his irritation at her having beguiled him with
false promises. He had placed so much reliance on her
influence over the mind of the English monarch, that he
thought my marriage would have taken place that very
year. He imagined she had merely wished to protract her
stay at Hanover. This storm lasted six weeks ; at the end
of which the royal couple were reconciled. My recovery, in
the mean time, was very slow. I was confined to my room
for two months.

The narrow mind of the Queen my mother inclines her
to jealousy. The great distinction with which I was honoured by the King, excited her displeasure against me ;
she was besides influenced by one of her ladies, a daughter
of the Countess Fink, whom I shall henceforth call Countess
Amalia, to distinguish her from her mother. This young
person had, unknown to her parents, formed an intrigue
with the Prussian minister at the court of London. His
name was Wallenrodt.[1] He was a true coxcomb, of a short
clumsy figure ; who served the Prussian interests merely
by his buffoonery. She had secretly contracted herself to
this envoy ; and her plan was to become my governess, and
to accompany me to England. To insure her success, she
had used her best efforts to ingratiate herself with the Duke
of Gloucester, and had made him believe she was my

[1] Johann Ernst von Wallenrodt, who had been Prussian ambassador to
the Hanoverian court since 1719, from which he was in the habit of
sending alarmist reports (Krauske, op. cit., 162).

101

favourite ; on which acount he had shewn her great attentions. But it was also necessary to get rid of my governess ;
and to effect this, she incessantly strove to irritate the
Queen against her and me.

Countess Amalia had an all-powerful influence over the
Queen, and availed herself of her foibles to obtain her own
ends. Every day I was ill-used, and the Queen constantly
upbraided me for the kind attentions which the King
shewed me. I no longer dared to caress him without
trembling, and in fear of being harshly dealt with : the
case was the same with my brother ; it was enough that the
King ordered one thing, for the Queen to forbid it. Sometimes we were absolutely at a loss to know what to do. But
as we both felt more affection for the Queen, we agreed to
obey her commands. This was the source of all our misfortunes, as will be seen by the sequel of these memoirs.
My heart bled, however, at not being allowed to express the
vivacity of my sentiments to the King : I sincerely loved
him ; he had done me a thousand kindnesses ever since I
was born : but as I was to live with the Queen, I was
obliged to conform to her will.

The Queen presented the King, in the beginning of the
year 1726, with a prince, who was christened Henry.[1] As
soon as she recovered, we went to Potsdam, a small town
near Berlin. My brother was not of the party : the King
was displeased with him, because he would not submit to his
will. He incessantly scolded him, and his animosity was so
inveterate, that all the well-disposed courtiers advised the
Queen to make the Prince submit to his father, which she
never would allow before : this gave occasion to a rather
ludicrous scene.

The Queen ordered me to write many things to my
brother, that the King was not to know of, and to send him
the draught of a letter which he was to address to his father.

[1] Friedrich Heinrich Ludwig, born in January 1726. He was to
establish a particularly close rapport with Frederick the Great. He was a
brilliant general as well as a man of cultivated taste. He died in 1802.

I was sitting between two Indian cabinets, writing these letters, when I heard the King coming. A skreen which was placed before the door, gave me time to thrust my papers behind one of those cabinets. Madam de Sonsfeld took the pens, and seeing the King already approaching, I put the inkstand into my pocket, and held it carefully, lest it might be overturned. After having addressed a few words to the Queen, the King suddenly turned towards those cabinets, and said, " They are very beautiful ; they belonged to my late mother, who valued them very much." At the same time, he went up to open them. The lock was spoiled : he pulled the key as much as he could, and I every moment expected my letters would appear. The Queen delivered me from this apprehension, to throw me into another. She had a beautiful little Bolognese dog, and I had one also : the two animals were in the room. " Will you decide our dispute ? (said she to the King) My daughter says her dog is prettier than mine ; and I maintain the contrary."—The King laughed, and asked whether I was fond of mine ?—" Heartily (answered I) ; for he is very clever, and of an excellent disposition." The King, pleased with my reply, embraced me several times ; which obliged me to let go my inkstand. The black liquid immediately ran all over my clothes, and was beginning to drop about the room. I did not dare to stir from the place, lest the King should perceive it. I was half dead with fear : but the King at length delivered me from my embarrassment by retiring. The ink had penetrated through all my garments : we were forced to have them bleached ; and we laughed very much at the occurrence. Meanwhile the King was reconciled to my brother, who joined us at Potsdam. He was the most amiable prince that could be seen ; handsome, well made, of an understanding superior to his years, and possessed of every quality that forms a perfect prince. But I am now arrived at more serious events, and at the source of all the misfortunes which that beloved brother and myself have undergone.

In the year 1717, the Emperor had established an East-India Company at Ostend, a seaport town of the Netherlands. The trade had begun with two vessels only ; and, notwithstanding the obstacles opposed by the Dutch, the success was so great that the Emperor granted the Company the privilege of trading to Africa and the East-Indies for thirty years, excluding all his other subjects from that trade.[1] As commerce contributes most to render a country flourishing, the Emperor had entered into a secret treaty with Spain in the year 1725, by which he engaged to oblige England to restore Gibraltar and Port Mahon to Spain. Russia afterwards acceded to that treaty. It was not long ere the maritime powers became sensible of the secret intrigues of the Court of Vienna ; to oppose the ambitious views of the House of Austria which tended only to ruin their commerce, their principal strength, they concluded an alliance between themseves ; to which France, Denmark, Sweden, and Prussia, afterwards acceded. This is the very treaty which was signed at Charlottenburg, and which I have already mentioned.

The Emperor, seeing that he could not maintain himself against so formidable a league, was obliged to take other measures and to attempt to break this league. General Seckendorff appeared extremely proper for the execution of his designs at the court of Berlin. It has already been observed, that this minister was intimate with Grumbkow ; he knew the selfish and ambitious disposition of his friend, and had no doubt he should bring him over to the interests of the Emperor. He began by writing to him, and endeavoured to penetrate into his sentiments ; he even made him some overtures respecting the circumstances in which his sovereign was placed. This correspondence had begun the year before, and Seckendorff's letters had been accompanied with very handsome presents and liberal promises. The

[1] The Charter of the Ostend Company was granted by Charles VI in 1722 in contravention (at least according to the Maritime powers) of the Treaty of Westphalia.

venal soul of Grumbkow was not long in yielding to such great advantages. Circumstances favoured his design. The alliance of the courts of Berlin and Hanover was beginning to decline. The King, my father, was highly offended at my marriage being delayed ; to this were added other matters of complaint. The Prussian monarch delighted in increasing his regiment of giants : his recruiting-officers took, *nolens volens*, every tall man whom they found in foreign dominions.

The Queen had obtained from the King her father, that the Electorate of Hanover should furnish a certain number every year. The Hanoverian ministers, bribed perhaps by the anti-Prussian party, at the head of which was Lady Darlington, neglected to execute the orders of the King of England. The Queen often remonstrated on this subject ; but was answered by some frivolous excuses. The King was highly offended at the little attention that was shewn to him ; and Grumbkow instigated him to such a degree, that, to be revenged, he ordered his officers to carry off from the electorate of Hanover every man they should meet of a size proper to serve in his regiment. This violence excited a violent outcry. The King of England demanded satisfaction, and required that his subjects should be set free : but the King of Prussia persisted in keeping them ; which caused a misunderstanding between the two courts, that soon increased into open hatred.[1] The state of affairs, at his arrival at Berlin, was therefore such as Seckendorff could wish. The pains which Grumbkow had taken beforehand to prejudice the mind of the King, facilitated his negociation. He was well received by the King, who had particularly

[1] Wilhelmina is here probably anticipating events which took place in 1729, when Hanoverian troops, in answer to an alleged siezure of tall Hanoverian soldiers, seized a field of disputed territory as well as some Prussian officers. The dispute nearly led to war. It is documented in an amusing anonymous publication, *A letter from an English traveller to his Friend at London, relating to differences between the Courts of Prussia and Hanover* (London, 1730). At this stage relations between the two courts were still good.

known him when he was in the Saxon service, and had always manifested great esteem for him. A numerous train of *heiduks*, or rather of giants, whom the Emperor sent to the King, tended farther to secure to him a favourable reception, and the compliment he delivered from his master completed the business. " As the Emperor," said he, " studies only to please your majesty on every occasion, he allows your majesty to enlist in Hungary, and has given orders to find out the tallest men in his dominions, to be offered to your majesty." This obliging behaviour, so different from that of the King his father-in-law, affected the Prussian monarch, but not sufficiently. Seckendorff rightly judged, that some time would be required to win him entirely from the grand alliance. He endeavoured to insinuate himself gradually into the mind of the King, and knowing his foible, he did not fail to draw him into the snare. He almost every day gave him magnificent entertainments, to which he admitted only his creatures and those of Grumbkow. The conversation constantly turned upon the juncture of Europe at that time ; and the cause of the Emperor was artfully pleaded. At length, in the midst of wine and good cheer, the King was induced to renounce some of the engagements he had entered into with England, and to connect himself with the House of Austria. He promised the latter, that the troops he was to furnish to England by virtue of one of the articles of the treaty of Hanover, should not act against the Emperor. This promise was kept very secret. The King was not yet determined to break the grand alliance, as he still hoped to conclude my marriage. It was only towards the end of the following year, of which I am going to speak, that he took off the mask. The Queen was in the utmost despair to witness the train which affairs were taking ; she was a personal sufferer. The King used her ill, and constantly reproached her with the procrastination of my marriage ; he spoke of the King her father in abusive terms, and studied to mortify her on every occasion.

Seckendorff's credit encreased daily. He obtained so great an ascendancy over the King, that he appointed to all offices. The Spanish gold had gained over to his interests most of the domestics and generals about the King ; so that he was informed of all his proceedings. As the double marriage agreed upon with the British monarch would have been a serious obstacle to his views, he resolved to break it off, by sowing discord in the family. For this purpose he employed some of his secret emissaries. A thousand false reports made every day to the King of my brother and me, irritated him so much against us, that he treated us very harshly and made us suffer martyrdom. My brother was represented to him as an ambitious and intriguing prince, who wished for his death that he might sooner be sovereign ; who had no affection for the army ; and who loudly declared, that when he should be master he would disband the troops ; who was prodigal in the extreme, and, in short, of a disposition so opposite to the King's, that it was but natural that this monarch should hate him. I was not better treated : I was painted as being insufferably haughty, intriguing, and imperious ; serving as an adviser to my brother, and speaking with very little respect of the King. As he wished very much to see his daughters settled, Seckendorff also insinuated himself in this respect. He prevailed with the Margrave of Ansbach, a young prince of seventeen, to come to Berlin to see my second sister. This prince was then very amiable, and excited great hopes. My sister was beautiful as an angel, but she had a narrow mind and numberless caprices. She had supplanted me in the favour of the King, by whom she was spoiled. The bitter sorrows which assailed her after her marriage have corrected her faults. The youth of the parties prevented the immediate solemnization of their marriage ; it was celebrated two years after, as I shall state in its time.

The Queen had always flattered herself, that the arrival of the King of England, who was to revisit his German dominions that year, would re-establish the former harmony between the two courts : but an unforeseen event destroyed all her hopes, for she received the mournful intelligence of the death of her royal father. He had left England in perfect health, and, contrary to custom, had endured the voyage uncommonly well. He felt indisposed near Osnabruck. All the remedies that were administered proved useless ; and at the end of four and twenty hours he expired, in an apoplectic fit, in the arms of the Duke of York his brother.[1]

This death plunged the Queen into a profound grief. The King himself appeared affected. Notwithstanding all the prejudices which he had entertained against the English monarch, he had always considered him as a father, and even stood in awe of him. This monarch had been careful of him in his infancy, when the King Frederick I had taken refuge at Hanover, against the persecutions of the Electress Dorothea, his mother-in-law. Their regrets were still greater when they learned, shortly after, that the British monarch had really intended to conclude my marriage, and to solemnize it at Hanover. The Prince his son was proclaimed King of Great Britain, and the Duke of Gloucester assumed the title of Prince of Wales.

In the mean time, the frequent debaucheries into which Seckendorff betrayed the King, began to prey upon his health ; his hypochondria returned with all its melancholy symptoms : and Mr Francke, the famous methodist,[2]

[1] Prince Anhalt-Dessau regarded the death of George I as an " *Österreichisches Mirakel* " (Droysen, op. cit., 411), and considered that reconciliation between the English and Prussian courts was henceforth impossible. Frederick William personally detested his brother George II.

[2] August Herman Francke (1667–1727), the German Pietist, was one of the most significant figures of the early German Enlightenment. His " Orphanage " founded in Halle in 1698 became a model for educational establishments and teaching methods throughout Protestant Europe in the eighteenth century. Frederick William actively protected Francke. His attachment to Francke's belief in the power of Grace combined with an understanding of the value of rational education and action are essential in order to comprehend his attitudes.

and founder of the orphan-house in the university of Halle, contributed much to increase it. This clergyman delighted in making scruples of conscience respecting the most innocent actions. He condemned every diversion, even hunting and music, as damnable. Nothing was to be spoken of but the word of God; any other discourse was prohibited. It was always he who acted the fine speaker at table, where he performed the office of lecturer, as in the dining-room of convents. The King preached a sermon to us every afternoon; his valet began to sing a hymn, in which we all joined; we were forced to listen to this sermon with as much attention as if it had been that of an apostle. My brother and I were often inclined to laugh, and sometimes we could not help bursting out. But we were instantly overwhelmed with all the anathemas of the church, to which we were obliged to attend with a contrite and penitent air, which we found it difficult to affect. In short, the tedious Francke made us live like the monks of La Trappe. This excess of bigotry led the King to thoughts still more extraordinary : he resolved to abdicate the crown in behalf of my brother. " He would (he said) reserve ten thousand dollars a year for himself, and retire with the Queen and his daughters to Wusterhausen. There (added he) I shall worship God, and superintend my farm ; whilst my wife and daughters regulate the concerns of the house."—" You are clever (said he to me) ; you will take care of the linen and washing : Frederica, who is avaricious, shall be the storekeeper ; Charlotte shall go to market to provide and purchase provisions ; and my wife will nurse the little ones, and cook." He even began to write some instructions for my brother, and to take several steps, at which Grumbkow and Seckendorff felt seriously alarmed. They vainly used all their rhetoric to dissipate these singular ideas : but as they saw that the projects of the King proceeded from his temper, they feared he might execute them, if he were not opposed, and resolved to try to divert his thoughts.

The court of Saxony having been in strict alliance with that of Austria, they turned their views to that quarter, and persuaded him to take a journey to Dresden : and as one idea commonly brings another in its train, this project gave birth to that of marrying me to Augustus King of Poland.[1]

This monarch was then forty-nine years old. He had always been famous for his gallantry : he possessed shining qualities, but they were tarnished by great faults. His excessive love of pleasure made him neglect the happiness of his people, and his attachment to the bottle betrayed him, when intoxicated, into indignities which will for ever be an indelible stain upon his memory.

Seckendorff, in his younger days, had been in the Saxon service ; and, as I have already observed, Grumbkow was on very good terms with the King of Poland. They both applied to Count Flemming,[2] a favourite of the Polish monarch, to endeavour to open a negociation on that subject. Count Flemming was a man of superior merit ; he had frequently been at Berlin, and knew me very well. He was delighted with the proposal, and sounded the King of Poland upon it. The monarch appeared favourably inclined to the alliance, and sent the Count to Berlin to invite the King of Prussia to pass the Carnaval at Dresden. Grumbkow and his Pylades imparted their designs to the King. Charmed to meet with so brilliant an establishment for me, he gladly assented to their wishes : he returned a very obliging answer to Count Flemming, and set out for Dresden in the middle of the month of January, 1728.

My brother was extremely chagrined at not being of the party. He was to remain at Potsdam during the absence

[1] Frederick Augustus II, Elector of Saxony, known as Augustus the Strong (1670–1733). He was elected to, or rather he seized, the Polish throne in 1696, from which he was for a short while deposed by Charles XII of Sweden.

[2] Jakob Heinrich von Flemming (1667–1728). He had previously accompanied William of Orange to England in 1688 and had also served at the Prussian court before becoming one of Augustus's closest advisers. His involvement in the " Clement " plot makes it difficult to understand Wilhelmina's sympathetic remarks about him.

of the King ; which did not at all please him. He acquainted
me with his disappointment ; and as I delighted in nothing
so much as in promoting his pleasure, I promised to contrive
it so that he might follow the King.—We returned to
Berlin, where the Queen held her drawing-rooms as usual.
I saw at court the Saxon minister, M. de Suhm, whom I
knew extremely well, and who was friendly to my brother.
I delivered the Prince Royal's compliments to him, and
mentioned to him the regret of the prince at not having
been invited to Dresden. " If you wish to do him a favour,
(added I) contrive it so that the Polish monarch may
prevail with the King of Prussia to send for him." Suhm
immediately dispatched an express to his court to acquaint
the King his master with my wishes. The latter did not fail
to induce my father to send for my brother, who received
orders to join him ; which he did with uncommon pleasure.

The reception given to the King of Prussia was worthy of
the two monarchs. As the Prussian monarch was not fond
of ceremonies, every thing was regulated according to his
inclinations. He had requested to be lodged at the house of
Count Wackerbart, for whom he entertained a high esteem.
The mansion of this general was superb ; the King found an
apartment truly royal. Unfortunately, it was consumed by
fire the second night after his arrival. The conflagration
was so sudden and violent, that it was not without extreme
difficulty that the King was saved. The beautiful mansion
was reduced to ashes.[1] The loss would have been very
considerable to Count Wackerbart, had not the Polish
monarch presented him with the Pirna palace which still
excelled in sumptuousness.

The Court of Dresden was then the most brilliant in

---

[1] Pöllnitz in his *Memoirs* (English edition, 1739, II 91) also describes
the fire at the house of General Count von Wackerbart : " His Majesty
was in Bed when the Fire burst out with such fury that he had just time
to make his escape in his Night-Gown, and to save a little box in which
there were papers of consequence ; for the Floor of his Bed-Chamber fell
in, the moment after the King had gone out of it. An Officer, his Wife
and her Maid-Servant perished in the flames."

Germany. Its magnificence was carried to excess. As it was the seat of all pleasures, it might justly be styled the island of Cytherea. The women were all lovely, and the courtiers uncommonly polite. The monarch kept a kind of seraglio of the most beautiful females of his dominions. At his death it was calculated that he had three hundred and fifty-four children by his mistresses.[1] The whole court was modelled after his example : luxury there had its throne, and the two presiding divinities were Bacchus and Venus. The King of Prussia was not long there before he forgot his devotion ; the debauches of the table and the wines of Hungary, soon revived his good humour. The obliging manners of the Polish monarch made him contract an intimate friendship with that Prince. Grumbkow, who did not forget his interest in the midst of pleasure, wished to avail himself of these good dispositions to inspire the King with a taste for mistresses : he imparted his design to the monarch of Poland, who undertook its execution.

One evening when they had sacrificed to Bacchus, the King of Poland insensibly led the King of Prussia to a very richly decorated room, the furniture and ornaments of which were of exquisite taste. The King of Prussia, delighted with what he saw, stopped to contemplate all its beauties ; when on a sudden a tapestry was rolled up, which procured him a very novel sight. It was a lovely female in a state of nudity, carelessly reclined on a couch. Her beauty excelled that of the finest pictures of Venus and the Graces ; her body seemed of ivory, whiter than snow, and better shaped than that of the Venus de Medicis at Florence. The closet which contained this treasure, was illuminated with so many wax tapers that their dazzling light added a new splendour to the beauty of the nymph.

The authors of this comedy had no doubt but this object would make some impression upon the heart of the Prussian monarch ; they were however disappointed. Scarcely had

[1] In fact Augustus acknowledged only ten of his certainly very numerous offspring—Paul Haake, *August der Starke* (Berlin, 1926) 198.

the King cast his eyes on the fair one, than he turned about with indignation ; and seeing my brother behind him, he rudely pushed him out of the room, and left it immediately after in a violent irritation against the trick they had attempted to practise upon him. He mentioned it to Grumbkow in very angry terms that evening, and declared that if such scenes were repeated, he would leave Dresden instantly. The case was different with my brother. In spite of the King's vigilance, he had had time to contemplate the Venus of the closet, who did not cause him so much horror as she had done to his father. He obtained her in a singular manner of the Polish monarch.

My brother had fallen passionately in love with the Countess Orczelska, who was at once a natural daughter and a mistress of the King of Poland.[1] Her mother was a French milliner at Warsaw. Countess Orczelska owed her fortune to Count von Rutowski her brother, whose mistress she had been, and who had introduced her to the King of Poland her father, who, as I have already observed, had so many children that he could not provide for them all. However the monarch was so struck with the charms of the Countess, that he immediately acknowledged her as his daughter ; his passion for her was unbounded. The attentions of my brother for this lady inspired him with a bitter jealousy. To break off this intrigue, he offered him the beautiful Formera on condition that he should renounce Countess Orczelska. My brother promised whatever was required, to obtain possession of the handsome Formera who was his first mistress.

My father, in the meantime, did not forget the object of his journey. He entered into a secret treaty with King Augustus, the conditions of which were nearly these :— The King of Prussia engaged to furnish a certain number

[1] Pöllnitz (op. cit., 119) describes Anna, Countess Orczelska, as " born in Warsaw, of one Renard, a French Woman and bred up in the Roman Catholic faith . . . . She is fond of Magnificence, Expense and Pleasures. One of her many Diversions is to dress up in Men's Apparel . . . many Ladies would have been glad of a Lover so handsome." (See Plate).

of troops to the King of Poland to force the Poles to render the crown hereditary in the electoral House of Saxony. He promised to marry me to the Electoral Prince, to lend him four millions of dollars, and to give me a considerable portion. The King of Poland, on his part, was to assign Lusatia to him as a mortgage for the four millions. A dowry of two hundred thousand dollars was to be settled for me upon that province, and after the King's death I should be permitted to reside where I might choose. I was to have the free exercise of my religion at Dresden, where a chapel was to be built for me. Lastly, all these articles were to be signed and confirmed by the electoral Prince of Saxony.[1] As my father had invited the King of Poland to Berlin to be present at the review of his troops, the signature of the treaty was delayed to that time. The Polish monarch had solicited this delay, to prepare the mind of his son and to persuade him to consent to what was required of him.

The King my father left Dresden, highly satisfied with his journey ; as likewise was my brother. They were both equally zealous in launching out before us in praise of the King of Poland and his court.

While all these things were going forward, I was cruelly persecuted at Berlin by the Countess Amalia, who was continually sowing discord betwixt the Queen and me. Her ill usage was incessant. I submitted with deference to the unjust proceedings of the Queen ; but those of her favourite drove me at times into a violent rage. The Countess treated me with an insufferable haughtiness ; and though she was but two years older than myself, she yet pretended to direct my conduct. Notwithstanding all the provocations I received from her, I was obliged to constrain myself and to put on an air of civility, which was more painful than death ;

---

[1] Frederick William's treaty with Augustus involved no marriage with Wilhelmina nor hers with anyone else. Principally an exchange of mutual guarantees was involved ; in addition Frederick William insisted that Augustus grant full rights to Protestants in both Saxony and Poland. This Wilhelmina interprets as a private chapel in Dresden (Droysen, op. cit., IV, iii, 15–19).

for I detest dissimulation : my sincerity has been the frequent source of the many sorrows I have experienced. It is however a failing which I do not wish to lay aside. My maxim is, that we ought always to follow the straight path ; and that we cannot grieve when we have nothing to reproach ourselves with.

A new monster was starting up as a favourite, and sharing the good graces of the Queen with Countess Amalia. Her name was Ramen : she was one of the waiting-women of the Queen, and the same who unexpectedly assisted her in her labour when she was delivered of my sister Amalia. This woman was a widow ; or, rather, she followed the example of the Samaritan woman, and had as many husbands as there are months in the year. Her pretended devotion, her affected charity for the poor, and the care which she had taken to cloak her dissolute life, had induced Madam de Blaspil to recommend her to the Queen. She began to insinuate herself into her good graces by her dexterity at several works which amused her Majesty : but it was only by the reports which she made her about the King that she reached the high degree of favour which she was then enjoying. The Queen placed a blind confidence in this woman, whom she trusted with her affairs, and her most secret thoughts. Two rivals for glory could not long agree. The Countess Amalia and Mrs. Ramen became sworn enemies : but as they were afraid of each other, they concealed their animosity.

Shortly after the King had returned from Dresden, Count Flemming, accompanied by Princess Radzivill his consort, arrived at Berlin as envoy-extraordinary of the King of Poland. The Countess was a young person without education, but very lively and ingenious ; extremely agreeable, though not handsome. The King noticed her very much, and ordered the Queen to do the same. Countess Flemming manifested a great attachment for me. I felt a real friendship for her husband, who had known me from infancy. As he was advanced in years, the Queen had given him leave to visit me whenever he chose : he assiduously availed himself of this permission, and came every morning with his lady, who paid me very great attentions. My dress was highly ridiculous. My hair and my garments were, by order of the Queen, in the same fashion as they had been worn by my old grandmother in her youth. The Countess de Flemming represented to her Majesty, that they would laugh at me at the court of Dresden, if they saw me thus accoutred. She made me dress in the new style, and every one allowed that I was no longer the same person and appeared much handsomer than before. My shape began to be fine and slender, which improved my appearance. The Countess repeated a thousand times a day to the Queen, that I must become her sovereign. As both the Queen and myself were unacquainted with the treaty of Dresden, we took her observations for mere jests. The Count resided two months at Berlin, and came to take leave of me the day before his departure, under repeated assurances of a sincere respect. " I hope," said he, " I shall soon be able to give your Royal Highness proofs of my inviolable attachment, and render you as happy as you deserve to be. I think I shall have the honour of seeing you again in a short time, with the King my master." I did not understand the meaning of his words ; I simply thought he would apply to promote my marriage with the Prince of Wales. I returned him a very obliging answer ; and he withdrew.

We set out for Potsdam a few days after. I should have been vexed with this journey at any other period ; but I was glad to leave Berlin at that time. I hoped to regain the good graces of the Queen, who had been so much prejudiced against me, that she could no longer endure me.

The affairs of England were in a tolerably tranquil state. The Queen, my mother, was incessantly pursuing measures to effect my marriage, without making any progress in the business ; while she suffered herself to be imposed upon by every idle promise. All this put her into an ill humour against me. She would say : " if you had been better educated, you would have been married some time ago." During the absence of Countess Amalia, I hoped to dispel all these prejudices which were of her suggesting : but I was disappointed. The mind of the Queen was so embittered against me, that my situation was not more comfortable at Potsdam than it had been at Berlin. The Queen was even on the point of complaining to the King of my governess and myself, and of entreating him to intrust the care of my person to another : but she was withheld by fear. She knew the particular regard which the King professed for Madam de Sonsfeld ; this made her apprehensive that the attempt would not be crowned with success. Count Fink himself, to whom she mentioned it, dissuaded her very much from venturing on such a step. This general was unacquainted with the ambitious views of his daughter, and his probity besides was too strict to approve of them. He earnestly addressed the Queen, on behalf of myself and of Madam de Sonsfeld, and urged so many representations on the harshness of her behaviour towards her and me, that she relinquished her intention. She even talked to me in the afternoon, and told me all the grievances which she sustained on my account. She condemned the confidence which I reposed in my governess ; a confidence which, she said, she altogether disapproved of. She also regretted that I blindly followed the advice of that lady ; and added many similar complaints. I cast myself at her feet ; and observed that the knowledge which I had of the character of Madam de Sonsfeld, would not allow me to keep any thing from her ; that I entrusted her with my own secrets, but never with those of others ; and that this very knowledge of her merit induced me to follow her advice, as I was sure she would never give me any but what was good ; that besides I was only obeying the commands which I had received from her Majesty. I entreated her to do justice to Madam de Sonsfeld, and not to drive me to despair by withdrawing that kindness with which I had always been honoured.

The Queen was somewhat disconcerted at my answer. She was searching for some ill pretence to complain of my behaviour. I made many submissions, and was at length pardoned. Two days after I was more in favor than ever, and Madam de Sonsfeld, whom she had studiously mortified, was better treated.

I should now have been perfectly tranquil, had not my brother disturbed my peace. Ever since his return from Dresden, he was plunged into a gloomy melancholy. This change of his disposition operated upon his health ; he was visibly falling away, and frequently fainting ; which made us fear he had become consumptive. The Queen and myself did all in our power to divert him. I loved him passionately ; whenever I enquired into the cause of his sorrow, he attributed it *to the ill treatment he met with from the King*. I endeavoured to comfort him in the best manner I could ; but in vain. His disease at last increased so rapidly, that it was necessary to inform the King of it. His Majesty ordered the surgeon of his regiment, to watch over the health of the Prince, and to examine into his illness. The report which the surgeon gave of the state of my brother greatly alarmed the King. He said that the Prince was very ill ; that he had a sort of slow fever, which would terminate in a consumption, if he did not take care of himself, and use some remedies. The heart of the King was naturally good : although Grumbkow had filled his mind with strong prejudices against the poor prince, and notwithstanding the just causes of complaint, which he thought he had against him, nature pleaded for him with a voice too powerful to remain unheard. The King upbraided himself, as having thrown his son into his present deplorable condition, by numerous sorrows and vexations, to which he had subjected him : and he endeavoured to atone for the past, by lavishing his caresses and kindness upon him : but all this was of no avail, and the cause of his disorder remained undiscovered. At length it was conjectured, that it proceeded from love. He had been inclined to libertinism since he had resided at Dresden. The constraint under which he lived prevented his abandoning himself to it ; and his constitution could not bear up against this privation. Some officious persons informed the King of it, and advised him to have the Prince married, else his life would be in danger, or he might indulge in excesses which would ruin his health. The King answered, in presence of some young officers, that he would give one hundred ducats to the person who should inform him, that his son was afflicted with a disgraceful malady. The endearments and kindnesses which he had shown him, gave way to reprimands and rebukes. Count Fink and Colonel Kalkstein were ordered to watch more strictly than ever the conduct of the Prince. But it was not till a long time after that I was acquainted with these circumstances.

The death of the British monarch had completely disengaged the King, my father, from the grand alliance. He at last concluded a treaty with Austria, Russia, and Saxony.[1] He, as well as the two latter powers, engaged to assist the Emperor of Germany with ten thousand men, whenever he should want them. The Emperor, on his part, engaged to guarantee to Prussia the duchies of Berg and Jülich. The Queen was excessively vexed at seeing all her plans miscarry : neither could she conceal her resentment, the whole weight of which fell upon Seckendorff and Grumbkow. The King frequently mentioned his treaty with the Emperor at table, and never failed to reproach the King of England ; and his invectives were always addressed to the Queen. Her Majesty immediately vented her's against Seckendorff. Her vivacity would not suffer her to keep within bounds : she treated this minister in a very harsh and offensive manner, sometimes imprudently reminding him of certain traits in his past conduct, which should have been passed over in silence. Seckendorff, in the mean while, could hardly contain his resentment : but he listened

[1] The Secret Treaty of Berlin, 1728. Wilhelmina gives the essential clauses quite accurately.

to the Queen's abuse with a feigned moderation, which
highly pleased the King. But there was nothing lost, for
he knew how to revenge himself otherwise than by words.

As the time appointed for the visit of the King of Poland
drew near, we returned to Berlin in the beginning of May.
The Queen there found letters from Hanover, which informed her that the Prince of Wales had resolved to go
incognito to Berlin, with an intention of availing himself of
the tumult and confusion that would prevail in that
metropolis, during the residence of the King of Poland, to
obtain a sight of me. This news gave unspeakable joy to the
Queen ; and she immediately communicated it to me. As
I was not always of her opinion, my satisfaction was not
equal to her's. I have always possessed some share of
philosophy : ambition is no failing of mine ; I prefer
happiness and tranquillity to grandeur : I hate constraint of
any kind ; I am fond of the world and its pleasures : but I
approve not of dissipation. My character, such as I have
described it, did not suit the court for which the Queen destined me. Of this I was fully sensible, and it made me
afraid of being settled in England.

The arrival of several ladies and gentlemen from Hanover
made the Queen suppose that the Prince of Wales was
among them. There was neither ass nor mule but what she
took for her nephew ; she would even have sworn that
she had seen him in the crowd at Mon-Bijou. But a second
letter from Hanover convinced her of her mistake : she
was informed that the rumour had been spread, in consequence of some jocose remarks which the Prince of Wales
had made one evening at table, and which had occasioned
the belief that he would go to Berlin.

The King of Poland arrived on the 29th of May. He
immediately paid a visit to the Queen ; who received him
at the door of her third anti-room. The Polish monarch
gave her his hand, and conducted her into her audience-
hall, where we were presented to him. This monarch,
who was then fifty years old, had a majestic appearance and

countenance ; affability and politeness shone in every movement, and were visible in all his actions. His constitution was much impaired for his age. In the gratification of his excessive debaucheries, he had met with an accident in his right foot, which impaired his walking, and rendered him unable to stand for any length of time. The wound was always kept open, and extremely painful. It had even been mortified, and the foot had only been saved by the amputation of two toes. The Queen immediately offered him a chair, which he would not accept for a long while, but at last, by dint of entreaties, he took a stool ; and the Queen sat down upon another opposite. As we remained standing, he made many apologies to my sisters and me about his unpoliteness. He examined me very attentively, and said something obliging to every one of us. He left the Queen, after an hour's conversation. She wished to attend him out of the rooms ; but he would not allow it.

The Prince Royal of Poland[1] came soon after, to pay his respects to the Queen. This Prince is very tall and stout ; his face is regularly handsome, but not prepossessing. An air of embarrassment accompanies all his actions, and, in order to conceal this embarrassment, he has recourse to a very disagreeable forced smile. He speaks little, and does not possess the talent of making himself affable and obliging like his father. He may even be taxed with inattention and rudeness. Under this uninviting exterior, however, he conceals great qualities, which have displayed themselves since he became King of Poland. He values himself on being a truly honest man, and his whole attention is devoted to the happiness of his subjects. Those who incur his displeasure, might still consider themselves fortunate if they were in any other country. Far from doing them any harm, he dismisses them with large pensions : he never has forsaken those on whom he had once placed his affection. He leads a very regular life, and cannot be reproached with any vice ; and the good understanding which prevails

[1] Later Augustus III (1696–1763).

121

between him and his spouse merits the greatest praise. This Princess was uncommonly plain, and had no accomplishment to make amends for her want of beauty.—The Prince did not stay long with the Queen. After this short visit we sunk again into our nothingness, and passed the evening, as usual, fasting and in solitude ; I say *fasting*, for we had scarcely as much as would assuage our hunger. But let us reserve the description of our way of life for some other place.

The King and the Prince of Poland supped each in private. The next day, which was Sunday, we all went after church into the state-rooms of the palace. The Queen, accompanied by her daughters, the Princesses of the blood, and her court, entered the gallery at one end ; and the two Kings approached by the other. I never beheld a finer sight. All the ladies of Berlin, magnificently attired, ranged themselves in a row along the gallery. The King, the Prince of Poland, and their retinue, which consisted of three hundred great personages of their respective courts, Polanders as well as Saxons, were superbly dressed. The contrast between them and the Prussians was striking ; the latter were simply clad in regimentals ; and their singular appearance excited attention. Their coats are so short, that they could not have served as fig leaves to our first parents ; and so strait, that they did not dare to move for fear of rending them. Their summer small-clothes are of white linen, as well as their spatterdashes,[1] without which they must not appear. Their hair is powdered, but not curled, and twisted behind with a ribband into a queue. The King himself was dressed in the same manner. After the first compliments, the strangers were all presented to the Queen, and then to me. Prince John Adolphus of Weissenfels, a Lieutenant-General in the Saxon service, was the first to whom I was introduced ;[2] many others followed, such as

[1] Gaiters.

[2] Johann Adolf, titular Duke of Weissenfels, and not even certain of his succession to this minor title. Wilhelmina seems to make too much of him in these pages. He really was most insignificant.

Count de Saxe and Count von Rutowski, both actual sons of
the King ; M. de Libski, since then Primate and Arch-
bishop of Cracow ; Counts Manteuffel, Lagnasco, and
Brühl, favourites of the King ; Count Solkofski, favourite of
the Electoral Prince ; and several other persons of the first
distinction, whom I pass over. Count Flemming was not of
the number : he had died three weeks before at Vienna,
universally regretted.

We dined in state. The table was long ; the King of
Poland and my mother sat at one end ; my father had the
King of Poland on one side, and the Electoral Prince on the
other. Next in order were the Princes of the blood and the
strangers. I sat near the Queen having my sister near me ;
and below us the Princesses of the blood according to their
rank. Many toasts were drank, but little was said, and the
dinner was altogether very tiresome. After the repast,
every one retired to his apartment. In the evening the
Queen held a grand drawing-room. The Countesses
Orczelska and Bilinska, natural daughters of the King of
Poland, came to court ; as well as Mrs. Potge so famous for
her dissolute manners. The first, as I have already observed, was mistress to her own father ; a circumstance
which makes one shudder with horror ! Though not a regular beauty, she possessed an agreeable person : her shape
was a perfect model, and there was a something altogether
prepossessing in her air and manner. Her heart was not
enslaved by her superannuated lover : she loved her
brother Count von Rutowski, who was the son of a Turkish
female that had been a waiting-maid to the Countess
Königsmark, mother to the Count de Saxe. Countess
Orczelska was uncommonly magnificent in her dress,
particularly in jewels, the King having presented her with
those of his late Queen. The Polish gentleman who had
been presented to me in the morning, were much surprized to hear me pronouncing their uncouth names, and to
see that I knew them again. They were delighted with my
attentions, and declared aloud *that I must be their Queen.*

The following day there was a grand review. The two Monarchs dined together in private, and we did not appear in public. The day after there was a grand illumination in the town, which we were permitted to see; I never beheld any thing more beautiful. All the houses of the principal streets were decorated with mottos, and illuminated with such a prodigious number of coloured lamps, that one's eyes were completely dazzled. Two days after this we had a grand ball in the state-rooms : we drew for partners, and the King of Poland happened to be mine. The next day there was a fête at Mon-Bijou : and the green-house was illuminated, which had a very pretty effect.

Festivities ceased at Berlin, and recommenced at Charlottenburg, where we had several splendid entertainments. I had but little share in them : the bad opinion which my father entertained of the sex in general, kept us under great restraints ; and the Queen was forced to be incessantly on her guard, by reason of his jealous disposition. On the day fixed for the departure of the Polish monarch, the two Kings had a friendly dinner (*table de confiance*). It is thus called, because none but chosen friends are admitted. The table is constructed in such a manner, that it may be let down with pulleys. No servants attend ; dumb-waiters placed near the guests supply their place. Every one writes on the top of the waiter what he wants ; the dumb-waiter is let down, and is hoisted up again with what was demanded.[1] The repast lasted from one o'clock in the afternoon till ten at night. Frequent libations were made to the god of wine, of which the effects were visible in the two monarchs. On leaving the table they went to the Queen : and here two hours were passed at play. I played with the

---

[1] An anonymous description of Frederick William's visit to Dresden (summarised by P. Haake in *Forschungen zur Brandenburgischen und Preussischen*, XLVII, 1935, 362) relates how he had seen a " dumb waiter " for the first time, and that he was so impressed by it that he requested Augustus to send the inventor, one Karl Friedrich Pöppelman, to instal one in Berlin. Clearly Augustus obliged.

King of Poland and the Queen. The monarch said many obliging things to me, and cheated on purpose to give me the opportunity to win. When the game was over, he took leave of us, returned to his libations, and set out that very night; as I observed before. The Duke of Weissenfels had been very assiduous about me all the time of his stay at Berlin. I had considered his attentions as the mere effects of politeness, and never could have supposed that he dared to entertain the idea of marrying me. He was a younger son of a house which, though very antient, does not rank among the illustrious houses of Germany; and though my heart was free from ambition, it was also free from meanness. I did not harbour the smallest suspicion concerning the real sentiments of the Duke. I was however mistaken; as will be seen hereafter.

I have not mentioned my brother since our departure from Potsdam. His health began to return: but he affected to be worse than he really was, that he might be excused from appearing at the state-dinner which was to be given at Berlin, as he did not wish to yield precedency to the Electoral Prince of Saxony; which the King my father would certainly have required. He arrived the Monday after. The pleasure which he felt on meeting again with Countess Orczelska, and the good reception she gave him when he visited her in secret, completed his cure. In the mean time, the King my father set out for Prussia. He left my brother at Potsdam, and gave him leave to go twice in a week to Berlin, to pay his respects to the Queen. We passed our time very agreeably during the King's absence. A great concourse of strangers rendered the court very brilliant; and the King of Poland sent his most skilful amateurs to the Queen. Among these were the famous *Weiss*, whose performance on the lute has never been surpassed; and those who come after him, will only have the glory of imitating him; *Buffardin*, celebrated for his excellence on the flute; and *Quantz*, a performer on the same instrument, a great composer, and whose taste and exquisite skill drew from the flute sounds equal to those of the finest voice.[1]

[1] The orchestra at Dresden was the most famous in Germany, especially as Frederick William had disbanded the Berlin orchestra at his accession. Silvius Leopold Weiss (1686–1750), a German composer, is said to have been the last great lute-player of the eighteenth century. Pierre Gabriel Buffardin (1690–1768) was the first flautist of the Dresden orchestra and the teacher of Joseph Joachim Quantz (1697–1773). Quantz first played for Frederick in 1728 and became his teacher, composing for him some 300 flute concertos and at least another 200 works for the instrument. He is also of great importance to music historians as the author of one of the few existing books on the performance of eighteenth-century baroque music, much referred to today.

IV

Purgatory — A new and disastrous match is planned — My brother is cruelly used — Plans for a secret visit are marred by the Queen's indiscretion — Insult added to insult — A truly comical scene — The King poses a desperate ultimatum — A new suitor is proposed.

WHILST our days were gliding away in tranquil pleasures, the King of Poland was endeavouring to persuade his son to sign the articles of the treaty which concerned my marriage : but all his intreaties proved vain ; the Prince constantly refused his signature. The King of Prussia having no security for the advantages stipulated on his and my behalf, annulled all that had been agreed upon, and broke off the match. It was not till a considerable time after that the Queen and myself were informed of the circumstance. My mother was glad that this negociation had failed : she was still intriguing with the French and English ministers, who acquainted her with all their proceedings ; and as she kept spies near the King, she in her turn communicated to them all that was reported to her. But the King, on his part, had likewise his spies about the Queen : Mrs. Ramen her favourite waiting-woman was his faithful emissary. The Queen kept nothing from this woman ; she every night trusted her with her most secret thoughts, and with whatever she had done during the day. The wretch instantly communicated this information to the monarch through the infamous Eversmann, and the contemptible Holtzendorff, a new monster high in the King's favour. Mrs. Ramen was even connected with Seckendorff : this I heard from my faithful Meermann, who saw her every day entering that minister's house in the dusk. Count de

Rottemburg, the French ambassador, had long since suspected that there were traitors who acquainted Seckendorff with all his plans ; he set so many people to watch him, that he discovered Mrs. Ramen's practices. He would have informed the Queen of her perfidy, had it not been for the English envoy M. Dubourgay[1] and the Danish minister called Lövener ; they were all three in a terrible passion at being thus duped. Count Rottemburg one day mentioned it to me in very bitter terms : " the Queen (said he) has disconcerted all our plans. We are resolved not to confide in her any more : but we shall apply to you, Madam : we are convinced of your discretion, and you will give us as much information as her majesty."—" No, Sir," answered I, " I beg you will never trust me with any secret ; I am very sorry when the Queen communicates any thing to me : I wish to have nothing to do with state affairs ; they come not under my department, and I trouble myself only with my own concerns."—" Our schemes are however for your happiness," replied the Count, " for the happiness of your brother, and of the whole nation."—" I am inclined to believe you," said I ; " but I do not care for the future ; my ambition, fortunately, is limited, and my ideas on those matters are perhaps widely different from those of others." This was the way in which I freed myself from the importunities of that minister. The King, in the mean time, was exceedingly offended at the intrigues of the Queen ; but, in spite of his violent temper, he dissembled his anger. On the other hand, Grumbkow and Seckendorff were not a little perplexed at my marriage with the King of Poland being broken off. To attain their ends, it was absolutely necessary that they should find an establishment for me. They rightly thought, that as long as I remained unmarried, the King would not fully enter into their views. My father was still wishing for my marriage with the Prince of Wales, and unwilling to break entirely with the King of England. They therefore set their heads together to concert a new plan.

[1] Brigadier Charles Dubourgay, English Envoy in Berlin, 1724–30.

Frederick the Great and Wilhelmina as children, 1714

Frederick William I

Sophia Dorothea, mother
to Wilhelmina

In the mean time, the King returned from Prussia ; and six weeks after we attended him to Wusterhausen. Our happiness at Berlin had been too great to be lasting ; from the paradise in which we had lived we fell into purgatory. Our sufferings began a few days after our arrival at this dismal place. The King had a private conversation with the Queen : my sister and myself were sent to an adjoining room. Although the door was closed, I soon conjectured, from the tone of their conversation, that they were having a violent quarrel. I even heard my name frequently repeated ; at which I felt greatly alarmed. The conversation lasted an hour and a half ; at the end of which the King left the room in a furious passion. I immediately went to the Queen, whom I found in tears. As soon as she saw me, she embraced me, and held me a long time inclosed in her arms without uttering a single word. " I am in the utmost despair, (said she at length) the King wants to marry you, and he has fixed upon the worst match that could possibly be found. He intends to unite you to the Duke of Weissenfels, a poor younger son, who lives on the bounty of the King of Poland : my grief would kill me, if you should have the meanness to consent to it." I fancied myself in a dream, so strange did the Queen's information appear to me. I wished to dispel her fears by remarking that the King could not possibly be serious ; and that he had only said so to make her uneasy. " But, good heavens ! " added she, " he will be here in a few days at latest, to solicit your hand : you will need some fortitude ; I shall support you as much as I am able, provided you will second me with your own efforts." I promised religiously to conform to her will ; being firmly resolved not to marry the person who was destined for me. I confess I made very light of it : but I altered my opinion that very evening ; the Queen having received letters from Berlin which confirmed that *delightful* intelligence. I passed a dreadful night, foreseeing the terrible storms that would ensure, and the cruel misunderstanding which would be introduced into the family. My brother, who was a sworn enemy to Seckendorff and Grumbkow, and entirely in favour of England, remonstrated with me in very strong terms on the subject.—" You will ruin us all," said he to me, " if you contract this ridiculous marriage. I clearly see that your resistance will overwhelm us with sorrows ; but it is better to endure any thing than to fall into the power of our enemies : we have no support but England ; and if your marriage with the Prince of Wales be broken off, we are all undone." The Queen and my governess used the same language : but I stood in no need of their exhortations ; reason sufficiently pointed out what I had to do.

The *amiable* prince, destined to be my husband, arrived on the 27th of September, in the evening. The King came to inform the Queen of his arrival, and ordered her to receive him as a prince who was to be her son-in-law ; for he was determined to betroth me to him immediately. This intelligence occasioned a fresh quarrel, which terminated without any alteration in the sentiments of either party. The next day being Sunday, we went to church in the morning ; the Duke did not take his eyes off me during the whole service. I was in a great agitation. Ever since this business had been started, I had not enjoyed any repose either night or day.

When we returned from church, the King presented the Duke to the Queen. She did not open her lips, and turned her back upon him. I had run off to avoid his approach. I could not eat any thing ; and the alteration of my face, joined to the offensiveness of my behaviour, gave sufficient indications of what was passing in my heart. In the afternoon, the Queen had another dreadful interview with the King. As soon as she was left alone, she sent for Count Fink, my brother, and my governess, to deliberate with them concerning what she was to do. The Duke of Weissenfels was known to be a prince of great merit, but of no very extensive genius : all were of opinion that the Queen should address herself to him. Count Fink under-

took the commission. He represented to the Duke, by
order of the Queen, that she would never consent to her
daughter's marriage with him ; that I felt an insupportable aversion for him ; that he would indubitably create
much discord in the family if he persisted in his design ;
that the Queen was determined to affront him in every
possible way, if he continued obstinate ; but that she was
persuaded he would not drive her to such extremities ;
that she had no doubt but, like an honest man, he would
desist from his pursuits rather than render me unhappy ;
and that, in this case, there was nothing that she would
leave undone to give him convincing proofs of her esteem
and gratitude. The Duke requested Count Fink to tell the
Queen, that he was actually captivated with my charms,
that, however, he should never have dared to aspire to the
happiness of obtaining my hand, had he not been induced to
indulge confident hopes : but that, since the Queen and
myself were averse to him, he would himself be the first to
dissuade the King from his project ; and that the Queen
might be perfectly at ease in regard to his pretensions.
Indeed, he kept his word, and wrote to the King pretty
nearly what he had told Count Fink ; with this single
difference, that he requested the monarch, in case the
hopes which his majesty still entertained of bringing about
my marriage with the Prince of Wales should vanish, to
give him the preference before any prince that might sue
for me, excepting, however, crowned heads.

The King, surprised at the Duke's behaviour, went a
moment after to the Queen, and vainly endeavoured to
persuade her to consent to my establishment. Their
quarrels were renewed ; the Queen wept, screamed, and
intreated the King so much, that he agreed not to pursue
matters farther at this time, on condition, however, that she
should write to the Queen of England for a positive
declaration with regard to my marriage with the Prince of
Wales.—" If the answer be favourable," said the King,
" I break any engagement but what I have entered into

with England : but if it be not couched in positive terms, the English may rely upon it, I shall not be their dupe any longer ; they will find me determined ; and, in that case, I insist upon being at liberty to marry my daughter to whom I choose. Do not flatter yourself, madam, that your tears and screams will prevent me from following my own plans. I leave you the care of persuading your brother and your sister-in-law ; they will settle our quarrel." The Queen declared herself ready to write to England, and doubted not but the King her brother and the Queen her sister-in-law would comply with her wishes. " That we shall see," said the King, " I once more tell you, that I shall be inexorable to your daughter, if I am not satisfied ; and as for your dissolute son, do not expect that I shall ever marry him to an English princess. I want no daughter-in-law that gives herself airs, and fills my court with intrigues as you do ; your son is but a saucy boy, who wants to be corrected rather than married : I detest him ; but I shall know how to *tame* him ; (this was the usual expression of the King). By heavens ! if he does not change for the better, I shall treat him in a manner which he does not expect." He added many more abuses against my brother and myself, and then withdrew.

When he was gone, the Queen considered on the step she was going to take. We presaged nothing good from it, being aware that the King of England would never consent to my marriage without that of my brother. As the Queen loved to flatter herself, she felt angry at us for making her apprehensive of obstacles ; and when I represented to her the sad situation to which she and I should be reduced, if the answer from England were not conformable to her wishes, she flew into a passion, and said, " that she clearly saw I was already intimidated and resolved to marry the corpulent John Adolphus ; but that she had rather see me dead than married to that prince ; that she would curse me a thousand times, if I were capable of forgetting myself so far ; and that if she could think that I had the smallest intention of doing so, she would strangle me with her own hands." In the mean time, she sent for Count Fink to consult with him. This general having made to her the same representations as I had ventured to do, she began to be alarmed ; and after having reflected for some time, she suddenly exclaimed : " A thought strikes me, which I consider as infallibly calculated to relieve us ; but it rests with my son to insure its success. He must write to the Queen of England, and give her his solemn promise to marry her daughter, on condition that she promotes the marriage of the Prince of Wales with his sister. This is the only way to make her consent to our wishes." My brother entered just at that moment : the Queen proposed the matter to him, and he readily consented. We all kept a gloomy silence, and I disapproved very much a step which I foresaw would prove fatal, but which I could not avert. The Queen urged my brother to write his letter immediately. To this she added one of her own, and sent them both off by a messenger whom M. Dubourgay, the English minister, dispatched secretly. She wrote another letter, which she showed to the King, and which was sent by the mail. The Duke of Weissenfels freed us also from his irksome company ; which afforded us time to breathe, but did not remove our fears.

The King was constantly with Seckendorff and Grumb-kow ; they had frequent revels together. At one of their drinking parties, a large goblet was introduced, in the shape of a mortar, which the King of Poland had presented to my father. This mortar was silver gilt, and engraved ; it contained another goblet, silver gilt, the lid of which was a gold bomb set in diamonds. These two goblets, which were handed round, were several times emptied. Heated by wine, my brother fell on the neck of the King, and repeatedly embraced him. Seckendorff wished to prevent it ; but he rudely repulsed him, and continued caressing his father, assuring him that he felt the tenderest affection for him ; that he was convinced of the goodness of his heart ; and that he ascribed the disgrace with which he constantly over-whelmed him to the wicked counsels of certain individuals who endeavoured to profit by the discord which they sowed in the family : that he would love and respect the King, and be submissive to him as long as he lived. This ebulli-tion gave great satisfaction to the King, and procured my brother some relief for a fortnight. But to this short calm succeeded fresh storms. The King began anew to treat him in a most cruel manner. The poor prince had not the smallest relaxation. Music, reading, sciences, and arts, were prohibited as crimes : no one was allowed to speak to him : he scarcely durst visit the Queen ; and led the most tedious life possible. Notwithstanding the King's prohibi-tion, he applied to the sciences, and made great progress in them. But the solitude in which he lived, made him plunge into dissoluteness ; as his governors did not dare to follow him, he entirely abandoned himself to debaucheries.

One of the pages of the King, named *Keith*,[1] was the pandar of his vices. This young man had found means to insinuate himself so much, that the Prince was passionately fond of him, and gave him his entire confidence. I knew nothing of his irregularities, but I had noticed some familiarities which he had with this page, and I often reproached him about it ; representing to him that such manners were unsuitable to his rank. But he excused himself, saying that as the young man reported to him all that passed, he was induced to treat him kindly ; particu-larly as the information he conveyed to him, saved him from many vexations. In the meantime, I felt uneasy in regard to myself : my fate was just on the eve of being de-cided. The Queen, by her set speeches, increased the

---

[1] Peter Christoph Karl von Keith (1711–55), descended from a Scot-tish family which had settled in Prussia having first resided in Sweden. Keith was married to a daughter of Baron Knyphausen, minister of Frederick William, who most strongly supported the Queen's party. He managed to escape to England after the failure of the Crown Prince's plot in 1730, but after Frederick's accession he returned to Berlin, where he became Director of the Academy of Sciences.

aversion which I had always felt for the Prince of Wales. The portrait which she drew of that Prince, was not to my taste. " He has," she observed, " a good heart, but a very narrow mind ; he is rather plain than handsome, and even a little deformed. Provided you can have the complaisance to put up with his debauches, you may then govern him entirely, and you may be more king than he at his father's death. Look what a part you will have to perform : upon you will depend the good or ill destiny of Europe, and the rule of the English nation."

This language showed that the Queen was not acquainted with my true sentiments. A husband such as she described the Prince her nephew would have suited her. But the principle which I had adopted respecting marriage, differed much from hers. I maintained, that a happy union ought to be founded upon mutual esteem and regard. I would have chosen reciprocal affection as its basis, and that my complaisances and attentions should flow from this source. Nothing appears difficult to us for those we love : but can there possibly be love without any return ? True affection suffers no division. A prince who has mistresses, grows attached to them ; in proportion as his love increases, his affection diminishes for her who ought to be its legitimate object. What esteem, what regard, can be entertained for a man who suffers himself to be governed, and neglects his affairs and his country, to abandon himself to dissolute pleasures ! I wished for a real friend, to whom I might give my confidence and my heart ; towards whom I could feel both esteem and inclination ; who might insure my felicity ; and whom I might render happy. I foresaw that the Prince of Wales would not suit me, as he did not possess the qualities which I required. The Duke of Weissenfels, on the other hand, pleased me still less. Independent of the inferiority of his rank, the disproportion of our ages was too great. I was nineteen, and he forty-three. His figure was rather disagreeable than prepossessing ; he was short, and excessively corpulent : his manners were polished ; but he was brutal in private, and very dissolute. The state of my poor heart may easily be conjectured. There was no one but my governess who was acquainted with my real sentiments; and to none but her could I make them known.

In the end, the Queen marred all by her haughtiness. Grumbkow had purchased a beautiful house at Berlin with the money he had received from the Emperor. He had adorned and furnished it at the expense of all the crowned heads. The late King of England and the Empress of Russia had been contributors to its embellishments. He solicited the Queen to give him her portrait, which he said would be the greatest ornament of his house. The Queen readily granted his request. She was just sitting to the famous *Pesne*,[1] one of the most distinguished painters: this portrait was intended for the Queen of Denmark. As the head only was finished, when she left Berlin for Wusterhausen, she gave orders to the painter to take a copy for Grumbkow; originals being never given but to Princesses. Grumbkow one day came to return his thanks to the Queen, and expressed the lively satisfaction he felt at possessing so perfect a painting. " It is Pesne's master-piece," added he : " it is impossible to see a greater likeness, or a more highly finished portrait." The Queen said to me in a low voice : " I am afraid there has been some mistake ; and that he has got the original instead of the copy ! " At the same time she asked him whether it was so ? " As the portait which the King," answered he, " has vouchsafed to give me is an original, it is but just I should have that of your Majesty equal to the King's. I have got it from the painter : it is a perfect performance."—" And by whose orders ? " replied the Queen ; " for I honour no private person with

---

[1] Antoine Pesne (1683–1757), born in Paris, came to Berlin in 1710, where he remained for the rest of his life. He was the only court artist not dismissed by Frederick William in 1713, who most surprisingly was himself an enthusiastic amateur painter ; several paintings by him survive, mostly portraits and genre pieces. Pesne, apart from executing very fine portraits in the Venetian manner, painted frescoes in many of the larger houses in Berlin.

an original picture, and it is not my intention to distinguish you from others." She was going to turn her back upon him, but he stopped her, beseeching her to leave him the portrait. She refused it in a very disdainful manner, and used many invectives against Grumbkow. While the King was amusing himself hunting, the Queen related the whole scene to Count Fink. The latter, glad to play a trick to Grumbkow, against whom he had a private resentment, urged the Queen to make him sensible of the insolence of his behaviour. It was therefore determined, that after her return to Berlin, she should send several of her domestics to Grumbkow, to demand her portrait, and to tell him, at the same time, that she would not give him either original or copy, until he conducted himself more becomingly towards her, and had learnt to pay her the respect which was due to her as his sovereign. The plan was put in execution the very next day, when we returned to town. No sooner was the Queen arrived at Berlin, than she hastened to give her orders accordingly, lest she might meet with any opposition. Grumbkow, who perhaps had been informed of the Queen's intention through Mrs. Ramen, listened, with a taunting air, to the message which the valet of the Queen delivered to him. " You may," said he, " take back the Queen's portrait, I have those of so many great princes, that I may easily console myself for the loss of her's." He however informed the King of the humiliation which he had endured, and painted it in the blackest colouring. Neither he, nor any of his family, appeared any more in the Queen's drawing-room. He spoke of her in very disrespectful terms and his envenomed tongue displayed all its eloquence in ridiculing her : and happy indeed would it have been for her Majesty, had he stopped there ; but he shortly after took a more effectual revenge, as will be seen in the sequel. Some well meaning persons interfered to conciliate the affair. Grumbkow made a parade of the respect he entertained for whatever belonged to the King, by muttering a kind of apology to the Queen ; to which she returned a condescending answer, which apparently put an end to their quarrel.

As the answer from England was long in coming, the Queen began to grow uneasy. She had daily conferences with M. Dubourgay, which for the most part tended to no purpose. At length, at the end of a month, the anxiously expected letter arrived. That which the Queen of England had written to be shown to the King, ran thus :—" The King my husband is well disposed to unite more closely the ties of alliance which his late royal father had contracted with the King of Prussia : and to promote the double marriage of his children : but he cannot state any thing positive till he has proposed the business to Parliament." This was evidently only an evasive answer. The other letter was not more satisfactory : it contained exhortations to the Queen, to support with firmness the persecutions of the King respecting my marriage with the Duke of Weissenfels ; and stated that the match was too little formidable to create so much alarm, and that it could only be a feint of the King. The letter to my brother was nearly in the same terms.

Never did Medusa's head cause greater astonishment than the reading of these letters did to the Queen. She would have passed them over silently, and written a second time to England, to endeavour to obtain more favourable replies, had not M. Dubourgay informed her that he was charged with the same commissions for the King. The Queen expressed, in severe terms, her dissatisfaction at the behaviour of his court towards her : and requested the ambassador to inform the King her brother, that if he did not change his sentiments, all would be lost. The King my father arrived a few days after. As soon as he entered the Queen's room, he asked whether the answer was come ? " Yes, (said the Queen, boldly assuming an air of satisfaction ;) and it is such as you wish." At the same time she gave him the letter ; which the King took ; and after having perused it, returned it in a passion. " I see," said he,

" that they still want to deceive me ; but I will not be their dupe." He then left the room, and went to Grumbkow, who was in his antichamber. His conference with that minister lasted two long hours ; after which he came again to the room where we were with an open and cheerful countenance. He said nothing more about the matter, and behaved uncommonly well to the Queen. She suffered herself to be blinded by the caresses of the King, and fancied that things were going on uncommonly well. But I was not deceived : I knew the King, and feared his dissimulation more than his violence. He staid only a few days at Berlin, and returned to Potsdam.

The year 1729 opened with a new transaction. M. de la Motte,[1] an officer in the Hanoverian service, came secretly to Berlin, and took up his residence with M. de Sastot, a chamberlain of the Queen, his near relation. " I am intrusted," said he to his friend, " with commissions of the greatest importance, but which require the utmost secrecy, and oblige me to keep my journey very secret. I have a letter for the King : but I am expressly commanded to have it delivered into his own hands. I have not applied to any person here, as I am not acquainted with any one. I therefore flatter myself, that as a friend and a relation, you will assist me in this business, and get my dispatches transmitted to the King." This confidential opening inspired M. de Sastot with curiosity ; he intreated La Motte to acquaint him with the motive of his journey. After a long resistance on the part of the latter, he at last learned of him, that he was sent by the Prince of Wales to inform the King that the Prince had resolved to escape from Hanover, unknown to the King his father, and to come to marry me. " You perceive," added La Motte, " that the success of the plan depends on its being kept secret. However, as I have been ordered not to inform the Queen of it, I leave to you

[1] This is probably August de la Motte, later a favourite of George III, who was to triumph with Sir George Eliott at the Siege of Gibraltar in 1783.

the care of acquainting her with the matter, if you think her sufficiently discreet." Sastot answered, that not to run any risk, he would consult Madam de Sonsfeld on the subject. I had a few days before been attacked with a severe cold. Sastot found Madam de Sonsfeld with the Queen, giving her majesty an account of the state of my health. As soon as he could speak to her, he acquainted her with the arrival of La Motte, and the intelligence he had communicated to him ; requesting her to advise him whether he ought to tell it to the Queen. Both Sastot and Madam de Sonsfeld knew full well that the Queen kept nothing from her dear Mrs. Ramen, and that, consequently, Seckendorff would not fail to be immediately informed of what had happened. But at length after mature deliberation, they resolved to confide it to the Queen. It is impossible to conceive an idea of the pleasure with which her majesty received the intelligence. She could not conceal her joy either from the Countess de Fink or Madam de Sonsfeld. They both exhorted her to be discreet, and warned her of the fatal consequences that might ensue, if the project happened to be divulged. She promised every thing ; and turning to my governess : " Go," said she, " prepare my daughter for this news : I shall visit her to-morrow to speak to her : but, above all, do your best that she may soon be able to leave her room." Madam de Sonsfeld immediately came to me. " I do not know," said she, " what is the matter with Sastot ; he is like a madman ; he dances, he sings, and all for joy, he says, about some good news which he has received, and which he is ordered not to divulge." I paid no attention to what she said ; and as I made no answer :—" I am however anxious," continued she, " to know what it may be, for he says, madam, that it concerns you."— " Alas ! " said I, " what good news can there be for me in my situation ; and whence could Sastot get any ? "— " From Hanover," answered she ; " and, perhaps, from the Prince of Wales himself."—" I see no very great happiness in that," replied I, " you perfectly well know my sentiments on the subject."— " It is true, madam," answered she, " but I am afraid Heaven will punish you for slighting a Prince, who, sacrificing himself for you, incurs the displeasure of the King his father, and exposes himself to the ill-will of all his family for the sake of coming hither to marry you. What is it you would be at ? You have no choice left. Do you prefer the Duke of Weissenfels, or the Margrave of Schwedt ? or will you not marry at all ? Indeed, madam, you break my heart ; and after all, you do not know your own mind." I could not forbear smiling at her earnestness, not supposing that what she had been telling me was so certain.—" The Queen has probably received letters similar to those she had six months ago, and this is doubtless the cause," said I, " of the long arguments you are using with me."—" By no means," replied she ; at the same time informing me of La Motte's journey. I now saw that the affair was serious, and the inclination to laugh gave way to a gloomy sorrow, which did not tend to restore my health.

The Queen came to see me the next day : and after having embraced me several times with tokens of the most lively affection, she repeated all that Madam de Sonsfeld had told me the day before. " At length you will be happy ! what a joy for me ! " During all this time I kissed her hands, which I bedewed with my tears without returning an answer. " But you weep," added she, " what is the matter ? " I felt some reluctance to lessen her satisfaction. " The mere thought of quitting you, madam," said I, " gives me more pain than all the crowns of the world could give me pleasure." She was affected at my answer, and after tenderly caressing me, withdrew.

The Queen held a drawing-room that evening. Her evil star brought M. Dubourgay, the English minister, to court. The ambassador as usual, communicated to her majesty the letters he had received from his court, and insensibly entered into conversation on their contents with the Queen ; who, forgetting all her promises, imprudently informed him of the design of the Prince of Wales. M. Dubourgay appeared surprised, and asked, whether it was perfectly certain ?—" So certain," said the Queen, " that La Motte has been sent hither to acquaint the King with the business." M. Dubourgay, shrugging his shoulders, replied : " how unfortunate I am, madam ! Your majesty has trusted me with a secret that should have been kept from me as much as from Seckendorff. Indeed ! I am much to be pitied, since I must this very evening send a messenger to England to inform the King of the project of his son ; which his majesty will, no doubt, take measures to prevent ; but I cannot act otherwise." The consternation of the Queen may easily be imagined. She used all her efforts to divert Dubourgay from his design : but the minister was inexorable, and withdrew immediately. The Queen was left a prey to despair. Unfortunately, she had likewise trusted the secret to her favourite Ramen. Seckendorff, who had been acquainted with the business through this woman, had gone to Potsdam to dissuade the King from returning any answer. Countess Fink told me all this the following day. The mine was sprung : nothing was now more urgent than to prevent the Queen's imprudence reaching the ears of her royal husband. The King came to Berlin the week after. In spite of Seckendorff's insinuations, his majesty sent for La Motte, whom he received very kindly, expressing his impatience at seeing the Prince of Wales. He gave him a letter for the Prince, and requested La Motte to set off as fast as he could to hasten his arrival. But matters were completely altered. The King's delay and the Queen's imprudence gave time to the messenger of the ambassador to arrive in England. As his dispatches were addressed to the secretary of state, the latter obliged the King to send an express to Hanover to order the Prince of Wales over to England without delay. The messenger reached Hanover a moment before the departure of the Prince for Berlin. As the order was addressed to the ministers, the Prince was forced to obey and to set out for London, while the King and

Queen of Prussia expected him at Berlin with joyful eagerness. But their joy was soon converted into grief by the arrival of an express, which informed their majesties of the Prince's sudden departure for England.[1]

But it is time to unravel this mystery. The English nation was ardently wishing for the presence of the Prince of Wales in his future kingdom. The British monarch had repeatedly, but vainly, been urged on this subject. He did not wish to have his son in England ; because he foresaw that his presence would give rise to parties, that might become prejudicial to his authority. He however saw, that he could not long delay complying with the wishes of the nation. He therefore secretly ordered his son to go to Berlin, and to marry me, with an express injunction of secrecy as to the part his majesty had taken in this business. This contrivance was a decent pretext to quarrel with the Prince, and to leave him at Hanover, without the nation having any right to complain. The indiscretion of the Queen of Prussia, and the arrival of Dubourgay's messenger, marred the project, and compelled the King of England to comply with the wishes of the nation. Poor La Motte fell a sacrifice ; he was confined for two years in the fortress of Hameln, and afterwards broke. But after his release, the King my father took him into his service, where he is still commander of a regiment. All this rendered our situation worse. The King was more than ever incensed against the British monarch his brother-in-law, and resolved from that instant to break with him, if my marriage were not concluded.

We shortly after followed the King to Potsdam, where he

---

[1] The Duke of Gloucester went to England for the first time in December 1728. He was created Prince of Wales on 9 January 1729. Droysen (op. cit., 44) quotes a letter of George II dated 16 December 1728, in which he asks about Colonel de la Motte, who, he had heard, had had an unauthorized audience with the king of Prussia and had apparently handed him a letter. The answer was returned that de la Motte had been meddling in the marriage affair and that he had been ordered to return to his regiment.

had a violent fit of the gout in both feet. This illness, added to the vexation of seeing his hopes vanished, put him into an insupportable humour. The pains of purgatory could not equal those we endured. We were obliged to be in the King's room by nine o'clock in the morning : we dined there, and durst not leave it on any account. The King passed the whole day in abusing my brother and me. He called me the *English baggage*, and my brother the *rascally Frederick*. He forced us to eat and drink things we disliked, or which disagreed with our constitutions ; this ill-judged severity sometimes made us throw up in his presence all we had in our stomachs. Every day was marked by some unlucky event : we could not lift up our eyes without beholding some ill-fated being tormented in one way or other. The impatience of the King would not suffer him to lie in bed. He was placed in an armchair upon casters, and rolled about all over the palace. His arms rested on crutches. We followed this triumphal car every where, like unfortunate captives undergoing their punishment. The poor King was really suffering violent pains, and the overflowing of a black bile caused his intolerable humour.

One morning, when we entered his room to pay him our respects, he sent us all back. " Get you gone," said he, in a passion, to the Queen, " with your confounded brats ; I wish to be alone." The Queen would have replied, but he bade her be silent, and ordered dinner to be served up in her room. My mother was vexed, but we were delighted ; for my brother and myself were actually as meagre as jades through the want of food. But we had scarcely sat down to dinner, when one of the King's valets came running, quite out of breath, calling out to the Queen : "For heaven's sake, madam ! come quickly ; the King is about strangling himself." The Queen immediately ran to his assistance. She found the King with a rope about his neck, and on the point of suffocation, if she had not timely saved him. His brain was affected : the heat of his fever, however, abated towards night, when he found himself somewhat better.

We were all exceedingly rejoiced at it, hoping that his humour would be less violent : but we were disappointed. At table he told the Queen that he had received letters from Ansbach, informing him that the young Margrave intended to be at Berlin in May, to marry my sister ; and that he should send M. de Bremer, his governor, to carry to him the betrothing ring. He asked my sister whether she was pleased ; and how she would regulate her house when married ? My sister was in the habit of speaking her sentiments freely, and even telling him his own faults, without his being offended. She therefore told him, with her usual frankness, " that she would keep a good table, well provided with all sorts of delicacies, which," added she, " will be superior to yours : and if I have children, I shall not use them ill as you do, not force them to eat food that disagrees with them."—" What do you mean ? " replied the King : " what fault is there in my table ? "—" The fault is," said she, " that there is not enough to satisfy one's hunger ; and that the little there is consists of coarse vegetables, which we cannot digest." The King had already begun to be angry at her first answer ; the last put him into a furious rage : but his passion vented itself upon my brother and me. He first threw a plate at the head of my brother, who avoided the blow ; he then threw one at me, which I also avoided. A pelting storm of abuse followed. He flew into a rage at the Queen, scolding her for the bad education she gave to her offspring ; and turning to my brother, " you ought to curse your mother," said he ; " she is the cause of your being so ill-bred. I had a tutor," added he, " who was an honest man. I shall never forget a story which he told me when I was very young. ' There was,' said he, ' a man at Carthage, ' who had been condemned to death for several crimes he had committed. When he was lead to exicution, he asked leave to speak to his mother, who was instantly sent for. He approached her, as if he wanted to whisper something to her, and bit off part of her ear with his teeth. I do this, said he to his mother, to set

145

you up as an example to all parents who neglect bringing their children up in the practice of virtue.' You may make the application ; " continued the King, still addressing my brother : and as the latter did not return any answer, he went on abusing us till he was no longer able to speak.

We arose from table ; and as we were obliged to pass close by him, he aimed a blow at me with one of his crutches, which I luckily avoided ; else it would have felled me to the ground. He pursued me for some time in his rolling car ; but those who dragged it gave me time to fly to the room of the Queen, which was at a great distance. I reached it half dead with fear, and in such a tremble, that I sunk on a chair unable to support myself any longer. The Queen had followed me ; she did all she could to comfort me, and to persuade me to go back to the King. His plate and crutches had so alarmed me, that I could scarcely be induced to return. When we went back, we found him conversing calmly with his officers. But scarcely had I entered the room, when I was taken ill and forced to return to the Queen's apartment, where I had two fainting fits. I stayed there for some time. The waiting woman of the Queen, after having considered me attentively, exclaimed : " Good heavens ! madam ! what ails you ? What a plight you are in ! It is horrible ! "—" I do not know what I ail," said I ; " but I am very ill." She brought me a looking-glass, and I was very much surprised to see my face and breast covered with red spots. I ascribed it to the violent emotion into which I had been thrown, and thought no more of it : but as soon as I returned to the King's room, the rash disappeared, and I again fell into a swoon. It proceeded from my having to cross a long suite of excessively cold rooms. In the night I had a violent fever ; and the next day I was so ill, that I let the Queen know I could not stir out. She sent me word, that I must come to her, dead or alive. My reply was, that a rash with which I was covered rendered my compliance impossible. Her commands to move were, however, repeated. I was accordingly dragged to her room, where I had a succession of fainting fits ; and in the same state I was carried to the King. My sister, seeing me so very ill, and supposing me on the point of death, pointed me out to the King, who had not taken any notice of me. " What ails you ? " said he to me : " you are very much altered ; but I shall soon cure you." At the same time he made me empty a large goblet of very old hock, of great strength. Scarcely had I swallowed it, when my fever increased, and I began to be delirious. The Queen saw that it was necessary to send me to my room : I was therefore carried to my bed, and laid upon it in full dress, being strictly ordered to reappear at night. But I was not long there, before I had a dreadful paroxysm. Dr. Stahl, the physician, took my illness for a violent fever, and ordered me several remedies quite contrary to my case.[1] I continued delirious all that day and the next. When I recovered my senses, I prepared for death. In my short lucid intervals, I ardently wished to die : but when I saw Madam de Sonsfeld and my good Meermann weeping near my bed, I endeavoured to console them by telling them that I was weaned from the world, and that I was going to enjoy a repose which no one could disturb. " I am," said I, " the cause of both the Queen's and my brother's sorrows. If I am to die, tell the King that I have always loved and respected him, that I have no fault to reproach myself with towards him ; that therefore I hope he will give me his blessing before I quit this world. Tell him that I beseech him to treat the Queen and my brother more gently, and to bury all discontents and animosities against them in my grave. It is the only boon I wish him to grant me ; and my only cause of uneasiness in my present state."

I lingered forty-eight hours between life and death, at

---

[1] Georg Ernst Stahl (1659–1734), Professor of Medicine at Halle. Apparently he was the founder of German " vitalism ", the doctrine that the origin of life derives from a vital principle, rather than from a physical or chemical source.

the end of which the small-pox manifested itself. The King had not inquired after me all the time I had been ill. When he was informed that I had the small-pox, he sent Holtzendorff, his surgeon, to see how I was. This brutal fellow repeated to me a hundred harsh things from the King, and added some of his own. I was so ill, that I paid no attention to what he said. He confirmed, however, the account which had been given to the King of my health. His apprehension that my sister might be attacked by this infectious malady, suggested to him all possible precautions to prevent it, but in a manner extremely harsh towards me. I was immediately treated as a prisoner of state ; every approach to my chamber was sealed up, except a single communication. The Queen, her domestics, and my brother, had strict orders not to visit me. No one was left with me but my governess and my poor nurse Meermann, who was pregnant, and, notwithstanding that, attended me night and day with unparalleled zeal and attachment. My bed was in an excessively cold chamber. The broth I had served up to me was nothing but water and salt ; and when something better was asked for me, the answer was, that the King had said, " it was good enough for me." When I slumbered a little towards morning, I was suddenly awakened by the noise of drums : the King would rather have witnessed my death, than have ordered the drums to cease. To complete my misfortune, my good Meermann fell ill. As the pains she suffered prognosticated a miscarriage, she was transported to Berlin. My second waiting-woman was sent for ; who being every day inebriated, was unable to attend me. My brother, who had already had the small-pox, did not forsake me : he came, by stealth, twice a day to see me. As the Queen did not dare to visit me, she was every moment secretly sending to hear how I was. For nine successive days I continued in great danger ; all the symptoms of my disorder appeared to prognosticate death ; and all who saw me thought that if I escaped with life I should be horribly disfigured : but my career was not yet run ; I was reserved to experience all the adversities which will be detailed in the sequel of these memoirs. I had the small-pox three times over ; as soon as it was dry, it began afresh. Yet I was not marked, and my complexion grew much finer than it had been.

In the mean time, M. de Bremer arrived at Potsdam from the Margrave of Ansbach. He presented the betrothing-ring to my sister, and her promise of marriage was taken without any ceremony. The King also recovered from his gout ; and this return of health dispelled his ill-humour, of which I now became the sole object. Holtzendorff came from time to time to see me by order of the King : but never without delivering some unpleasant message. He always studied to heighten these messages by using the most mortifying expressions. He was a creature of Seckendorff, and so great a favourite with the King, that every one bent the knee before him. He used his credit merely to do mischief, and had not even the merit of being expert in his profession. The King was behaving somewhat better to my brother, at the instigation of Seckendorff and Grumbkow, who entirely ruled the mind of the monarch. The sudden changes in the sentiment of the King to which they had been exposed, kept them in awe. They rightly feared, that the British monarch might at last consent to the double marriage ; in which case, their plans would be overthrown : they were not ignorant of the efforts of the Queen, who was continually intriguing with the court of St. James's ; and they were informed of the letter which my brother had sent to England ; they therefore formed the most abominable project to prevent all reconciliation with the English monarch. This was to establish open discord in the royal house of Prussia, and to force my brother by dint of ill-treatment from the King to come to some violent resolution, which might involve both him and me in guilt. Count Fink opposed this project. My brother had a great regard for him, and his office of governor gave him a certain authority over the Prince which might prevent his taking any step prejudicial to his interests. They therefore represented to the King, that my brother, being above eighteen, stood no longer in need of a mentor ; and that, by depriving the Prince of Count Fink, the King would put an end to the intrigues of the Queen, whose minister he was. The King approved of their arguments : the two governors were both most graciously dismissed with considerable pensions, and resumed their military employments. Two officers were assigned to the Prince in their stead, as companions : one was Colonel de Rochow, a man of great probity, but of a very narrow capacity ;[1] the other, Major de Keyserling, a very honest man too, but very giddy, and a great talker, who pretended to be witty, and was nothing but a library in confusion.[2] My brother liked them both very well, but Keyserling, being the youngest and very dissolute, obtained of course the preference. My beloved brother passed all his afternoons with me : we were reading and writing together, and applied ourselves to the cultivation of our understanding. I must confess, that our compositions frequently were satires, in which our fellow creatures were not spared. I remember that, having read the *Roman Comique* of Scarron, we made a very pleasant application of it to the imperial faction : we nick-named Grumbkow *la Rancune*, Seckendorff *la Rapinere*, the Margrave of Schwedt *Saldagre*, and the King *Ragotin*.[3] I certainly was highly reprehensible thus to weaken the respect which I owed to the King : but I do not intend to gloss over my failings, or to exculpate myself. Whatever causes of complaint children may have against their parents, they never ought to forget

[1] Friedrich Wilhelm von Rochow (1689–1759). In 1745 he married the sister of the ill-fated Katte.

[2] Dietrich, Freiherr von Keyserling (1698–1745). Later a member of Frederick's Rheinsberg coterie. It was he who brought Voltaire to Frederick in 1737.

[3] The *Roman Comique* by Paul Scarron, published in 1651, enjoyed great popularity all over Europe at this time. It relates the escapades of a group of strolling players in the French provinces. Ragotin, for instance, was the dwarf of the company, whilst La Rancune was a misanthrope, who was universally hated.

their duty to them. I have frequently reproached myself for the errors of my youth in this respect : but the Queen, instead of chiding, encouraged us by her applause to continue those malicious satires. Madam de Kamecke, one of her ladies, was not spared in them. Although we had a great esteem for that lady, we could not help noticing her foibles, and amusing ourselves with them. As she was very lusty and of a figure resembling that of Madam *Bouvillon*,[1] we gave her that name. We often joked about it in her presence which made her wish to know who that Madam Bouvillon might be, that was so much talked of : my brother made her believe we were speaking of the *camerara-major* of the Queen of Spain. After our return to Berlin, my mother one day held a drawing-room when the court of Spain happened to be mentioned, Madam de Kamecke took that opportunity to observe, that the *camerara-majors* were all of the family of *Bouvillon*. Those who heard her, laughed in her face ; and for my part, I thought I should have been suffocated. She perceived that she had said something silly, and inquired of her daughter, who had read a good deal, what it might be ? The latter explained the mystery. Madam de Kamecke was very angry with me for having jeered her ; I had much difficulty to pacify her.

A satirical disposition is far from estimable : the vice insensibly becomes habitual, and in the end we spare neither friend nor foe. Nothing is more easy than to turn

---

[1] Madame Bouvillon was the somewhat debauched mother of one of the actors in the *Roman Comique*, who " proceeded to take off her handkerchief from her neck, and thereby discovered to her lover at least ten pounds of exuberant flesh ; that is to say, near the third part of her bosom, the rest being distributed in two equal portions under her arm pits . . . Then she began to complain, that something troubled her in her back, and therefore moving herself about in her harness, as if she had itched, begged of Destiny to thrust his hands down her stays to scratch her. This the youth immediately obeyed her in, trembling all the while, but whilst he was employed in pleasing her behind, she diverted herself with him before, handling his sides through his waist-coat, and asking him often, If he was not ticklish ? " (trans. T. Brown and others, 1892, 233).

people into ridicule ; every one has some foible. It is amusing, I confess, to see an indifferent person wittily bantered : but the idea that we ourselves are exposed to the same fate, is far from pleasing. How blind we poor mortals are ! we descant on the failings of others, and never reflect on our own. I have entirely weaned myself from this vice ; I no longer employ my satirical talent except against persons of an evil disposition, whose empoisoned tongue deserves a retort of its own venom. But I return to my subject.

As the arrival of the Margrave of Ansbach was drawing near, and this Prince had not had the small-pox, the King and Queen thought proper to send me back to Berlin. But before I set out, I went to the King. He received me as usual, that is, extremely ill, and abused me without pity. The Queen fearing lest he should proceed to greater extremities, shortened the visit, and reconducted me herself to my room. I returned the next day to Berlin, where Countess Amalia had just been betrothed to M. de Viereck, a minister of state ; death having carried off M. de Wallenrodt, her former admirer. The intelligence had been conveyed to her some time before, while she was on duty with the Queen on a drawing-room day. As the Countess did not even know of Wallenrodt being indisposed, she was so shocked at his sudden death, that she fainted before the whole court ; which betrayed her intrigue with him. This accident had greatly impaired her credit with the Queen, who was not sorry to be rid of her. The King and Queen arrived at Berlin a few days after me. The nuptials of my sister were solemnized with great pomp ;[1] and she left us a fortnight after her marriage. Upon this I escaped from my solitude, and shortly after attended the Queen to Wusterhausen, where the quarrels respecting my marriage were renewed : we had no other topic from morning till night. The King starved my brother and myself : as he

[1] The marriage of Frederica Louise with the Margrave of Ansbach took place in May 1729.

himself performed the office of carver, he helped every one at table except us ; and when by chance there was a bit left in any dish, he spit in it to prevent our tasting of it. We lived on nothing but coffee and milk, and dried cherries, which entirely vitiated my stomach. My share of insult and invectives, on the contrary, was extremely liberal : the most abusive language was used towards me all the day, and that in presence of every one. The displeasure of the King was even carried to so great a length, that he ordered both my brother and myself never to appear in his presence but at the times of dinner and supper. The Queen used to send for us secretly, when the King was amusing himself with hunting : she posted her spies in the fields, who came to inform her whenever the King was seen at a distance, that she might have time to send us back. Owing to the negligence of some of these intelligencers, the King, one day, was very near catching us with the Queen. There was but one door in the room, and he came so suddenly that to avoid him was not in our power. Fear armed us with resolution : my brother hid himself in a corner where there was a certain convenience ; and as for me, I crept under the bed of the Queen, which was so low that it required great efforts to get under it, and I was forced to recline in a very irksome posture. We had scarcely got to our retreats when the King entered. As he was very much fatigued with the chace, he cast himself on the bed, and slept for two hours. I was just ready to be suffocated under the bed, and could not help advancing my head sometimes to breathe. The scene must have been truly comical to any disinterested spectator : at length the King left the room ; and we quickly crept out of out holes, intreating her Majesty not to expose us any more to such dilemmas.

Perhaps it will be thought strange that we took no steps to be reconciled to the King. I several times proposed it to the Queen : but she never would consent ; observing, that the King's reply would be, that if I wished for his good graces, I must marry either the Duke of Weissenfels, or the Margrave of Schwedt ; which would only render my situation worse, as I could not comply. To this argument I had nothing to answer, and was of course obliged to submit.

A few tranquil days succeeded this calamitous time. The King went to Lübben,[1] a town small of Saxony, to have an interview with the King of Poland. Here Grumbkow and Seckendorff, supported by this monarch, drew from my father a formal promise of my hand to the Duke of Weissenfels, to whom I was solemnly pledged. The King of Poland engaged to confer some advantages upon him ; and my father thought that, with an income of fifty thousand dollars a year, I might live very respectably with him. In his road, he stopped at Dahme, a small borough belonging to the Duke as his apanage ; where he was splendidly regaled with Hungary wine, which did not fail to invigorate his friendship for the Duke. All these underhand dealings were however kept so secret, that we did not learn them till some time after.

The King, on his return, recommenced his ill-usage ; he never saw my brother without threatening him with his cane. The Prince repeatedly told me, that he would endure every thing from his father except blows ; and that if ever he proceeded to that extremity with him, he would withdraw from his power by flight.

Keith the page had obtained a commission in a regiment quartered in the Duchy of Cleves. I had been extremely pleased at his departure, hoping that my brother would lead a more regular life : but I was disappointed. Keith was succeeded by a second favourite, infinitely more dangerous. This was a young man, a Captain-Lieutenant of the Horse-Guards (*gens d'armes*), named Katte.[2] He was a grandson of Field-Marshal Count Wartensleben. Having been destined for the law, his father, General Katte, had given

---

[1] Frederick William was in Lübben between 11 and 25 October to review the Saxon army—Krauske (op. cit., 433).

[2] Hans Hermann Katte (1704–30) ; unlike Keith he was to pay with his life for his part in the Crown Prince's plot.

him an university education, and then sent him on his travels in foreign parts ; but as there was no favour to be hoped for from the King but for military men, he entered the army against his expectation. He continued however to devote himself to study : a good understanding, much reading, a thorough knowledge of the world, and the select company which he still frequented, had given a polish to his manners which at that time was somewhat rare at Berlin. His figure was rather disagreeable than prepossessing ; his eyes were almost hid under two large black eyebrows ; his countenance carried in it a certain ominous trait that seemed to mark his future destiny : a tawny complexion and a face marked with the small-pox added to his deformity. He affected to be a free-thinker, and led a most dissolute life : with these vices he combined great ambition and much levity. Such a favourite was not calculated to reclaim my brother from his errors. It was only on my return to Berlin a few days after the King had returned from Lübben, that I heard of this new attachment. We had enjoyed some tranquillity for a short time, when it was disturbed by a new event.

The Queen received from my brother a letter, which was clandestinely delivered to her by one of her domestics. That letter has made so strong an impression on my mind, that I am still able to state nearly its contents. It ran thus :—

" I am in the utmost despair. What I had always dreaded has at length happened. The King has entirely forgotten that I am his son, and treated me like the meanest of men. I was entering his room this morning as usual ; as soon as he perceived me, he seized me by the collar, and beat me with his cane in the most cruel manner. I vainly endeavoured to defend myself ; he was so overpowered by passion, that fatigue alone made him give over. I am driven to extremes ; I have too much honor to submit to such treatment ; and I am determined to put an end to it one way or other."

155

The perusal of this letter plunged the Queen and myself into the most poignant affliction : but my alarm was greater than hers. I understood the meaning of the last line better than she did ; and I rightly judged that my brother's determination *to end his sufferings one way or other*, alluded to an attempt to escape. I availed myself of the grief in which I beheld the Queen to represent to her that she had better give up my marriage. I made her sensible that the King of England did not intend that I should marry his son ; that if such had been his intention, he would have acted differently ; that, in the mean time, the King grew more and more irritated against her, and against her son and me; that having once begun to cane my brother, his behaviour towards us would continually grow worse, and might at last drive the Prince-Royal to fatal extremities. That I confessed I should be the most unfortunate being on earth, if I were forced to marry the Duke of Weissenfels ; but that I clearly saw that one of us must be sacrificed to the hatred of Seckendorff and Grumbkow ; and that I had rather be the victim myself than my brother ; that, finally, I saw no other way of restoring harmony in the family. The Queen fell into a furious passion against me. " Do you wish to break my heart," said she, " and to kill me with grief ? Never mention it again, I charge you ; and be persuaded, that if you were capable of such a meanness, *I should curse you, I should deny your being my daughter, and never suffer you to appear before me.*" She uttered these last words with so much energy and agitation that I was frightened. The consideration that she was in a state of pregnancy heightened my terror. I endeavoured to appease her by assuring her, that I never would do any thing that should cause her the least sorrow.

Madam de Bülow, first maid of honour to the Queen, had obtained that favor, which had been enjoyed by Countess Amalia, who had been married shortly after my sister. She was goodnatured and obliging, injuring no one, but fond of intriguing, and indiscreet. The Queen employed her to obtain and convey information, and to communicate with M. Dubourgay, and M. Knyphausen,[1] the first cabinet minister. The latter, a man of talents, and of great ability in the conduct of affairs, was a sworn enemy to Grumbkow, and, consequently, of the English party. The Queen sent him my brother's letter, and asked his advice how she might prevent the violent usage of the King. Knyphausen was acquainted, through Madam de Bülow, with the practices of Mrs. Ramen. He knew that this woman was intimately connected with Eversmann, the great favorite of the King ; he was sensible that the Queen's confidence in that woman was the principal cause of our sufferings, as she exasperated the King by the accounts, true or false, which she and her companion gave him of my brother and me. He thought it was necessary to obtain the good-will of these two individuals at any price. He only mentioned Eversmann to the Queen, as he thought it too dangerous to name Mrs. Ramen ; and he advised her majesty to endeavour to bring him over to her interest, by promising him, on the part of the King of England, a sum of money sufficient to tempt him. The Queen approved of this advice, and mentioned it to M. Dubourgay. After many difficulties, the ambassador sent five hundred dollars to Eversmann ; and upon Knyphausen's entreaties, he clandestinely transmitted a like sum to Mrs. Ramen. They both promised wonders : but when they had got the money, they informed the King of the circumstance, and deceived the Queen and M. Dubourgay with false confidences. This intrigue of the Queen provoked the King in the highest degree ; he fancied himself betrayed, since she was beginning to bribe his domestics. We shall see the effects of his resentment in the year 1730, upon which I am going to enter.

The King spent his Christmas at Berlin. He was in

---

[1] Friedrich Ernst von Knyphausen (*d.* 1731). A privy councillor, he was banished from Berlin on 30 August 1730 for being too zealous an English partisan.

excellent humour all the time ; and though he did not treat my brother and me with kindness, he yet did not abuse us. We had found means to appease my brother, and we were all in the utmost security, since the good behaviour of the King had destroyed all suspicion. But who can search the secret recesses of the human heart ?

My father returned to Potsdam. Some days after, Count Fink received a letter from him, with a separate order not to open it but in the presence of Field-Marshal Borck and Grumbkow. At the same time, he was commanded, upon pain of death, not to mention any thing to any one. The two ministers, whom I have just named, had received similar injunctions with orders to repair to the Count de Fink. When they were met, they read the letter which enclosed one to the Queen. That to Count Fink ran thus :

" After Borck and Grumbkow have got to your house, you must all three go to my wife. Tell her, that I am informed of her intrigues ; that I disapprove of them, and am weary of conniving at them ; that I do not intend to continue the dupe of her family, by whom I have been unworthily treated ; that, once for all, I am determined to marry my daughter Wilhelmina ; but that, as a last favour, I will allow the Queen to write once more to England, and demand a formal declaration of the British monarch about the marriage of my daughter. Tell the latter, that in case the answer be not conformable to my wishes, I shall insist upon marrying her to the Duke of Weissenfels or the Margrave of Schwedt ; that I leave her the choice ; that the Queen must pledge her honour, that she will no longer oppose my wishes ; and that if she continues to provoke me by her contradictions, I shall break with her for ever, and banish her and her unworthy daughter, whom I shall disown for my child, to Oranienburg, where she may weep over her obstinacy. Perform your duty as faithful servants, and endeavour to induce the Queen to comply with my wishes. I shall acknowledge your service. But in the contrary case, I shall resent your conduct by punishing you and your families. I am your affectionate King.

WILLIAM."

They immediately went to the Queen, who by no means expected such a visit. I was with her when she was informed that those three gentlemen had a message to deliver from the King. I told her, that I foreboded it concerned me. She shrugged her shoulders, and said : " never mind, we shall need fortitude, and I do not fear the want of it." At the same time she passed into her audience-room, where the gentlemen were waiting. Count Fink explained the motive of their visit, and gave her the letter of the King. After she had perused it, Grumbkow began to speak, and endeavoured to prove to the Queen, by long political arguments, that the interests and honour of the King required that she should submit to his will in case the answer from England were not conformable to his wishes ; and (following the example of the fiend, when he wanted to tempt our Lord) he adduced passages of Holy Writ to obtain her assent. He afterwards argued, that a father had a greater right over his children than a mother ; and that when parents disagreed, the children ought preferably to obey the father ; that a father had a right to marry his daughter against her inclination, and that, finally, the Queen would be completely in the wrong, if she did not yield to these arguments.

The Queen refuted the last proposition by quoting Bethuel's answer to Abraham's servant, who was demanding his daughter in marriage for Isaac his master : *We will call the damsel, and enquire at her mouth.* " I know that wives ought to be submissive to their husbands' " added she, " the latter, however, ought to require nothing but what is just and reasonable. The proceeding of the King is not of this stamp. He wants to do violence to my daughter's inclination, and to render her unhappy for the remainder of her days, by marrying her to a brutal debauchee, a younger son, who is merely a general in the King of Poland's service, without any dominions and without the means to support his character and rank. What advantage can such a match procure to the state? None. On the contrary, the King will be obliged to support a son-in-law, who will depend upon him for his maintenance. I shall write to England, agreeably to the King's commands : but though the answer should not be favourable, I shall never consent to the marriage which you have proposed to me ; and I had rather see my child in the grave than unhappy." And stopping on a sudden, she declared that she felt indisposed, and that she was entitled to a little more attention in her situation. " However I blame not the King," continued she, looking at Grumbkow, " I know to whom I am indebted for his bad treatment." With these words, she left the room, casting upon him a glance which sufficiently shewed how highly she was incensed against him. She came back to her room in a state of stupor. When we were alone, she related this conversation to me, and shewed me the letter of the King. It was couched in terms so violent and harsh, that I shall not recal them. Its perusal cost us a flood of tears. The Queen perceived that there was but little to be hoped for from England ; but that she should at least gain time till an answer was returned. She resolved to use her best efforts to obtain a favourable one, and ordered me to write to my brother, to acquaint him with what was passing, and to send him the draught of a second letter he was to write to the Queen of England. I wrote it much against my will. This was its purport.

" Dear Sister and Aunt ;
Though I had once before the honour of writing to your majesty, and stating the sad situation in which my sister and myself are placed ; yet I am not discouraged by the rather unfavourable answer with which I have been honoured : I cannot imagine that a Queen whose merit and virtues are the theme of universal admiration, can forsake a sister who

*Portrait of a Grenadier by
Frederick William I*

*Self-portrait.   The King was an
enthusiastic amateur painter*

The 'Tabakskollegium' of Frederick William I

Friedrich Wilhelm von Grumbkow

Field-Marshal von Seckendorff,
Austrian Ambassador at Berlin

Leopold, Prince of Anhalt-Dessau

Rudolf Wilhelm Eversmann, Castellan
the Castles in Berlin, a favourite
Frederick William I, and an enemy
Wilhelmina

is tenderly devoted to her, by refusing to promote the marriage of my sister with the Prince of Wales, after it had been so solemnly stipulated by the treaty of Hanover. I have already pledged my word of honour to your majesty never to marry any other but the Princess Amelia your daughter. I renew this promise, in case your majesty consents to the marriage of my sister. We are reduced to the most miserable condition, and all will be lost if your majesty should still hesitate to return a favourable answer. I shall then be exonerated from all the engagements I have taken, and obliged to obey my father by accepting of any match he will chuse to propose. But I am convinced that I have no disappointment to fear, and that your majesty will maturely weigh what I have stated, being, &c."[1]

My brother did not hesitate to transcribe this letter. The Queen wrote two ; one was shown to the King, and the other contained an account of what had happened, and the enumeration of the strong motives that ought to induce the court of England to comply with my father's wishes. All these letters were dispatched by a messenger, by the King's express commands, that the answer might arrive the sooner : he had even calculated, that though the wind should prove contrary, the messenger might yet be back in three weeks.

Ten days had elapsed since the departure of the messenger, and the alarm of the Queen increased in proportion as the time passed away. As no one prognosticated any favourable reply from England, and as the Queen was informed, from all quarters, that the King would know no bounds to his rage if the answer was too long delayed ; she earnestly

[1] The actual text of this letter is printed by W. Oncken in " Sir Charles Hotham und Friedrich Wilhelm im Jahre 1730 ", in *Forschungen zur Brandenburgischen und Preussischen Geschichte*, 1894, VII 81. The tenor of the letter given here is correct, except that Sophia Dorothea was further instructed to inform Queen Caroline that no conditions should be attached to the marriage and that an answer was expected by 1 February. The letter is dated 17 December 1729.

revolved in her mind what ought to be done to prevent any fatal extremity.

Countess Fink, Madam de Sonsfeld, and myself, spent a whole afternoon in her closet in search of expedients. We agreed, at length, that she should affect to be ill : but the difficulty was to impose upon the King. If the wicked Mrs. Ramen had any knowledge of the trick, matters would rather be made worse than rendered more propitious. We dared not to inform the Queen of all the atrocities which we knew of that woman ; for she was so taken with her, that she would have betrayed us to her. However, there was no other means left but that. It was not probable that the Queen would be harassed when confined by illness, and in a state of pregnancy ; time was thus gained for the messenger to return. We therefore persisted in this opinion, but we gave the Queen to understand that if she did not keep the matter secret, it would only render our condition more miserable. Countess Fink even represented to her, that there were traitors among her domestics, who reported every thing to the King and Seckendorff ; that she knew to a certainty that secret conversations had been repeated at Seckendorff's, which she had had with the Queen, and which could only have been divulged by individuals who had listened at the doors. She unreservedly praised several of the Queen's domestics, and affected not to mention Mrs. Ramen ; adding : " Such as appear the most attached to you, madam, are perhaps the very persons who betray you." The confusion of the Queen showed that she had perfectly understood what was meant, but she pretended that she had not noticed it, and promised us inviolable secrecy. The farce of her illness was postponed to the next evening. The Queen began to complain in the morning, and, to excite more alarm, she affected to faint. In the evening, at table, we managed our gestures and countenances so well, that every one, even Mrs. Ramen, was deceived. The next day the Queen continued in bed, and used all the necessary grimaces to induce the belief that

she was very ill. She ordered me to acquaint my brother
with what we were about, to prevent his being alarmed at
this feigned malady. My mind was far from being at ease.
Notwithstanding the aversion I felt for the Prince of
Wales,[1] I clearly perceived that, of the three evils with
which I was threatened, this was doubtless the least, and
through the malignity of my stars I saw myself reduced to
wish for what I should have dreaded at any other time.
The Queen used to get up at night to sup with us in her
bed-chamber : but it was the physician who was instigated
to induce her to make the effort. Five days had gone by in
this manner. But whether Mrs. Ramen had discovered the
trick, or the Queen had entrusted her with the secret, we
were assailed by a fresh hurricane. A second embassy,
composed of the same individuals who had harangued the
Queen the first time, came from the King on the 25th of
January ; a day which I shall never forget. The message
which these gentlemen had to deliver was far more violent
than the former, and the letter of the King so terrible, that
it made that which she had received before appear com-
paratively mild.

" The King," they said, " will hear no longer of any
alliance with England. Whatever answer may come thence
is perfectly indifferent to his majesty, and will not alter his
intention to marry his daughter to the Duke of Weissenfels,
or the Margrave of Schwedt. The King insists upon being
obeyed ; he will even cause your majesty to feel the weight
of his resentment, if he meet with any resistance to his will.
His majesty declares, that in that case he will be separated,

[1] John Percival, later Lord Egmont, in his diary, 5 April 1730
(*Historical Manuscripts Commission*, 1920, I 92). " . . . the Prince had
lately engaged a mistress in his neighbourhood, a Papist, and had taken
a house and furnished it just over against her father's ; and that her
father's name is La Tour, the man in the playhouse [who] plays the
hautboy. That the discourse is the Prince has bought her for fifteen
hundred pounds. I was very sorry to hear it, and do heartily wish the
project of his marriage with the Princess Royal of Prussia may come to
effect, upon which I am persuaded that his Royal Highness will forsake
this kind of life."

banish you to the place assigned for your dowry, confine the Princess in a strong castle, and disinherit the Prince Royal : that, after having maturely weighed the matter, he thinks the disobedience of his family dangerous for his subjects, since, instead of setting them the example of submission, it does the reverse. His majesty is therefore resolved to perform an act of justice in his own house, to prevent the bad consequences which your want of respect might produce." The Queen answered in a few words. " You may tell the King, that I shall never consent to the misfortune of my daughter ; and that as long as I have a spark of life, I shall not suffer her to accept either of the husbands proposed." They would have replied, but the Queen begged them not to trouble her with any observations, as they would never draw from her any other resolution. The next day she kept her bed, pretending to be ill.

The answer from England arrived at length : it was still in the same style. The Queen my aunt wrote, that the King her husband was much inclined to my marriage with his son, provided the marriage of my brother with his daughter took place at the same time. The letter addressed to my brother contained nothing but idle compliments. The Queen my mother was highly offended at this behaviour ; she immediately acquainted me with the edifying intelligence. The vexation to which she was a prey made us fear for her health. In the mean time she could not help transmitting to the King the letter she had received, to which she added one in her own hand-writing, couched in the most affecting terms. The King had been instantly informed by Mrs. Ramen of the contents of the letters ; he returned them to the Queen unopened. Eversmann was the bearer of them. He came to the Queen in the evening, and told her that the King was in a violent rage against her and me ; that he had sworn, more than once, that he would have recourse to the most rigorous measures imaginable to reduce us to obedience, if we did not submit with a good grace ; that he was in a frightful humour, of which every one that approached him was the victim, particularly my brother, whom he had treated in the most barbarous manner, having covered him with blood by beating him, and dragging him by the hair through the room. I was not present. But after the wretch had sufficiently enjoyed the killing anguish which his account caused to the Queen, he came to me. " How long," said he, " do you intend to keep disunion alive in your family, and incur the wrath of your father ? I advise you as a friend : submit to his will, or be prepared for the most dreadful scenes. There is no time to be lost ; give me a letter to the King, and set yourself above the bawlings of the Queen, I do not say this of my own head, but by command." Whoever puts himself in my place, will judge of what was passing in my heart, when I saw myself so infamously treated by this scoundrel. I was a thousand times on the point of answering him as he deserved : but I perceived it would only be making things worse. I contented myself with telling him, very coolly, that I knew the good heart of the King too well to suppose that he would render me unhappy ; that I was sorry to have incurred his displeasure ; that I was ready to make any submission to regain his good graces, having never been wanting in that respect and affection which a daughter owes to her father. In ending these words, I turned my back upon him, and sat down greatly agitated in the farthest corner of the room.

But the scene was not over yet, Eversmann also addressed Madam de Sonsfeld. " The King commands you," said he, " to prevail with the Princess to marry the Duke of Weissenfels ; he lets you know, that in case she cannot be brought to give him her hand, he leaves her at liberty to marry the Margrave of Schwedt : but that if you suppose you ought to obey the orders of the Queen preferably to his, he will show you that he is your sovereign, and send you to Spandau, where you are to live upon bread and water. This is not all : your family shall also feel the weight of his wrath ; while, on the other hand, they shall be loaded with favours, if you listen to the calls of duty."

" The King," answered Madam de Sonsfield, " has entrusted me with the education of the Princess. I shed many tears before I would accept of the office, and I did it solely to obey the orders of the King. It does not become me to give her any advice, or to interfere with her marriage ; I shall speak neither for nor against either of the matches the King proposes to her. I shall implore heaven, that it may guide her to chuse that which may be the best, and shall then submit to whatever the King shall be pleased to order relative to me and my family."—" All this is well and good," replied Eversmann, " but you will see what will happen and what you will gain by your obstinacy. The King has taken violent resolutions. He gives the Princess three days to determine. If, at the end of that time, she does not yield, he will send her to Wusterhausen, whither the two princes are to come. He will force his daughter to chuse one of them ; and if she will not do it with a good grace, she is to be shut up in a room with the Duke of Weissenfels ; after which she will be but too happy to marry him."

Madam de Kamecke, who was present, and had hitherto kept silent, could not contain herself any longer. She bitterly railed at Eversmann, reproaching him with telling untruths, and having fabricated what he had said. Her zeal even betrayed her into animadversions upon the King. Eversmann, on his part, sneeringly maintained that facts would soon confirm what he had asserted. " But," said Madam de Kamecke at last, " Is there no other convenient match in the world for the Princess, than the two that are proposed ? "—" If the Queen," answered he, " can find a better one exclusively of the Prince of Wales, perhaps the King may enter into some composition with her, although he ardently wishes to make the Duke his son-in-law."

The Queen, who sent for us all, put an end to this impertinent conversation. Countess Fink was sitting at the head of her bed, endeavouring to calm her agitation. The Queen immediately perceived by our countenances, that we had been vexed. We related our conversation with Eversmann, and she told us that which she had had with the same personage. We had a long conference about what was to be done in a conjuncture so critical. Madam de Kamecke offered some advice, which was followed ; namely, to consult Field-Marshal Borck,[1] a man of uncommon probity and uprightness. He was sent for the next day. The Queen told him what had happened the day before ; adding, " I ask your advice as a friend ; speak without reserve, and according to your conscience."—" I am excessively sorry," answered the Field-Marshal, " to witness the discord which reigns in the royal family, and the cruel distresses which your majesty endures. No one but the King of England could have put an end to them ; but as his answers are still the same, all hopes must be given up in that quarter. What Eversmann has told you yesterday, Madam, concerning the violence which the King meditates against the Princess does not appear to be destitute of foundation. I learned last night, that the Margrave of Schwedt is here incognito ; one of my domestics has seen him. Curiosity has induced me to inquire privately whether it be true ; and I have been assured that he has been in town these three days : he is lodged in a small house in the new town, which he never leaves but in the dusk, that he may not be known. I have this day received letters from Dresden, which I may show to your majesty, by which I am informed, that the Duke of Weissenfels left it secretly to repair to a small town a few miles distant from Wusterhausen. Your majesty knows the humour of the King : when once excited to a certain point, he is no longer himself, and his passion betrays him into fatal excesses ; which are so much

---

[1] Adrian Bernhard von Borck (1668–1741), a Prussian minister and general, who had earlier been sent by Frederick William to Vienna to receive confidential inquiries from Prince Eugene concerning the " Clement " plot.

the more to be dreaded at present, when he is constantly beset with wicked people, who give him no time to cool. Far from irritating him by any refusal, you must endeavour to gain time, and parry his first violence by fixing on a third match for the Princess. Your majesty risks nothing by the proposal. Seckendorff and Grumbkow are too much inclined for the Duke of Weissenfels, to suffer the Princess to marry any other. Grumbkow has his particular views : he wishes to get rid of the Prince of Anhalt, and to give his place to the Duke. The King will be appeased by your condescension, Madam, and give you time to make a final attempt in England."

The Queen appeared satisfied with this advice, and after having conferred some time about the match that was to be proposed to the King, the choice fell upon the hereditary Prince of Brandenburg—Kulmbach (Bayreuth). The Field-Marshal undertook to have the King informed underhand of this change. " At all events (said he to the Queen), if these measures are of no avail, your majesty will at least have the satisfaction of seeing the Princess your daughter well established. The Prince of Bayreuth is extremely well spoken of ; he is of an age proportioned to that of the Princess, and at the death of his father, he will inherit the sovereignty of a very fine country." The Queen approved and adopted the Field-Marshal's ideas.

The King came two days after to Berlin. He immediately went to the Queen. Rage and fury were painted in his eyes. I was not present. The Queen, still affecting to be ill, was in her bed. The passion and wrath of the King were excessive ; he overwhelmed her with all the abuse and insults that came across his mind. She suffered this first ebullition to pass over, and then attempted to soften him by the most tender and most affectionate discourse. But nothing would appease him. " Chuse," said he, " between the two matches I have proposed ; if, however, you wish to please me, you will determine in favor of the Duke."— " Heaven forbid ! " exclaimed the Queen. " Well, then," continued the King, " I care little for your consent : I am going to the Margravine Phillippa (this Princess was mother to the Margrave of Schwedt) to settle the marriage of your unworthy daughter, and arrange matters with her for the wedding."

He immediately left the Queen, and hastened to the Margravine. After the first compliments, he informed this Princess of the motive of his visit, and ordered her to assure the Prince her son, that in spite of the Queen's opposition, he would render him master of my person. He also charged the Margravine with the preparations for the wedding, which was to take place in a week's time. The Margravine had been extremely delighted with the beginning of the King's address ; but the end made her alter her sentiment. " I acknowledge as I ought," said she, " the favor your majesty does to my son by chusing him for your son-in-law : I feel the value of the happiness which you destine for him, and the advantages which would accrue to him and to myself. This son is dearer to me than life ; there is nothing that I would leave undone to insure his happiness : but, Sire, I should be inconsolable if it were to be against the will of the Queen and the Princess. I cannot consent to a marriage, which would render the latter unfortunate, knowing the antipathy which she manifests for my son ; and if he were mean enough to wish to marry her against her inclination, I should be the first to blame his conduct, and should in future consider him as a base, degenerate man."—" Would you rather," replied the King, " have her to marry the Duke of Weissenfels ? "—" Let your daughter marry whom she chuses, provided my son or I be not the instruments of her misfortune."

As the King could not overcome the firmness of the Margravine, he withdrew. I was the very same evening acquainted with these circumstances by a note which the Margravine sent me secretly, requesting me to inform the Queen of its contents. I was filled with admiration and gratitude for so generous a proceeding. I expressed these sentiments in the answer which I returned to her note ; and I shall never forget the obligations which I owe to her for so noble a conduct. Meanwhile, the continual agitations of my mind undermined my health ; I grew remarkably thin. I have observed before, that I was rather lusty ; and now I was so diminished, that my body measured only half a yard in circumference. I had not yet made my appearance before the King ; as the Queen did not wish to expose me to the treatment which my brother had experienced. The latter was in the utmost despair. I felt his sufferings more than my own, and I would willingly have sacrificed myself to have freed him from them.

I used to go every afternoon to the Queen, when the King was engaged elsewhere. She had contrived a labyrinth of skreens, ranged in such a manner that I could avoid the King unperceived, in case he should enter unexpectedly. The wicked Mrs. Ramen, who slept no more than the fiend, wishing to amuse herself at my expence, deranged this retreat without my being aware of it. The King surprised us one day. I sought to escape but unfortunately got entangled between those confounded skreens, several of which were overturned, so that I could not get out. As soon as the King perceived me, he ran to lay hold of me to beat me. Seeing the impossibility of avoiding him, I planted myself behind my governess. The King pushed her so, that she was obliged to draw back : but when she had got against the chimney, she could get no farther. I was still behind Madam de Sonsfeld, betwixt the hammer and the anvil. The King, looking over Madam de Sonsfeld's shoulder, overwhelmed me with a torrent of abuse, and endeavoured to seize me by my cap while I was on the ground half roasted. The scene would have taken a tragical turn, had it continued much longer ; my clothes were already beginning to burn. The King tired with bawling and struggling, put an end to it by going away.

Madam de Sonsfeld, though frightened, displayed her

firmness on this occasion ; she remained all the time before me immoveable like a post, fixedly looking at the King. The next day, my father was more enraged than ever. The poor Queen was treated very roughly. He threatened my brother and me, that he would beat us unmercifully in her presence, and send me instantly to Spandau. The Queen had not yet mentioned the Prince of Bayreuth, hoping still to appease him : but seeing that his passion had reached its acme, she hesitated no longer in following the advice of Field-Marshal Borck. " Let us both be reasonable, said she, " I consent to break off the match with the Prince of Wales, since you assure me that your tranquillity is at stake ; but, in return, you must no more mention those hateful marriages you propose. Find a convenient establishment for my daughter, a husband with whom she may live happy ; and, far from opposing your wishes, I shall be the first to second them." The King immediately grew calm, and, after having considered for some time, " your expedient is not bad," he answered, " but I do not know of any match better suited for my daughter, than those which I have proposed : if you can suggest any other, I will attend to your suggestion." The Queen named the hereditary Prince of Bayreuth. " I am satisfied," said the King, " there is but one trifling difficulty which I think it well to inform you of : that is, that I shall give neither portion nor clothes to my daughter ; and that I shall not be at the wedding, since she prefers your wishes to mine. Had she married to my fancy, I should have treated her better than any of my children. She may chuse which of us two she will obey." " You absolutely reduce me to despair," exclaimed the Queen ; " I do every thing in my power to oblige you, and you are never satisfied. You wish to kill me, and to see me in the grave. Well then, my daughter may marry your dear Duke of Weissenfels ; I shall not oppose it ; but I curse her if she marries him in my life-time." " Well ! well ! madam, you shall be satisfied," said the King, " I will write to-morrow to the Margrave of Bayreuth on the subject, and shall show you my letter. You may mention it to your unworthy daughter. I give her time till to-morrow to determine the matter."

When the King was gone, the Queen sent for me. She embraced me with transports of joy, which I could not account for. " Every thing prospers to my wishes, my dear girl," said she, " at length I triumph over my enemies : we have nothing more to do with the big Adolphus, or the Margrave of Schwedt : you are to be married to the Prince of Bayreuth, and it is from my hand that you are to receive him." At the same time, she repeated the conversation which she had just had with the King ; the conclusion of which was not very agreeable to my mind. I remained quite stupified not knowing what answer to return. " Well ! are you not satisfied with what I have done for you ? " I answered, that I acknowledged as I ought, the favours she had done me ; but intreated her to give me time to consider what I ought to do. " How ! " replied she, " give you time ! I thought the matter would not want any deciding of yours, and that you would submit to my will." " I should not hesitate doing so, did not the King oppose insurmountable obstacles. Your majesty cannot require me to be married without the approbation of the King and the customary formalities. What idea would it give to the public, and what opinion would be entertained of me, if I left the parental roof in so unworthy a manner as the King hints at ? Under the circumstances in which I am placed, I can do nothing but inform the King that I am ready to give my hand to one of the three proposed Princes, provided your majesty and the King are agreed. But I shall not determine any thing before the sentiments of my father and mother coincide."—" Then you may marry the great sultan or the grand mogul," said the Queen, " and follow your own caprice. I should not have brought so many sorrows on my head, had I known you better. Obey the commands of the King ; it rests with you ; I shall not concern myself any more about what regards you ; and deliver me, I beg, of the trouble of your odious presence ; for I cannot bear it any longer." I wished to reply, but she bade me be silent, and ordered me to withdraw. I left the room in tears. Madam de Sonsfeld was then called in. The Queen made heavy complaints against me, and told her to use her endeavours to prevail with me to obey. " I insist," said she, " upon her marrying the Prince of Bayreuth. This marriage gives me as much satisfaction as that with the Prince of Wales would have done : I will not be disappointed ; and my daughter may rest assured, that I shall never forgive her if she starts any difficulties." Madam de Sonsfeld ventured the same representations which I had done, and boldly declared that she would not presume to advise me ; which much vexed the Queen. My brother, who had been present at the conversation, came to me, and tried to persuade me to obey. His patience was exhausted ; the King continued to use him ill ; and he was wearied with the delays of the English court. I think his resolution was already taken to escape. In spite of the solid arguments by which I justified my refusal, he grew angry, and used some harsh expressions which heightened my despair. All whom I consulted concerning my conduct, approved of it and encouraged me to continue firm, assuring me that it was the only way to get reconciled with the King, who would at length be appeased, and more easily induced to yield to the wishes of the Queen.

Madam de Bülow, seeing me in tears and much distressed at my brother's behaviour, endeavoured to comfort me. She assured me she had infallible means of reconciling the Queen : she only wished to let her first ebullition pass over, and engaged that as soon as she had spoken to her majesty, the Queen would alter her sentiments. The next morning the King showed to the Queen the letter he had written to the Margrave of Bayreuth. It was couched in very obliging terms. After having read it, he repeated in an angry tone all he had said the preceding evening ; to wit, that he would not be present at my wedding, nor give me any portion. To this the Queen submitted, and he left her, declaring that he was going to send her letter off. Such was indeed his intention : but Seckendorff and Grumbkow, who did not relish the measure, prevented its execution. The Queen was secretly informed of it the very same evening by Field-Marshal Borck. At length, Madam de Bülow found means to speak to the Queen. She told her, that M. Dubourgay and M. de Knyphausen had, after mature deliberation on seeing the extremity to which matters were reduced, resolved upon a last attempt in England by dispatching thither the English chaplain, who had taught me his language ;[1] that M. Dubourgay would give him very pressing letters to the British ministers concerning our situation ; and that this clergyman, from having seen me every day, would be able to give an exact description of my figure and disposition, and to paint the deplorable situation to which we were reduced. The Queen highly approved of this arrangement. She wrote to the Queen of England, bitterly complaining of her procrastinations, and reproaching her with the little friendship she manifested for her. The chaplain set off with his dispatches, loaded with presents by the Queen. He wept in taking leave of me ; and told me, saluting me in the English fashion, that he would deny his nation, if the English did not do their duty on this occasion.

In the mean time, the King appeared more calm : he behaved tolerably well to the Queen, mentioning nothing more about the matter. My brother's condition and my own were however not improved ; I did not dare to appear before the King. My poor brother, who could not help being about his person, was every day exposed to blows either with his fist or his cane. He was in the utmost despair, and I suffered more even than himself, to see him thus treated.

[1] One Dr Villa, who had given Wilhelmina English lesssons.

V

I dissuade Frederick from running away — The Queen's illness induces a temporary truce — Plans for a double marriage — I am loved by a 'madman' — The King insults the English ambassador — An exchange of letters.

About this time the King resolved to go to Dresden, to have an interview with the King of Poland.[1] His departure was fixed for the 18th of February. I had already taken leave of my brother in the Queen's room ; and having retired to my own, I was on the point of going to bed, when I saw a young man enter, magnificently dressed in the French style. I uttered a loud scream, not knowing who he was and concealed myself behind a skreen. Madam de Sonsfeld, equally terrified, went out to inquire who could have had the boldness to have come in at such an improper hour ? But, a moment after, I beheld her returning with the gentleman, who laughed immoderately, and whom I recognized to be my brother. His appearance was so

---

[1] Frederick William went to see Augustus at the end of February 1730 to discuss the possibility of war with Hanover, over their territorial dispute (see above, p. 105), which had not yet been settled (Droysen, op. cit., 78). In the negotiations described in this chapter Wilhelmina oversimplifies and inevitably places too much emphasis on her marriage ; in outline, however, her story is correct and serves to illustrate the utter confusion and inconsistency that existed in Anglo-Prussian relations at this time. On the wider front, Walpole was anxious to detach Prussia from the Austrian alliance which was threatening war with the signatories of the Treaty of Seville (principally England, Spain and France). This necessitated the removal of Grumbkow in Berlin from Frederick William's confidence and was the chief reason for Hotham's visit to Berlin. On the smaller front the animosity between Prussia and Hanover, as well as that between the two kings and their respective sons, led to complication and intrigue that inevitably meant that the marriage plans would break down.

changed by his French dress, that he actually seemed a different person. He was in the most cheerful humour. " I once more come, my dear sister," said he, " to bid you farewell ; as I know the friendship you have for me, I will not make a mystery to you of my designs. I go away, never more to return. I cannot longer endure the insults with which I am treated ; my patience is exhausted. The opportunity is favourable to free myself from an odious yoke : I shall make my escape from Dresden, and pass over to England ; and I doubt not but I shall deliver you from your thraldom as soon as I have got there. I therefore beg you will be calm. We shall soon meet in a place where mirth will succeed to our tears, and where we shall enjoy the pleasure of seeing each other in peace and be free from all persecution."

I remained immoveable ; but recovering from my first surprise, I remonstrated strongly with him on the step he was going to take. I endeavoured to make him sensible of the difficulty and dreadful consequences of such a step ; but seeing him unshaken in his resolution, I cast myself at his feet, which I bedewed with my tears. Madam de Sonsfeld, who was present, joined her intreaties to mine. We at length proved to him so clearly by dint of argument how fantastical his project was, that he gave me his word of honour he would not execute it.

A few days after the departure of the King, the Queen fell dangerously ill : this sudden attack brought her to the verge of the grave. Her sufferings were excessive, and, in spite of her fortitude, the violence of her pains extorted from her loud screams. As her illness had been gradually increasing, the King had returned to Potsdam before it was at its height. Madam de Kamecke, and Dr. Stahl first physician to the King, had acquainted him with the Queen's situation. His Majesty had even been informed, that her life was in danger, and that she would probably be obliged to submit to an operation very dangerous for her and her infant, if the illness did not abate soon. Mrs. Ramen, seconded by Seckendorff, contradicted these accounts, and sent word to the King that the Queen was not ill, and that it was a mere artifice. I did not quit the bed of her Majesty. The indifference which the King manifested for her, increased her sufferings. They at length grew so violent, that an express was sent to the King to intreat him to come, if he wished to find the Queen alive. He therefore came to Berlin in spite of Seckendorff's endeavours to prevent it. He brought Holtzendorff with him, that he might be accurately informed whether there was any truth in the Queen's malady. But as soon as he saw her, his suspicions were dissipated, and gave way to the bitterest grief. His despair was heightened by his surgeon's report. He shed abundance of tears, and told all who were around him, " that he should not survive the Queen, if she were snatched from him." The affecting expressions which she addressed to him, completed his despair. A thousand times, in the presence of her ladies, he implored her forgiveness for the vexations he had caused her, and showed that his heart had been less concerned than the wretches who had always prejudiced him against the Queen. Her Majesty availed herself of this opportunity to beseech the King to treat my brother and me with more lenity. " Make your peace," said she, " with these two children, and let me carry to the grave the consolation of seeing harmony restored in the family." The King sent for me. I cast myself at his feet, and said every thing I thought best calculated to soften him, and to interest him in my favour. My sobs stifled my speech ; and all who were present shed many tears. At length he lifted me up, and embraced me, apparently much affected with my situation. My brother came afterwards. The King simply told him, that he forgave him the past for his mother's sake ; that he ought to reform, and regulate his conduct by his will ; in which case he might rely upon his paternal love. The Queen was so rejoiced at her success in restoring harmony in the family, that, at the end of three days, she was pronounced out of danger. When free from uneasiness concerning the Queen, the King resumed his hatred against my brother and me. But fearing for her Majesty's health, which was still very precarious, he treated us kindly in her presence, and used us ill as soon as we had left her room.

My brother was even again exposed to his customary *endearments* with his fist and cane : we, however, concealed our sufferings from the Queen. My brother at length grew more and more impatient, and repeatedly told me, " that he was determined to make his escape, and only waited for an opportunity." His mind was so exasperated, that he would not listen to my exhortations, and vented his passion against me. One day, when I was using all my efforts to appease him, he said, " you are always preaching patience, but you will not put yourself in my place ; I am the most unfortunate being ; surrounded from morn to night with spies who put malicious constructions upon my words and actions. I am forbidden the most innocent recreations. I dare not read, I dare not touch an instrument,[1] and I enjoy those pleasures but by stealth and trembling. But what has driven me to despair, is the adventure which I lately had at Potsdam, of which I have given no account to the Queen, that I might not alarm her. As I was entering the room of the King in the morning, he instantly seized me by the hair, and threw me on the ground, and after having tried the vigour of his arms upon my poor body, he dragged me, in spite of my resistance, to a window, and was going to perform the office of the mutes of the seraglio ; for, seizing the cord with which the curtain is fastened, he drew it round my neck. Fortunately I had had time to get up from the ground ; I laid hold of his hands, and screamed as loudly as I could. A valet immediately came to my assistance, and snatched me from his gripe.

[1] Egmont (op. cit., 107) heard in October 1730 that Frederick William " had lately ordered a young woman, daughter to a clergyman, to be stripped to her shift, whipped and afterwards banished, only for having played on the harpsichord to the Prince his son in a concert ".

Every day I am exposed to the same perils ; my situation is so desperate, that nothing but desperate remedies will cure it. Katte is in my interest : he is attached to me, and will follow me to the farthest corner of the globe, if I chuse. Keith will also join me. These two friends will facilitate my flight ; I am concerting every thing with them for the execution of my plan. I shall not mention it to the Queen : she would infallibly tell it to Mrs. Ramen, and I should be undone. I shall secretly inform you of what is going on, and find means to get my letters safely conveyed into your hands."

This dreadful confidence plunged me into an agony of grief. The situation of my brother was so deplorable, that I could disapprove of his resolution, and yet I foresaw its terrible consequences. His plan was so badly contrived, and the individuals acquainted with it were so giddy, and so little calculated to conduct an affair of that importance, that it could not possibly succeed. I pointed out all this to my brother ; but he was so obstinately bent upon his project, that he would not credit what I told him ; and all I could obtain of him was, that he would delay its execution until answers should have been received to the letters sent to the court of St. James's by the English chaplain.

As the Queen was gradually recovering, the King returned to Potsdam. The expected letters arrived shortly after his departure. The chaplain had safely landed in his country, where he had acquitted himself of his commission, and represented our situation to the English ministers. The interesting portrait he had drawn of my brother and me had prepossessed the whole nation in our favour. He had even obtained an audience of the Prince of Wales, who had expressed the greatest eagerness to marry me, and had declared to the King his father, that he would never give his hand to any other princess. The solicitations of the Prince had been strongly backed by ministers, and the murmurs of the nation against the delays of the King had been so loud, that he determined at length to send Sir

Charles Hotham[1] his ambassador extraordinary to Berlin : and he was to set out immediately. This intelligence caused great joy to the Queen ; it also calmed a little the uneasiness given me by my brother, to whom I instantly imparted this good news. I availed myself of this momentary tranquillity to perform my devotions. On the Sunday, in coming from church, I found M. de Katte, who was waiting for me at the bottom of the staircase in the palace, and very imprudently handed me a letter from my brother. The apartment of Mrs. Ramen faced the stairs ; the door was open, and she was sitting so that she could see all that passed. " I come from Potsdam," said Katte to me : " I passed three days there *incognito*, to approach the Prince Royal. He has entrusted me with this letter, and charged me to deliver it into the hands of your royal highness. It is of great consequence, and he intreats you, madam, not to show it to the Queen."[2] I took the letter without returning any answer, and flew up stairs like lightning, angry at the rash step that had been taken. After having vented to my governess my resentment against Katte for the embarrassment into which he had thrown me, I opened the letter, and read as follows :—

" I am still in the utmost despair ; the tyranny of the King increases ; my patience is exhausted. You vainly flatter yourself that the arrival of Sir Charles Hotham will put an end to our sufferings. The Queen frustrates our plans by her blind confidence in Mrs. Ramen. The King is already informed, through this woman, of the news which are arrived, and the measures that are taken, at which he is

---

[1] Egmont (op. cit., 84), 21 March 1730, " was to-day well assured that Sir Charles Hotham is gone to Prussia to propose the double marriage so long talked of". Sir Charles Hotham, 5th baronet (*d.* 1739), was a Groom of the Bedchamber, but endowed with no diplomatic qualification other than that he was related to Lord Chesterfield by marriage.

[2] Katte admitted during his interrogation to having handed Wilhelmina a letter, stating also that she was most loath to receive it—C. Hinrichs, *Der Kronprinzenprozess* (Berlin, 1936) 64.

more and more exasperated. I wish the old slut was hanged
upon the highest gibbet ; she is the cause of all our misfortunes. The Queen ought no longer to be made acquainted with any intelligence : her weakness for that infamous
creature is unpardonable. The King will go to Berlin on
Tuesday ; it is still a secret. Adieu, my dear sister ; I am
wholly yours."

I had no doubt but Mrs. Ramen had already informed the
Queen that I had received a letter. I durst not shew it, and
knew not what pretence to invent to avoid it. At length I
agreed with my nurse, that she should not send me the
letter, though I should dispatch thirty messengers to her
with the order to find it ; that after having pretended to
have been anxiously looking for it, she was to say that I must
have inadvertently burnt it with some other papers which I
had thrown into the fire. To save her an untruth, I
actually committed the fatal epistle to the flames. The
Queen, fortunately, mentioned nothing about the letter ;
which relieved me from my anxiety. The sequel will
show how much uneasiness I suffered from Katte's imprudence.

Sir Charles Hotham arrived at Berlin on the 2d of May.[1]
The Queen was yet so weak, that she could not leave her
bed. Sir Charles Hotham would not acquaint her with the
object of his embassy, though she sent him word that she
wished very much to know it. He demanded an audience
of the King, who received him at Charlottenburg. The
Queen, anxious to know what he had to propose, sent some
of her domestics in disguise, to endeavour to discover what
turn her affairs were taking. Sir Charles Hotham, after
having assured his Prussian majesty of the friendship which
the King of England still entertained for him, told him that
he was ordered to demand me in marriage for the Prince of

---

[1] All editions of the *Memoirs* give 2 May as the date of Hotham's
arrival in Berlin. In fact he arrived exactly one month earlier and saw
the king for the first time on 4 April.

Wales ; and that, to cement the union of the two houses, he had no doubt but his Prussian majesty would also consent to the marriage of my brother with the Princess Amelia ; that his sovereign, however, would not object to my marriage being first celebrated ; and that it should rest with the King of Prussia to fix what time he thought proper for the nuptials of my brother.

The King, highly pleased with the proposal, replied to it in the most obliging manner. During the dinner, which was served up at the close of the audience, satisfaction shone radiant on his countenance ; the repast was uncommonly cheerful, and Bacchus, as usual presided at the feast. In the height of his good-humour, the King took a large goblet, and pledged Sir Charles Hotham, to the health of his son-in-law the Prince of Wales and mine. These few words had a different effect upon the guests. Grumbkow and Seckendorff were thunderstruck ; while the friends of the Queen and the other foreign ministers were triumphing. All, however, behaved alike ; they arose from table to congratulate the King, who was so delighted that he shed tears of joy.[1] After dinner, Sir Charles Hotham went up to the King, and intreated him not to divulge the proposals of marriage he had made to his majesty before he had had a second audience. The King felt somewhat surprised at the secrecy which was recommended ; signs of disapprobation clouded his brow. Seckendorff and Grumbkow, tired of the scene which they had witnessed, returned to Berlin, much abashed at seeing their projects ruined. The Queen, in the mean time, learned all this through her domestics.

I was quietly in my room, busy with my needle, and listening to my lecturer, who was reading to me. The ladies of the Queen's household, followed by a swarm of domestics, broke in upon me, and bending one knee,

---

[1] This dinner, where, according to Hotham's reports, " we all got immodestly drunk ", is confirmed by various documents given by Oncken (op. cit., 87). Since the marriage had not been discussed hitherto, Hotham claims to have been quite taken aback by the King's outburst.

eagerly exclaimed : " that they came to pay their compliments to the Princess of Wales." I really thought they were mad ; they stunned me with their noise ; their joy was so turbulent, that they did not know what they were about. They all spoke at once, they wept, they laughed, jumped about, and embraced me. At length, after the farce had continued for some time, they told me what I have just related. I was so little moved at the intelligence, that I said, continuing my work. " Is that all ? "—They left me, surprised at my indifference. Shortly after, my sisters and several ladies came to congratulate me. I was much beloved, and was more pleased with the proofs of attachment given me on this occasion, than with the cause of these felicitations. In the evening I went to the Queen. Her satisfaction may easily be conceived : she called me her dear Princess of Wales, and addressed Madam de Sonsfeld by the appellation of my lady. The latter took the liberty to suggest, that the Queen would do better to dissemble ; that as the King had not sent her any information concerning the business, he might be offended at her making so much noise about it ; and that the least trifle might yet ruin her hopes. Countess Fink having joined in these representations, the Queen reluctantly promised to moderate her joy.

The King arrived two days after. He mentioned nothing of what had passed, which gave us an unfavourable opinion of Sir Charles Hotham's negociation. He told the Queen the engagements he had entered into with the Duke of Brunswick-Bevern, who had demanded the second of my sisters in marriage for his eldest son ; and that he expected those two princes the next day. Seckendorff had contrived this match ; he carried his views much farther ; this alliance was merely an outline of the great plan he had formed. The Duke, brother-in-law to the Empress, was at that time but an apanaged prince, the Duke of Blankenburg being presumptive heir to the duchy of Brunswick. I shall not attempt his portrait : it will be sufficient to state, that this prince had the love and esteem of the virtuous ; his son treads in his steps. As the Queen was near her time, the betrothing of my sister took place without any ceremony. Seckendorff was the only foreign minister invited.

In the mean time, Sir Charles Hotham had almost every day secret conferences with the King. The conclusion of the double marriage depended only on one condition which the King of England required of the Prussian monarch, namely, that he should sacrifice Grumbkow. The English ambassador represented, that this minister, being entirely devoted to the court of Vienna, was the sole author of the continual animosity between the two families ; and that, in concert with a Mr. Reichenbach,[1] an Austrian *chargé-d'affaires* in England, he was plotting the most infamous intrigues. Sir Charles Hotham added, that some of Grumbkow's letters to this Reichenbach had been intercepted ; and that he was ready to prove his assertions by laying these letters before his majesty. He continued to urge the conclusion of the double marriage, affirming that his sovereign would be satisfied, if my brother were only betrothed to his daughter ; and that the King of Prussia should be at liberty to fix the time for the wedding. He did more ; his sovereign offered to give a portion of £100,000 sterling to the English Princess, and required none with me.

---

[1] Reichenbach was in fact the Prussian envoy in London, where he had been for some ten years. He was, however, in the pay of Grumbkow and Seckendorff. Hotham's object was to try to secure his removal, as well as that of Grumbkow in Berlin, and Oncken claims that the marriage was no more than a ploy for that purpose. Egmont writes (op. cit., 100), 10 August 1730 : " A short time ago, Sir Charles Hotham was sent to Berlin to endeavour a reconciliation with that Court. He was ordered to insist with that King that Reichenberg [*sic*], his Resident here, a saucy fellow, and who has long promoted a difference between the two Courts, should be recalled, but that King constantly refused it, saying what we laid to his charge was all lies. At length Sir Charles pulled out of his pocket a letter of Reichenberg's intercepted . . . wherein was several false informations of our Court, and particularly concerning the Princess Amelia, whose disorders he writ were fits of madness, than which nothing is more false. The King took the letter, and instead of reading it, threw it at Sir Charles's head, commanding him not to speak any more about recalling his Minister."

Offers so handsome had some effect upon my father. He answered, that he should not hesitate to sacrifice Grumbkow if he could be convinced, by his own hand-writing, of the detestable intrigues of which he was accused ; that he accepted with pleasure the alliance of the Prince of Wales ; and that he should consider of his proposals concerning the marriage of my brother. A few days after, he informed Sir Charles Hotham that he also consented to the latter, on condition, however, that my brother should be appointed vice-regent of the Electorate of Hanover, and should be maintained there at the expence of the British monarch until he should inherit the kingdom of Prussia at his death. The English ambassador answered, that he would communicate this proposal to his court ; but that he could not flatter the King with the prospect of obtaining his demand.

Every mail brought Sir Charles Hotham letters from the Prince of Wales. I saw several which the ambassador had transmitted to the Queen. " I intreat you, my dear Hotham," said the Prince, " to hasten the termination of my marriage.[1] I am in love like a madman ; my impatience is unparalleled." I thought these sentiments very romantic. The Prince had never seen me, and knew me only by character. I could not help laughing at his expressions.

On the 23d of May 1730, the Queen was delivered of a Prince, who was christened Augustus Ferdinand ; and had the Brunswick family for sponsors.[2]

The insinuations of Sir Charles Hotham appeared to have made some impression upon the King. He scarcely addressed a word to Grumbkow, and affected to speak ill of him in the presence of persons whom he knew to be his friends.

On the 30th, the King set out for the camp of Mühlberg ; whither he had been invited by the Polish Monarch. The whole Saxon army was assembled there, and went through

[1] " *Faites bientôt une fin de mon mariage* " is what Wilhelmina wrote. " Conclusion " might be a better translation. For the Prince's real behaviour in London, see above, p. 163 n.

[2] August Ferdinand (1730–1813), the last of Sophia Dorothea's fourteen children.

the evolutions and manœuvres described by the celebrated *Chevalier Folard*.[1] The regimentals, liveries, and equipages, were of uncommon magnificence : the tables, a hundred in number, sumptuously served ; and this camp was reported to exceed in splendour that of the gold cloth under Louis XIV.

My brother came to take leave of me on the eve of his departure. He was again dressed in the French style, which I thought ominous. I was not mistaken. " I come to bid you farewell," said he, " under the greatest anguish, as I shall not see you again for a great length of time. I have delayed my project of sheltering myself against the King's violence ; but I never lost sight of it. Your intreaties prevented its execution the last time I went to Dresden : but I must not procrastinate it any longer ; my situation grows worse from day to day : if I miss this opportunity, I shall perhaps not meet with so favourable a one for a considerable time. Yield to my wishes ; do not oppose my resolution any longer ; the attempt would be fruitless." Madam de Sonsfeld and myself were not a little surprized, that wishing to contradict him bluntly, I asked how he would contrive his escape ? I found his plan so fantastical, that I made him confess its absurdity. My governess, on her part, remonstrated that this step would destroy the good intentions of the King of England ; that, before the Prince undertook any thing, he ought to await the conclusion of Sir Charles Hotham's negociation ; that if this were broken off, he would still be at liberty to have recourse to extremes ; and that if, on the contrary, it proved successful, his situation must of course be improved. These arguments determined him at length to give us his word of honour that he would not make the attempt :[2] we separated highly satisfied with each other.

[1] Jean-Charles, Chevalier de Folard (1669–1752), a famous French military tactician and writer, highly regarded by Frederick the Great.

[2] In fact Frederick did make an unsuccessful attempt to escape from Mühlberg. Together with Katte he tried to procure horses to ride to the fair at Leipzig (see p. 210 below), but was prevented from doing so by

As soon as the King was at Mühlberg, efforts were made to counteract all the measures of Sir Charles Hotham. The latter had taken care to acquaint the Queen through Madamde Bülow with what had happened in his conferences with the King. The Queen had the weakness to mention it to Mrs. Ramen ; and the latter did not fail to convey her information to Grumbkow, who eagerly availed himself of it. His creatures were instructed to persuade the King, that the proposals of the English court were merely a trap to remove from his service those who were most faithfully attached to his Majesty ; that the British monarch aimed only at placing my brother on the throne, and seizing the government by means of the Princess he was to espouse ; that, fearing the vigilance of the loyal servants of his Majesty, the English cabinet would endeavour to remove them gradually that they might have no obstacle to their designs ; that, to obtain their end, they would subscribe to every one of the King's demands : that the blow could not be averted but by a constant refusal to assent to my brother's marriage, and by starting difficulties calculated to break off the negociation, without coming to a downright quarrel. The same observations were repeated to the King by so many different persons, who seemed to have no interest in them except what proceeded from their attachment to his Majesty, that they at length made some impression. The King was however advised to dissemble, and to wait for the answers from England, before he should throw off the mask. These detestable counsels excited him against my brother. As his suspicious disposition would not allow him to investigate the truth, he remembered the former attacks made against Grumbkow, which the latter had always repelled at the expense of his accusers, and by such thoughts he con-

---

a Saxon courtier, one Count Hoym. He also made overtures to Captain Guy Dickens, who was Hotham's secretary, begging him to make a further appeal to London. Both Dickens and Hotham had travelled with the King to Saxony. An unfavourable reply came on the night before the King and Frederick set off for Ansbach (see below, p. 211)— Hinrichs, op. cit., 47 ff.

firmed himself in the opinion, that his favourite must be innocent.

The King returned to Berlin in his disposition. The caresses of the Queen, whom he really loved tenderly, joined to a certain affection which he still preserved for his family, rendered him so uneasy, that being unable to continue silent, he opened his mind to M. de Lövener, the Danish minister, a man of much probity and great understanding, for whom he entertained a high esteem.

M. de Lövener, who was acquainted with the intrigues of Grumbkow and Seckendorff, not only took the part of Sir Charles Hotham, but also acquainted the King with many particulars calculated to dispel his doubts. He so clearly demonstrated what he had asserted, that the King, convinced by his arguments, promised to dismiss his favourite as soon as my marriage should be publicly announced : a remnant of suspicion would not allow him to make the sacrifice before he had obtained his demands. Sir Charles Hotham, informed by M. de Lövener of his conversation, expressed his dissatisfaction at it. He showed M. de Lövener his instructions, and told him that the King his master would not sign any of the stipulated articles, before he had received the satisfaction which he demanded. He was intreated to write to his employers that they should desist from that article : but to no purpose ; he would not attempt it, being convinced that the national honour was concerned.

The King having returned to Potsdam, the Queen held a drawing-room at Mon Bijou. Sir Charles Hotham, from motives of policy, did not appear. Grumbkow cut a miserable figure ; he looked as pale as death ; and, like an excommunicated person, he scarcely durst lift his eyes from the ground. He had retired to a corner of the hall, where neither the Queen nor any one spoke to him. To behold him thus humiliated made me reflect upon the vicissitudes of human affairs, and inspired me with commiseration for his misfortune. I did not wish to add to it by insult. I spoke to him and showed him the usual attentions.

M. de Lövener upbraided me for so doing ; adding withal, that the English Ambassador would be highly offended if he heard of my behaving thus to the mortal enemy of his King and Court. " Thus far," answered I, " I have no concern with either Sir Charles Hotham or his court, and need not regulate my behaviour according to their notions. I pity every unfortunate being. Grumbkow has caused me violent sorrows ; but I am too goodnatured to shew him the least resentment at a time when I see him overwhelmed and ready to sink. Besides, Sir, I think it bad policy to despise an enemy, when we think we have nothing more to fear from him. He may yet extricate himself, and become more formidable than ever. As for me, I wish him no other punishment than that he may no longer be able to do mischief." M. de Lövener has since told me, that he oftentimes thought of this conversation, in which I had too well predicted what happened shortly after.

When the King came back to Berlin, I found my brother more distressed than ever. Colonel de Rochow, who scarcely ever left him, sent word to the Queen, that he meditated an escape ; that he often mentioned it in the height of his vexation ; and that he was taking certain measures which confirmed his fears. At the same time, he promised to watch his proceedings so as to counteract his designs. This conduct of M. de Rochow was very praiseworthy ; but his very limited capacity betrayed him into great errors. He was actually in a critical situation ; if he opposed my brother, he incurred his hatred ; and if he suffered him to escape, he was exposing himself to the ill-will of the King, and perhaps running the risk of losing his head. These reflections intimidated him so much, that he went about Berlin, lamenting his situation from house to house ; and his secret soon became that of the fable. It was not long before it reached the Austrian party. The Queen, distressed at Rochow's information, mentioned it to me, knowing that I was perfectly acquainted with my brother's disposition. She consulted me about what ought to be done. I did not dare to acquaint her with the true state of affairs, being afraid of her foible for Mrs. Ramen, through whom my brother might be undone. I confessed that he was sinking into a dreadful melancholy ; that he had moments of irritation, at which I had frequently been frightened ; that he kept her majesty ignorant of the horror of his situation, that he might not give her any uneasiness : but that I did not think him capable of coming to the extremities which she apprehended. I observed, that plans were formed in the height of despair, which were left unexecuted when reflected upon coolly ; and I exerted myself to remove her fears.

The answers from England arrived in the mean time. They were such as the King could wish. Every one of his demands was granted, but still on condition that he should remove Grumbkow, before any article was signed. Sir Charles Hotham had received intercepted original letters of that minister. He informed the King of the circumstance, and demanded a secret audience. Seckendorff, who had his spies every where, was apprized of it. He got the start of Sir Charles Hotham, and had a prior interview with the King. He descanted on the pains which the Emperor had taken to gain his friendship, on the condescension with which he had granted him leave to recruit in his dominions, and on the guarantee he had given him of the duchies of Jülich and Berg ; adding, that it was very hard for the Emperor to see that, in spite of all his advances, his Prussian majesty abandoned him to side with his enemies. " I am a man of probity," continued he, " your majesty has always acknowledged me as such. I am personally attached to your majesty, and the excess of my devotion for your interests forces me to interfere in a very delicate affair : but the situation in which I see you, makes me shudder ; let what may happen, I shall have the consolation of having performed my duty by warning you of what is going on. The Prince-Royal is secretly plotting with England. Here are letters which I received from our minister at London ; here are others of the envoy of Cassel and some of my friends. The Queen of England has had the imprudence to show to several persons the letters which the Prince-Royal has written to her ; they contain formal promises of marriage, given unknown to your majesty. Besides, there is a rumour afloat in town, that he intends to escape. All these circumstances combined, appear suspicious. Grumbkow has received more detailed information on that subject, which he will be able to communicate to your majesty. As for the rest, sire, if you have the marriage of your daughter so much at heart, I am ordered by my court to offer you my assistance. I do not despair of success. That of the Prince-Royal appears too dangerous for you to consent to it. Consider, sire with how many inconveniences it will be attended. You will have a vain-glorious haughty daughter-in-law, who will fill your court with intrigues, the revenues of your kingdom will not be sufficient for her expences : and who knows whether she will not finally strip you of your authority ! Forgive me, sire ; my zeal is betraying me into undue warmth ; it is Seckendorff and not the envoy of the Emperor that speaks to you. The British ministers treat you as a child ; they allure you with a bauble, and seem to say : We give it you, if you are obedient and remove Grumbkow. What a stain to the glory of your majesty, if you fall into so palpable a snare ; and what dependance can your faithful servants have upon you, if they constantly see themselves at the mercy of foreign powers ? " He carried his hypocrisy so far as to shed tears, and acted his part so well, that his speech made a lasting impression. The King remained thoughtful and uneasy ; he replied very little, and left him soon after. He continued in a horrible humour the rest of the day. The next morning the 14th of July, Sir Charles Hotham had his audience. After having assured the King that his court granted all he had wished, he handed him Grumbkow's letters ; remarking, that he had no doubt but the King would dismiss him as soon as he had perused them ; that one of them was indeed in cyphers, but that persons had been found clever enough to decypher it. The King took the letters with an enraged countenance, threw them into Sir Charles Hotham's face, and lifted up his leg as if to give him a kick. He however recollected himself, and left the room without saying any thing, clapping the door in a violent passion. The English minister withdrew in as great a rage as the King. As soon as he got home, he sent for the Danish and Dutch ministers, to whom he related what had passed. He shewed the spirit of an Englishman on the occasion, and assured those gentlemen, that if the King had staid a moment longer, he should have forgot himself, and have demanded satisfaction. He interested them in his cause, which was that of all crowned heads. His character of ambassador having been violated by the affront, he declared that, his negociation being at an end, he should leave Berlin early the next morning. The Queen was informed of this distressing affair by a note which Sir Charles Hotham wrote to Madam de Bülow. Her grief may easily be conceived. The King, on his part, was a prey to bitter remorse. Being extremely sorry for his ebullition, he had recourse to the Danish and Dutch ministers, and intreated them to make matters up with the English ambassador. He commissioned them to apologize to the latter for the offence into which he had been betrayed, protesting that if he would stay, he would endeavour to obliterate it by the kindest treatment. The whole day passed in messages backwards and forwards, without obtaining any thing of Sir Charles Hotham, who remained inflexibly determined to depart. The King vented his ill-humour upon the Queen. He told her with a sneer, that " the negotiation being entirely broken off, he had determined to obtain for me the survivorship to the Abbess of Herford." For this purpose he instantly wrote to the Margravine Philippa, who was the abbess, and it may easily be supposed that she made no difficulty to grant his request. I think it was a mere feint of the King to induce the Queen to use her intercession with Sir Charles Hotham. As his uneasiness increased in proportion as the day advanced, he gave the

Danish and Dutch envoys full powers to offer a formal reparation to be made in their presence. M. de Lövener informed my brother of the circumstance, and besought him to write a note to the English minister to persuade him to accept of the expedient. My brother having mentioned the matter to the Queen, and obtained her assent, he wrote as follows :

" Sir ;
Having been informed by M. de Lövener of the ultimatum of the King my father, I have no doubt but you will yield to his wishes. Consider, sir, that my happiness and my sister's depend on the resolution which you will take ; and that your answer will ground the union or eternal disunion of the two families. I hope your reply will be favourable, and that you will not be deaf to my intreaties. I shall never forget your kindness, but acknowledge it all the days of my life by the perfect esteem with which, &c."

The letter was delivered to Sir Charles Hotham by Katte. This was his answer.

" Sɪʀ ;
M. de Katte has handed me a letter from your Royal Highness. I am penetrated with gratitude for the confidence with which I am honoured by your Royal Highness. Were it my own cause, I should even attempt impossibilities to prove my respect by my obedience to your Royal Highness's commands : but as the affront which I have received concerns the King my master, I cannot comply with your Royal Highness's wishes. I shall endeavour to give the best turn I can to the affair ; and though it interrupts the negociation, I yet hope it will not break it off entirely. I am, &c. '

The perusal of this letter was a thunderstroke to the Queen and me. I felt at that time as little disposed to my marriage with the Prince of Wales as before : but the Margrave of Schwedt, the Duke of Weissenfels, blows and insults, were all too fresh in my memory not to wish to be safe against them ; I was persuaded that my fate could not be as miserable in England as it would be at Berlin, where I saw nothing but abysses on all sides. My brother did not appear much distressed at the misfortune ; he shook his head and said : " turn abbess ; you will have an establishment. I cannot conceive why the Queen is grieving ; the misfortune is not very great. I am tired of all these intrigues ; my resolution is taken. I have nothing to reproach myself with in your respect ; I have tried every thing for your marriage. Extricate yourself as you can ; it is time for me to think of myself. I have endured enough. Do not harass me any more with intreaties and tears : they would be useless, as they have no longer any effect upon me." All this spoken in an angry tone rent my heart. His mind had been so irritated for some time, and he led a life so dissolute, that his former good sentiments seemed extinguished. I endeavoured to soothe him, and to argue with him. At length his harsh and disdainful remarks provoked my anger : I used some cutting expressions, which being retorted by observations still more severe, I remained silent, and hoped to make matters up after his passion had subsided.

He was to set out with the King early the next day to go to Ansbach, I therefore wished to effect a reconciliation that evening. I was too fond of him to separate on bad terms, and, by making the first advances, I wished to prevent, if possible, the step which he meditated. He listened very coolly to the many tender and kind things which I told him, and as I intreated him to pledge his word that he would not attempt any thing : " I have made many reflections," said he, " which have induced me to alter my sentiments : I do not think of escaping, and certainly shall return hither." I could not reply ; I had only just time to embrace him. The King having entered the apartment, my brother said, in a low voice : " I shall see you again to-night in your room." These words revived my hopes. I took leave of the King, and retired ; but I vainly waited for my brother. At length, at midnight, he sent me his valet with a note which contained nothing but excuses and protestations of friendship. This valet had been with my brother ever since he was born ; he was a man of talents and of unshaken fidelity. Unfortunately, he fell in love with one of the Queen's waiting-women, and married her. This woman having been gained over by Mrs. Ramen, used to wind all my brother's secrets out of her husband to tell them to this hag, who communicated them to the King. This we learned afterwards.

The King left Berlin, as I said, the following day, the 15th of July. The agitation of my mind would not let me sleep. I passed the night in conversing with Madam de Sonsfeld. As we foresaw what would happen, we could not refrain from tears. I was however obliged to constrain myself before the Queen. Her majesty did not notice my countenance, being busily employed in reading Grumbkow's intercepted letters, which Sir Charles Hotham had sent her. They were six or seven, all of the month of February, and written at the time when the Queen was afflicted with the dangerous malady which I have mentioned. Their contents were nearly these :

" Much noise is made here about the Queen, who is reported to be on the point of death. Let the court know, that she is as well as a fish in water ;[1] her illness is but a feint to move the King her brother. I have already instructed two of my emissaries[2] to inflame the fat man[3] against his son. Continue to inform me of whatever you may learn about his intrigues with the Queen of England."

In another it was said :

" I have requested the friend (Seckendorff) to acquaint the fat man concerning the correspondents of his son in

---

[1] The literal expressions used in the letter. (Authors' note.)
[2] They were valets, and frequently less than valets. (Author's note.)
[3] The King. (Author's note.)

England : write me on that subject a letter, that I may show and give it such a turn that the suspicions which it will excite may sooner lead us to our ends. Be not afraid. I shall know how to support you, and prevent all discovery ; for the fat man's heart is in my hands ; I do with it what I like."

Those of the month of March ran thus :

" I am much surprized, my dear Reichenbach, at the conduct of the English court, and particularly of the Prince of Wales. What do they intend by that embassy of Sir Charles Hotham ? and whence that eagerness to marry a Princess plainer than the Devil, whose face is covered with pimples ; who is disgusting and silly ? I am astonished that the Prince, who might chuse the most perfect Princess, should think of such a baboon. I pity the fate of the Prince : he ought to be warned of it. I leave that care to you."

The other letters were written in the same style. The character of their author is sufficiently manifested by those which I have inserted ; it will display itself more and more in the sequel of these Memoirs.

VI

A plaguy visit — My brother is arrested — We destroy implicating letters — The circumstances of my brother's flight — I am confined — A letter in a piece of cheese — I counterfeit illness with turpentine cakes — The conditions of Frederick's imprisonment and the unfortunate death of Katte.

SIR Charles Hotham left Berlin, as he had intended.[1] During the absence of the King, the Queen held a drawing-room four times a week at Mon-Bijou. I was glad to see M. de Katte there ; I was certain that, as long as he was at Berlin, my brother would make no attempt to escape. Katte one day came to tell me, that he was going to send an express to the Prince Royal, and asked whether I would not write to him, the conveyance being perfectly safe ? I was much surprized at his proposal. " You are very wrong, Sir," said I, " to venture such a thing. Consider the fatal consequence to which this express may lead, if the King be informed of it. Suspicious as he is, it may cause much trouble to my brother and ruin your fortune for ever. Though my friendship for my brother be very great, I certainly shall not write to him by that conveyance." He wished to urge me, but I turned my back upon him, terrified at what he had told me, and foreseeing that the step was taken from motives which I had long dreaded. A few days after, Madam de Bülow and some other well-meaning persons came to inform me, that Katte had divulged my brother's projects all over the town ; that he had even mentioned them before suspicious charac-ters. Proud of the Prince's favour, he loudly boasted of it, and dashed about with a box that contained the portraits of the Prince Royal and myself. This imprudence had render-

---

[1] He left on 11 July.

197

ed the mischief worse. I thought it necessary to inform the
Queen of it, that by her authority I might get the box out of
his hands, and oblige him to be silent. She was very angry
at his impertinance, and ordered Madam de Sonsfeld to
deliver him a rather unpleasing message, and to demand my
portrait. Madam de Sonsfeld acquitted herself of her commission that very evening. Katte apologized as well as he
could : but nothing that my governess urged, could induce
him to return my portrait ; he said, my brother had permitted him to copy it from an original in miniature with
which the Princess had presented the Prince Royal, and
which the latter had entrusted to him till his return. He
promised to be more discreet in future, and requested her to
tell the Queen that he besought her to be easy ; that as long
as he should enjoy the Prince's favour, he would endeavour
to avert any fatal resolution the Prince might take ; that he
sometimes entered into his views, to bring him more
easily back ; and that thus far there was nothing to be
apprehended.

The Queen was fond of flattering herself. This answer
dispelled her uneasiness for my brother. But the denial of
my portrait exasperated us both so much against Katte,
that we spoke to him no more.

One morning when I awoke, I was much surprised to see
Mrs. Ramen enter my room ; her apparition seemed to me
the sequel of an evil dream. She told me, she came only to
open her heart to me. Madam de Sonsfeld would have
withdrawn : but she requested her to stay, saying that the
business concerned her also : " you are sorry," continued
she, " that the Queen uses you ill ; rather thank heaven for
it ; were you her favourite the King would soon dismiss
you. As for me, I have nothing to dread on that head ;
I have taken my precautions before hand ; although my
favour should diminish, the King would not forsake me, and
would know how to support me. I know you are acquainted
with all my intrigues ; I do not deny them ; It rests with
you to warn the Queen of them. If you wish to incur the

resentment of the King by whose orders I act, he shall be instantly informed of the obstacles you thus oppose to his designs, and will have recourse to extremes against you. Besides, you know the narrow capacity of the Queen ; I shall immediately perceive that you have excited her against me, and find means to persuade her that all you told her were calumnies, and I shall thus retort on your head the harm which you intended to do me." She had been addressing us both : but now turning to me, she added : " you are going, Madam, to be plunged into a very great misfortune, make up your mind beforehand. You will not be able to extricate yourself from your trouble but by marrying the Duke of Weissenfels. Is marriage then so solemn a thing ? It is only here that so much noise is made about it ; believe me, a husband under the rule of his wife is a great convenience. As for the rest, be not uneasy concerning what the Queen will say ; I know her well, and I can assure you that if the King caresses her and distinguishes her a little in public, she will soon be consoled, and not care for the matter." I was enraged against this woman : had I followed my first impulse I should have thrown her out of the window to shorten her road. But I was obliged to dissemble my indignation. I answered, that I was perfectly resigned to the decrees of Providence ; that, for the rest, I should never do any one thing without consulting the Queen, and having her approbation. I thus terminated this plaguy visit, which filled me with horror at the conduct of the infamous woman. We could not help bewailing the fate of the Queen for having fallen into such hands.

But I return to Grumbkow. His countenance was very much changed since Sir Charles Hotham's departure ; an air of satisfaction reigned in his physiognomy. He assiduously paid his respects to the Queen, who treated him with politeness. One evening (it was on the 11th of August, a day remarkable on more than one account) as my mind had been extremely agitated, and an unusual melancholy had fastened upon it all the day, I did not sit long at cards, and took a walk with Madam de Bülow. After having taken a few turns, I sat down with her on a seat at the end of the garden. Grumbkow joined us. We were to perform our devotions on the following Sunday. Grumbkow was one of those who reject religion from the desire of satisfying their passions, and without previous inquiry. As he was not firmly grounded in his principles, he sometimes had violent upbraidings of conscience, and felt remorses which rendered him melancholy, and which he drowned in wine and good cheer. M. Jablonski, one of the chaplains of his majesty,[1] had passed the day with him, and had probably given him a lively description of hell. Grumbkow entered upon a long moral discourse, which in his mouth appeared to me like the gospel in that of the fiend. Passing afterwards to other matters, he said he was extremely sorry for the bad treatment I had experienced, and that which my brother had endured from the King. " The Prince-Royal," continued he, " ought to conform more than he does to the wishes of his father, who is the greatest monarch that ever reigned, and who combines the political with the moral virtues." I was afraid this conversation would lead him farther ; which I wished to avoid : I therefore rose, and walked very fast, taking the road to the house. I only answered respecting the King, and endeavoured to outdo him in the praises which he had lavished upon his majesty ; but he returned to his subject : " Your ascendancy over the mind of the Prince Royal is very great," continued he ; " you are the only person, madam, who can recal him to his duty ; he is a charming Prince, but he is badly advised."—" If my brother," answered I, " will follow my advice, he always will regulate his conduct according to the intentions of his majesty, provided he be acquainted with them." He wished to reply : but several ladies came up to me, and relieved me from my embarrassment.

---

[1] Daniel Ernst Jablonski (1660–1741), reformed court preacher in Berlin and a distinguished theologian. He corresponded extensively with Leibniz.

On the same evening, the Queen being before her toilette-table undressing, and Madam de Bülow sitting near her, they heard a terrible rumbling noise in the adjoining cabinet. This superb cabinet was decorated with rock crystal and other precious stones of high value, independent of gold and other articles of superior workmanship. Vases of ancient Japan and China porcelain had been placed between the compartments ; they were of an enormous size. The Queen at first supposed that the fall of some of them had occasioned the noise. Madam de Bülow looked into the cabinet, but, to her surprise, she found every thing in order. Scarcely had she shut the door, and left it, when the noise recommenced. She three times renewed her search, attended by one of the Queen's women ; and they always found everything in the most perfect order. The rumbling ceased, at length, in the cabinet ; but another more dreadful noise was heard in a passage which separated the apartments of the King from those of the Queen, and by which they communicated. No one ever entered there but the domestics about their majesties' persons, and centries guarded its entrance at the two ends. The Queen, anxious to know whence the noise proceeded, ordered her women to follow her with lights. Fear revealed the false attachment of Mrs. Ramen ; she would not go with the Queen, and ran away to hide herself in the adjoining room. Two other waiting-women and Madam de Bülow accompanied her majesty. Scarcely had they opened the door, when their ears were struck with dreadful groans followed by horrible screams, which made them shake with fear. The Queen alone remained firm. Having entered the passage, she encouraged her followers to search what it could be. They found all the doors bolted. After having removed the bolts, they searched the place without discovering any thing. The two soldiers were half dead with fright : they had heard the same groans close to them, but had seen nothing. The Queen asked whether any one had entered the King's apartments ? They answered in the negative. She returned to her room rather depressed, and related the adventure to me the next morning. Though she was far from being superstitious, she yet ordered me to mark the date, to see what that rumbling noise might have prognosticated. I am well convinced that there was nothing supernatural in the case. Yet chance would have it so that my brother was arrested that very evening, and on the return of the King he had the most afflicting scene with the Queen in that passage.

As there was no drawing-room that day, we had a concert at Mon-Bijou, at which the amateurs of music were permitted to assist ; and Katte never failed to be present. After having accompanied for a while on the piano-forte, I passed into the adjoining card-room. Katte followed me, requesting me for heaven's sake to hear him for a moment in behalf of my brother. At a name so dear I stopped. " I am excessively grieved," said he, " at having incurred the disgrace of her majesty, and that of your royal highness. You have been deluded by false reports. I am accused of confirming the Prince Royal in his intention to escape. I protest, madam, by every thing most sacred, that I have written to him and absolutely declined following him, if he attempted to fly ; and I answer for it with my head he never will make the attempt without me."—" I think your head is not very safe on your shoulders already," answered I ; " and if you do not reform very soon, I may perhaps see it at your feet. I must confess that the Queen and myself are both very much displeased with you ; I never could have supposed you would have been guilty of the imprudence to divulge my brother's intentions, and to confide his secrets to every one. You should make a better return for his kindness, and reflect on the irregularity of your behaviour ; particularly, Sir, it does not become you to have my portrait, and to make a boast of it. The Queen ordered you to return it, you ought to have obeyed her commands ; it would have been a reparation of your fault, and nothing but that can insure you her forgiveness and mine."—" As to the first

article," replied he, " I can take my oath, madam, that I
never spoke to any one but to M. de Lövener concerning the
Prince Royal. He is not a man of suspicious character, and I
do not suppose that the Queen will blame me for it. As to
the second, having myself taken a copy of the portrait of
your royal highness, and of that of the Prince Royal, I
thought it no harm to shew them to some of my friends,
particularly as I only shewed them as pieces of my own
workmanship : but I confess, madam, that I had rather
submit to death than give them up. As for the rest,"
continued he, " I have many enemies who envy the favour
with which I am distinguished by the Prince, and, finding
nothing reprehensible in me, have recourse to calumnies :
but I repeat it, madam, as long as I am with that beloved
Prince, I shall prevent his executing his designs, though,
after all, I cannot see that he would run any great risk.
What harm could befal him if he were taken in his flight ?
He is heir to the crown, and no one would be bold enough to
meddle with him."—" Indeed," said I, " you are playing a
dangerous game, and I am very much afraid I shall prove
too true a prophet."—" If I lose my head," answered he,
" it will be in a good cause : but the Prince will not forsake
me." I gave him no time to say more, and left him. It
was the last time I saw him ; I was far from thinking that
my sad predictions would be so soon fulfilled, having only
intended to intimidate him.

On the 15th of August, the King's birth-day,[1] when the
Queen received the compliments of the court, the drawing-
room was extremely crowded. I had again a long conversation with Grumbkow : he had dismissed morals, and resumed the playful style. As his wit is very lively, he entertained me very much. He again expatiated largely on the
praises of the King ; and seeing that I was attempting to
disengage myself from him, he told me, with an earnestness at which I was surprised, " You will shortly see,

[1] The King, whose birthday was in fact on 14 August, was of course
not in Berlin.

madam, how much I am attached to you, and how much I am devoted to your service." I returned a kind answer to this protestation, and was leaving him, when Madam de Bülow came up, and began to ply him with her wit : it was her habit ; she never could see him without making him the butt of her sarcasms. I had warned her more than once not to carry the joke too far, and to behave civilly to Grumbkow ; observing that she ought to follow the example of the Indians, who adore the devil, that he may not harm them : but she did not attend to my warnings. The contestation she had with him that night was very hot. Her antagonist ended it by saying to her, as he had said to me, " In a short time I shall convince you how much I am your friend." I thought there was a meaning hid under an expression so studiously repeated, and felt uneasy at it.

On the next day, the 16th of August, the Queen afforded me a very agreeable surprise. She gave a ball at Mon-Bijou, in honour of the King's birth-day. The dining-room was decorated with coloured lamps and devices, and the table represented a flower-garden ; every one found a present under his plate. We were all extremely cheerful, only Madam de Kamecke, Madam de Sonsfeld, Countess Fink, and Madam de Bülow, appeared distressed. They spoke not a word, and complained of being indisposed. Dancing was resumed after supper. I had not danced for the last six years ; it was something new, I enjoyed it to my heart's content, without paying much attention to what was passing. Madam de Bülow said several times, " It is late, I wish you would withdraw."—" For goodness' sake," answered I, " let me dance as much as I like this day ; perhaps I may not dance again for a long time."—" That may be the case, indeed ! " replied she. I made no reflection upon it, and continued to divert myself. She renewed her attack half an hour after. " Do give over," said she, in an angry tone : " you are so well employed that you cannot see."—" And you are so cross to-day," replied I, " that I do not know what to make of you."—" Do but look at the

Queen, and you will no longer find fault with me, madam."
Indeed the sight of the Queen, on whom I now cast my
eyes, chilled me with horror. She was as pale as death,
conversing, in a corner of the room, with the first lady of her
household, and Madam de Sonsfeld. As I felt more interested in my brother's fate than in any thing else, I immediately enquired whether it concerned him? Madam de
Bülow shrugged her shoulders, saying, " I don't know."
The Queen retired a moment after, and took me in her
carriage. She did not open her lips all the way to the palace.
The uneasiness her silence gave me, caused me terrible
palpitations of heart. As soon as I was in my room, I
tormented my governess to know what was the matter.
She answered, with tears in her eyes, " that the Queen had
enjoined her to be silent." I now thought my brother was
dead ; which plunged me into such violent grief, that
Madam de Sonsfeld thought it necessary to undeceive me.
She told me that Madam de Kamecke had that morning
received an express from the King, with letters for her and
the Queen, in which his majesty ordered her gradually to
prepare the Queen for the intelligence, that he had placed
the Prince Royal under arrest, for having attempted to
leave the country. My brother's misfortune threw me into
an agony of grief ; I passed the night in the most frightful
agitation. The Queen sent for me early in the morning to
show me the King's letter, which evidently betrayed his
rage. It ran thus :

" I have ordered the rascally Frederick to be arrested. I
shall deal with him as his crime and his meanness require. I
no longer acknowledge him for my son. He has dishon-
oured me and my house. Such a wretch does not deserve to
live."

I fainted at the perusal of this letter. The situation of the
Queen and mine would have moved a heart of stone. As
soon as the Queen recovered a little, she related to me
that Katte had been arrested. I shall here insert the par-

ticulars of his arrest, such as we learned them afterwards.

M. de Grumbkow having been acquainted with my brother's misfortune on the 15th, had not been able to conceal his joy, and had mentioned the matter to several of his friends. M. de Lövener, who had spies about Grumbkow's person, was informed of it. He immediately wrote to Katte, and advised him to set out instantly, or else he would infallibly be arrested. Katte availed himself of his advice, and wrote to Field-Marshal Natzmer, who commanded his regiment, for leave of absence, to go to Friedrichsfelde, to pay his respects to the Margrave Albert, which was granted. He had got a saddle made, in which he could conceal money and writings. Unfortunately for him the saddle was not quite ready, and he was obliged, to wait. He made, however, a good use of his time, for he burnt all his papers. His horse being at length saddled, he was going to mount it when the Field-Marshal, attended by a strong guard, came to ask him for his sword, and arrested him in the King's name. Katte delivered his sword without changing countenance, and was immediately conducted to prison. His effects were sealed in the presence of the Field-Marshal, who appeared more depressed than the prisoner. He had delayed more than three hours executing the orders of the King, to give Katte time to escape, and was extremely sorry to meet him yet at home.[1]

I return to the Queen. She inquired whether my brother had ever mentioned his design to me? I told her what I knew on the subject, and stated as an apology for not having communicated it to her, that I had been afraid it might commit her majesty in case my brother should actually make the attempt. I confessed, besides, that the assurances which Katte had given me had thrown me into a perfect security, and taken away the most distant expecta-

---

[1] The order for the arrest of Katte was given at Wesel on 12 August. The King was furious at what he considered a great delay and believed that Wilhelmina herself was responsible for warning Katte—Hinrichs (op. cit. 34).

tion of what I had just learnt. " But," said the Queen,
" do you know what is become of our letters ? "—" I have
frequently mentioned them to my brother, and he assured
me that he had commited them to the flames."—" I know
your brother too well," replied she, " and I durst lay any
thing that they are among Katte's effects. If that be the
case, we are undone." The Queen was right in her con-
jecture ; we heard, the next day, that there were several
chests belonging to my brother at Katte's, and that seals had
been put upon them. This intelligence made us shudder.
After having reflected some time, the Queen had recourse
once more to Field-Marshal Natzmer, who had rendered her
service in a similar case, as I have related above. She immediately sent for one of her chaplains, of the name of
Reinbeck,[1] to commission him to induce the Marshal to let
her majesty have the chest which contained the letters.
Reinbeck being ill, begged to be excused, which increased
the Queen's uneasiness. Chance, however, served her
better. Countess Fink came to see me the next morning. I
was surprised at the alteration of her face. After I had dismissed every one except Madam de Sonsfeld, she told me
that she was the most unfortunate person in the universe,
and that she was come to trust me with her sorrows.
" Judge, madam," said she, " of my embarrassment. Last
night, on my return home, I found a sealed chest addressed
to the Queen, which had been left with my servants, together with this note." She gave it me ; it contained only
these words :

" Have the goodness, madam, to give this chest to the
Queen ; it contains the letters which her majesty and the
Princess have written to the Prince-Royal."

" I cannot conceive," added she, " who can have played
me this trick ; for those who brought it, were masked. In
the mean time I know not what to resolve. I am sensible

[1] Johann Gustav Reinbeck (1683–1741), Halle priest and an influential religious figure at the Berlin court.

that by sending this fatal deposit to the King, I ruin the Queen ; and if I give it to her majesty, I shall be the victim of it. Either of these measures is so fatal, that I know not which to adopt." We spoke to her with so much energy, and urged her so earnestly, that we persuaded her to mention the circumstance to the Queen ; proving to her that she could not run any risk by doing so, since the chest was addressed to the Queen.

We repaired all three to her majesty's room. The satisfaction which the Queen felt at this good news, caused some alleviation of her grief ; but it was not of long duration. Our reflections dispelled it. We observed how difficult it would be to bring the chest secretly to the palace, as there were spies every where ; that, though this could be accomplished, it was to be feared that Katte would allude to it at his examination ; what then should be the lot of the Countess Fink ? She would find herself innocently implicated in this shocking affair, without the possibility of extricating herself. If she should act openly and send the chest publicly to the Queen, the King would immediately be informed of it, and force her majesty to become the instrument of her own misfortune, by giving the letters up. The case was critical ; there were precipices on all sides. At length, after having maturely weighed the arguments on both sides of the question, the last resource was determined upon as the least perilous, and leaving us, besides, the hope of hitting upon some expedient to get at the papers. The writing-desk, for such it was, was carried to the apartment of the Queen ; who immediately locked it up in presence of her domestics and of Mrs. Ramen. Our conferences were resumed in the afternoon. The Queen intended to burn the letters, and simply to say to the King, that as they were of no importance, she had thought it no harm to commit them to the flames. We all rejected this advice ; one proposed one thing, the other another, and the whole day passed in this manner without coming to a conclusion.

When I had retired to my room, I told Madam de Sonsfeld

that I had hit upon an infallible expedient, but which would be attended with great danger, if the Queen entrusted it to Mrs. Ramen. I gave her to understand, that if the seals could be removed without breaking, it would be easy to open the padlock of the desk : the letters might then be taken out without difficulty, and others might be written and put in their place. My governess approved my plan, we agreed with Countess Fink to propose it to the Queen, and to bind her by her word of honour not to mention any thing about the business.

This plan was executed the next day, as agreed upon. We all spoke so intelligibly, without naming any one, that the Queen remarked extremely well, that we were alluding to Mrs. Ramen. But her foible for this woman was such, that she made as though she had not understood us ; she promised however eternal secrecy, and was for this time as good as her word. In the afternoon we executed our scheme. The Queen dismissed her ladies and domestics, I remained alone with her. We met at first with a terrible obstacle. The writing-desk was so heavy, that neither the Queen nor I could move it ; which circumstance obliged her to confide in a valet, an old and faithful domestic of inviolable integrity and discretion. I tried for a long time to lift up the seal ; and trembled as I found it impossible. The valet, whose name was Bock, having examined the arms which were those of Katte, said with great exultation : " good heavens ! I have the very same seal about me, I found it a month ago in the garden of Mon-Bijou, I have carried it with me ever since, with the view to discover its owner." Having compared the impression with the seal, we found them exactly corresponding, and concluded that they were the arms of Katte. Having now removed the cords and the padlock, we proceeded to the examination of the letters. These demand a more detailed account.

I have already, in the course of this work, spoken of the rather disrespectful manner in which we had frequently mentioned the King. The Queen delighted in our satirical

remarks, and outdid us in that respect. Her letters, as well
as mine, were full of them. Hers contained besides, the
detail of the English intrigues, the illness which she had
affected the preceding winter to gain time ; and, in short,
secrets of the highest importance. Mine contained something more : for greater safety, I used to write indifferent
things with common ink, and those of consequence with
lemon-juice : by holding the paper over the fire, the characters appeared and became legible. Mrs. Ramen was commonly the subject of this mysterious writing. I railed
against her, and complained bitterly of her ascendency over
the mind of the Queen. We also agreed by that means about
what was to be told to or kept secret from her majesty.

My mind had been so agitated, that I had not thought of
the effect which those letters would have upon the Queen :
the idea struck me whan I opened the desk, and made me
shudder : a lucky incident however, extricated me ; the
chaplain Reinbeck was announced. The Queen could not
help seeing him, as she had sent for him the day before.
She was so agitated, that, in leaving the room, she said :
" for heaven's sake, burn all those letters ; let me not find
one on my return." I did not wait for the command being
repeated, and committed them instantly to the flames.
There were at least fifteen hundred, reckoning those of the
Queen and mine together. I had scarcely got over this fine
task, when her majesty came back. We now examined the
remainder of the papers ; there were letters of a great
number of persons, love letters, moral reflections, and notes
upon history, written by my brother, a purse with a
thousand pistoles,[1] several precious stones and jewels ; and,
finally, a letter from my brother to Katte, written in the
month of May, and containing these words :

" I am off, my dear Katte. My precautions are so well
taken, that I have nothing to fear. I shall go through
Leipzig, where I shall pass myself for the Marquis

[1] Pistole—gold coin worth about 18*s.*

d'Ambreville. I have already sent word to Keith, who is to go straight to England. Lose no time, for I expect to meet you at Leipzig. Adieu. Be of good cheer."

We cast all those writings into the fire, except the small compositions of my brother, which I have preserved. In the evening I set about re-writing the letters which were to be substituted. The Queen did the same the next day. We carefully used paper of each year to prevent any discovery. It took us three days to fabricate six or seven hundred letters ; these were a mere trifle compared with those we had burnt. We became fully aware of it, when we were about shutting the desk ; it was so empty, that this circumstance alone might have betrayed us. I proposed to continue writing to fill it ; but the anxiety of the Queen was so great, that she preferred cramming all sorts of things into it, rather than keep it open any longer. I objected to it as much as I could, but in vain. At length we restored the chest to its former state, and the change could not possibly be perceived.

The King arrived on the 27th of August, at five o'clock in the afternoon. His domestics had preceded him ; the Queen sent for them, and inquired about my brother : they protested their ignorance of his fate ; they had left him at Wesel, and did not know what had been done with him since. But it is proper to relate there the circumstances of his flight, such as I have learnt them of himself and of those who were with him.[1]

His first intention was to have made his escape from Ansbach.[2] His imprudence in speaking of his discontents

---

[1] This story is confirmed by a letter from Seckendorff to Prince Eugene, printed by F. Förster in *Friedrich Wilhelm I* (Potsdam, 1836–7) III 11 ; and also by a letter from the King to Anhalt-Dessau, —Krauske (op. cit., 456), 30 August : " . . . die *Brifschaften von Katte die sein fort aber es kommen wunderl[iche] sachen heraus* ".)

[2] The King had taken Frederick with him on his tour of southern and western Germany, where by visiting various minor German rulers he was demonstrating his commitment to the Empire. On 21 July he arrived at Ansbach, whose domains bordered on those of Bayreuth, to visit his daughter, the Margravine Frederica.

to the Margrave prevented it. This Prince, seeing him extremely irritated against the King, suspected his design and deranged his plan by refusing him horses which he asked for, under pretence of taking a ride in the country. The King had overstepped all bounds, and publicly ill-treated him in the presence of strangers. He had even repeated before those strangers what I had often heard him say : " *Had my father treated me as I do you, I should have ran away a thousand times for one : but you are a faint-hearted fellow, a mere coward.*" Unable to obtain his end during his stay at Ansbach, my brother was forced to wait for another opportunity which might offer on the road. The express sent by Katte reached the Prince at the distance of a few German miles from Ansbach. He immediately returned him an answer, informing him that he expected to effect his escape in two days ; that Katte was to meet him at the Hague, assuring him that his success was infallible, because, if he were pursued, he should find an asylum in some of the numerous convents on that road. His agitation made him forget to direct the letter to Berlin. Unfortunately, there was a cousin of Katte of the same name employed on the recruiting service ten or twelve German miles thence. The express went to him, and delivered him my brother's letter.

In the mean time, the King proceeded on his road to Frankfurt, and he and his retinue passed the night in the barns of a village. My brother, Colonel Rochow, and my brother's valet, slept in the same barn.

I have already stated, that Keith had obtained a Lieutenant's commission in the regiment of Mosel. The King had taken Keith's brother as a page in his place. This young man was as deficient in point of talents, as his brother was clever. The Prince Royal knowing this, had not entrusted him with his designs : but he thought that on account of his dullness he would be better calculated to facilitate his escape. He made him believe, that, having heard of some pretty girls in a neighbouring small town, he wanted to try his fortune there, and recommended him to awaken him for that purpose at four o'clock in the morning, and to have horses ready for him ; which was extremely easy, since there was to be a horse-fair in the place that very day. The page obeyed, but, instead of awakening the Prince, he called his valet. The latter, who had long been a spy of the King, suspected some mystery, and, to investigate the matter, he continued quiet, affecting to sleep. My brother, who was not perfectly easy on the point of so serious an undertaking, awoke a moment after. He rose, dressed himself, and, instead of his uniform, put on a coat in the French fashion, and left the barn. His valet, who had witnessed all this, immediately informed M. de Rochow. The latter, in his perplexity, ran to the generals in the King's retinue. Their names were Bodenbrok, Waldow, and Derschau, (the latter was of the imperial party, and a worthy friend of those who were at its head, after having conferred together, they went all over the village, in search of the Prince Royal. They found him at length in the horse-fair, leaning on a carriage. They were surprized to see him dressed in the French style, and very respectfully asked, " what he was doing there ? " The Prince answered very bluntly. He told me since, that he was in such a rage at being discovered, that, had he been armed, he should have driven those gentlemen back by main force. " For Heaven's sake, Prince," said Rochow to him, " change your dress : the King is awake and going to set off in hae an hour's time. What would be the consequence, were he to see you thus ? "—" I promise you," answered the Princlt " I shall be back before the King sets out ; I only wish of take a short walk." They were still disputing when Keiht came up with the horses. My brother seized one by the bridle, and was going to vault in the saddle : the gentlemen however prevented him ; they surmounted him, and obliged him *nolens volens* to return to his barn, where they forced him to dress himself in his uniform. He saw himself under the necessity of repressing his rage. General

Derschau and his valet acquainted the King that very day with what had happened. The King dissembled and concealed his resentment, having no sufficient proofs yet against my brother, and suspecting that he would not be satisfied with this first attempt.[1]

They all arrived in the evening at Frankfurt. The next morning the King received an express from Katte's cousin, who sent him the letters my brother had written to the Berlin Katte. These the King immediately communicated to General Waldow and Colonel Rochow, with orders to watch the conduct of his son, for whom he made them answerable with their heads, and to take him instantly to the yacht which had been prepared for the King, as he wished to go from Frankfurt to Wesel by water. These orders were executed without delay. All this took place on the 11th of August.

The King continued all the day at Frankfurt, and did not embark till the following morning. As soon as he saw my brother, he flew upon him, and would have strangled him, had not General Waldow came to his assistance. He dragged him by the hair, and threw him into such a pitiful plight, that these gentlemen being afraid of the consequences, intreated permission to take the Prince to another vessel ; which they at last obtained. His sword was taken from him, and from that instant he was treated as a state criminal. The King seized his effects and clothes ; my brother's valet secured his papers. He made amends for his former fault by throwing them into the fire in the presence of his master ; whereby he rendered us all a very great service. The King all this while was in such a rage, that he harboured the most fatal designs. My brother, on his part, appeared tolerably calm, hoping still to elude the vigilance of his guards.

[1] All this took place on the night of 4–5 August in the village of Steinfurth. Frederick's own description given to his interrogators is printed by Hinrichs (op. cit., 78–9). The only additional point he makes is that the King confiscated the horses which the younger Keith had obtained and had them incorporated into his own suite.

With these dispositions they reached Geldern. The King went before, and my brother followed him with his two guards. He intreated them so much, that they allowed him to enter Wesel at night. On coming to the floating bridge at the entrance of the town, he besought those gentlemen to permit him to walk in on foot, that he might not be known. They granted him this trifling favour, supposing it of no consequence : but as soon as he was out of the chaise, he made a second effort to escape, and began running with all his might. A strong guard commanded by Lieutenant-Colonel Borck, sent by the King to meet the Prince, overtook him, and conducted him to a house in the town close to the residence of the King ; who was carefully kept ignorant of this last attempt. The King himself examined the Prince the next day. There was no one with his majesty but General Mosel, an officer of fortune, whom his valour and merit had raised to that rank. The King's first question, and which he proposed in a furious tone, was this : " *Why have you attempted to desert ?* " (These were his very words.) " *Because,*" answered the Prince in a firm tone, " *you have not treated me as your son, but as a worthless slave.*"—" *Then you are,*" replied the King, " *nothing but a base deserter, without honour.*"—" *I have as much honour as you,*" said the Prince : " *I have only attempted what you told me a hundred times you would do, if you were in my place.*" Vexed at this last answer, the King, in a transport of rage, drew his sword, and was going to run him through. General Mosel perceived his intentions and placed himself between them, to parry the bow. " *Run me through, Sire,*" exclaimed he ; " *but spare your son.*"[1] These words arrested the King's fury. He ordered my brother to be reconducted to his house. The General remonstrated strongly with the King, and represented to him, " that he would always be master of the person of his son ; that he

---

[1] This story is unconfirmed in the sources, although General Mosel, who was commandant of the fortress at Wesel, was present at the interview, printed by Hinrichs (op. cit., 25–7).

ought not to condemn him without hearing him ; and finally, that he would committ an irremissible crime, if he became his executioner. He intreated his majesty at the same time to have him examined by honourable and loyal men, and not to see him any more, since he could not sufficiently master his passion to bear his presence." The King approved of these suggestions, and complied with them.

He remained but a few days at Wesel, and then prosecuted his journey to Berlin. Before he left Wesel he added General Derschau to the two other guards of my brother, and ordered them to follow him in four days, leaving them sealed instructions, in which the place was named whither they were to take him, and which they were not to open before they had got to the distance of some German miles from Wesel.

My brother was adored all over the country. The cruel treatment which he had experienced from the King, excused in some degree his attempts. Fears were entertained for his life from the well-known violence of the King. Several officers, who had at their head Colonel Gröbnitz, resolved to risk everything to set the Prince free. They had already procured him the dress of a peasant girl, and some ropes to let himself down from the window ; when General Derschau deranged these plans by getting iron bars fixed in the window. This General was a favourite of the King, to whom he reported every thing. Unfortunately, the favour- ites of the monarch were all men of wicked dispositions. This was a true imp of Satan, who injured the virtuous and oppressed the poor. The four days being elapsed, they set out with the Prince, and took him, according to the King's orders, to a small market-town, named Mittenwalde, three German miles from Berlin.

The reader is perhaps anxious to know what became of Keith. A page of the Prince of Anhalt, who had been present when the Prince Royal was arrested at Frankfurt, having reached Wesel four-and-twenty hours before the King, went to see Keith who had been his comrade, and very ingenuously told him my brother's misfortune. Keith fled the same evening, under pretence of going in pursuit of a deserter, and sheltered himself at the Hague in the house of Lord Chesterfield, the English Envoy. Colonel Dumoulin was sent after Keith, and used so much diligence that he arrived a quarter of an hour after him, and saw him at a window in the hotel of the British minister. Keith did not trust to the fine promises of Dumoulin, who had the mortification to see him the next day crossing the town in Lord Chesterfield's carriage, and going on board an English vessel to pass over to England.

I return to the interview between the King and the Queen. Her majesty was alone in the King's room when he arrived. The moment he saw her, though at a distance, he bawled out : " *Your worthless son is no more ; he is dead.*" —" *What !* " cried the Queen, " *have you the barbarity to kill him ? *"—" *Yes, I tell you,*" continued the King, " *but I want his writing-desk.*" The Queen went to fetch it ; I availed myself of that moment to see her : she was distracted with anguish, and continually crying : " *Heavens ! my son ! Just heavens ! my son !* " I fell breathless and fainting into the arms of Madam de Sonsfeld.

When the Queen delivered the desk to the King, he broke it into pieces, seized the letters, and took them with him. The Queen then returned to the room, where I was just recovering. She told us what had happened, and exhorted me to show some fortitude. Our hopes were a little revived by Mrs. Ramen, who assured the Queen that my brother was alive ; that she had her information from a good quarter. The King came back in the mean time. We all ran up to him to kiss his hands : but he scarcely cast his eyes upon me, when anger and fury overpowered him. He grew black, his eyes sparkled with rage, and he foamed at the mouth. " *Infamous baggage !* " said he to me, " *dare you show yourself before me ? Go and keep company with your rascally brother.*" In uttering these words, he seized me with one hand, and struck me several times in the face with his fist : one of his blows fell upon my temples so violently, that I fell backwards, and should have split my head against a corner of the wainscot, had not Madam de Sonsfeld broke my fall by seizing me by my head-dress. I remained senseless on the ground. The King, no longer master of himself, strove to renew the blows, and trample upon me ; but the Queen, my brothers and sisters, and all who were present, prevented him : they all surrounded me ; which gave Madam de Kamecke and Madam de Sonsfeld time to lift me up. They placed me in a window-seat which was close by ; but seeing that I continued senseless, they sent one of my sisters for a glass of water and some salts, with which they insensibly recalled me to life. As soon as I was able to speak, I reproached them for the pains which they took with me, death being a thousand times more agreeable than life in the situation in which we were. To describe its horror is impossible.

The Queen was uttering mournful screams : her fortitude had forsaken her ; she was wringing her hands in despair, and running disconsolate through the room. The face of the King was so greatly disfigured by his rage, that one could not look upon him but with terror. My brothers and sisters, the youngest of whom was four years old, were embracing his knees and endeavouring to move him by their tears. Madam de Sonsfeld was supporting my head, which was bruised and swollen by the blows I had received. Can a more affecting picture be conceived ?

The King, it is true, had changed his tone ; he confessed that my brother was still alive : but his horrible menaces of having him sentenced to death and myself confined between four walls for the remainder of my life, caused our dismay. He accused me of being the accomplice in the attempt of the Prince Royal, which he called high treason ; and of having had a love intrigue with Katte, by whom, he said, I had had several children. My governess, being unable to restrain herself on hearing such foul calumnies, had the courage to answer : " That is not true ; and whoever reported any thing like it to you has imposed upon your majesty." The King made her no reply, and recommenced his invectives. The fear of losing my brother wrought upon me, and I called out as loudly as my weakness would allow, that " I consented to marry the Duke of Weissenfels, if the King would grant life to my brother." The violent noise which the King was making prevented his hearing me. I was going to repeat the same declaration ; but Madam de Sonsfeld kept my mouth close with a handkerchief. I was struggling to remove the handkerchief, and turning my head round, when I beheld poor Katte crossing the palace-yard, attended by four horse-guards, who were conducting him to the King. Though pale and depressed, yet he took off his hat to bow to me. His and my brother's trunks, which had been seized and sealed, were carried after him. A moment after, the King was informed that Katte was brought. He left the room, exclaiming : " *Now I shall have a plea for condemning the rascally Frederick and the baggage Wilhelmina : I shall find motives sufficiently weighty to have them beheaded.*" Madam de Kamecke and Mrs. Ramen followed the King. The latter stopped him by the arm, saying, " If you wish to have the Prince Royal put to death, you ought at least to spare the Queen ; she is innocent of all this, you may believe me upon my word ; treat her gently, and she will do whatever you wish." Madam de Kamecke addressed him in a different manner : " You have hitherto," said she, " valued yourself on being a just, equitable monarch, and fearing God. The Lord has rewarded you for it, and loaded you with his blessings : but tremble to deviate from his holy commands, and dread the effects of Divine justice. It punished two sovereigns who shed, as you intend to do, the blood of their sons ; Philip II and Peter the Great died without male heirs ; their dominions have been a prey to foreign and intestine wars ; and those two monarchs, from having been the admiration of the world as great men, have become the execration of mankind. Recollect yourself, Sire ; the first impulse of your anger may still be pardoned, but it will be criminal if you do not endeavour to overcome it."

The King let her go on without interruption : he looked at her for a while, and when she had ceased speaking, he at length broke silence in these terms : " *You are very bold to address me in such language : however, I am not angry at it ; your intentions are good ; I admire your frankness, it increases my esteem for you : go and pacify the Queen.*"

This trait is so admirable on both sides, that to recount it is to bestow upon it the praises which it deserves. Indeed, the moderation of the King in the midst of his rage, and the courage of Madam de Kamecke to expose herself to his wrath, do them both infinite honour. We were all astonished at the imprudence of Mrs. Ramen, and her effrontery, to dare to speak of the Queen as she had done, before Madam de Kamecke.

When the King was gone, I was removed to an adjoining room, which he never entered. I trembled so much that I could not stand on my legs, and my agitation affected my nerves in such a manner, that I shall carry the sad remembrance of it about me all the days of my life. The King had sent for Grumbkow, the Judge-Advocate-General Mylius, and the Attorney-General Gerbert who filled this post ever since the death of Katsch, which had taken place a few years before. Katte immediately cast himself at the feet of the King, but the wrath of the monarch was rekindled at the sight of him : he kicked him, struck him with his cane, and gave him several blows in the face, which covered him with blood. Grumbkow intreated the King to moderate his passions, and to suffer Katte to be examined. He immediately confessed all he knew about the flight of my brother, and avowed himself his accomplice ; protesting, however, that they had never formed any design against the person of the King, or against the state ; that their plan had merely been to withdraw themselves from his anger, to go over to England, and to place themselves under the protection of that crown. When he was questioned concerning the Queen's letters and mine, he answered that he had sent them to her majesty, agreeably to the orders of the Prince Royal. He was also asked, whether I had been informed of their project? This he positively denied. Whether he had ever given me letters from my brother; and whether I had entrusted him with mine? He answered, that he recollected having given me a letter from my brother one Sunday when I was returning from the cathedral; that he was not acquainted with the contents; and that my letters had never passed through his hands. He confessed that he had several times been secretly at Potsdam to see the Prince, and that Lieutenant Spahn, of the King's regiment, had introduced him into the town disguised; that Keith was to accompany them in their flight; and that they had corresponded with him.

The examination being over, my brother's and Katte's effects were searched, but nothing of consequence was found. Grumbkow perused the Queen's letters and mine, and was disappointed at not finding what he was seeking. He angrily turned to the King, and said: " *Sire, these confounded women have duped us; I find nothing in these letters that can implicate them; and those which might give us some information most certainly are no longer in existence.*"

The King went back to the Queen.—" *I was not mistaken,*" said he to her majesty; " *your worthless daughter is implicated in the plot. Katte has confessed that he has given her letters from her brother. Inform her that I confine her as a prisoner to her room: I am going to give orders to double the guards. I shall have her severely examined, and send her to a place where she may do penance for her crimes. She may prepare to set out as soon as she has been examined.*" This was again spoken with rage and violence. The poor Queen protested of my innocence; she uttered a thousand imprecations against Katte for having asserted such an untruth, and ordered Madam de Kamecke to ask me how the matter stood. I was in a cruel embarrassment. It should be recollected, that I had not dared to show to the Queen the only letter which Katte had given me, because it contained invectives against Mrs. Ramen. I thought it was now all over with me, when I saw myself on the point of having the Queen also for mine enemy. Considering, however, that nearly twelve months had elapsed since, I determined to outface the matter. I therefore replied to Madam de Kamecke, " that the Queen had probably forgotten, that I had shown her that letter, which contained nothing mysterious ; that the manner in which Katte had given it me was tantamount to a justification, since he had delivered it to me publicly ; that I had indeed committed the letter to the flames, but that I had so distinct a recollection of it, that if the King commanded I could transcribe it word for word." My answer was immediately conveyed to the King, who retired a moment after to confer again with those who were still assembled in his room.

The Queen then came to me. Madam de Sonsfeld seconded me so well, that we persuaded her that she had been informed of the statement I had sent to the King. She transmitted me his orders under a flood of tears, strongly recommending an absolute silence concerning the writing-desk, and a resolute perseverance in denying the fact. We afterwards took an affectionate leave of each other ; she held me a long while encircled in her arms. I begged her to be calm ; assuring her, that I was perfectly resigned to the will of God and the King ; and that the greatest misfortune I dreaded was to be removed to a distance from her majesty. It required some violence to tear her from my arms, I was carried to my room in a sedan chair through a crowd of people, who had assembled in the palace-yard.

As the apartments of the Queen were on the ground-floor and the windows had been left open, the populace were spectators of the scene, and could distinctly hear and see every particular. As things of this kind are generally magnified, it was reported that I was dead, as well as my brother ; which caused much anxiety all over the town.

As soon as I had gained my room, the sentries at all the avenues were doubled, and the officer on duty went his round seven or eight times a day. Madam de Sonsfeld and Mrs. Meermann were the two faithful companions of my misfortune. I passed a wretched night ; the most dreadful thoughts rushed upon my imagination. My own fate did not create a moment's uneasiness ; my mind from infancy had been habituated to vexations and troubles, and I looked forward to death as the boundary of my sorrows. But the fate of so many individuals dear to me, gave me so much concern, that I suffered a thousand deaths for one, when I adverted to their respective situations. The next day I was unable to stir out of my bed ; I could not support myself on my legs, and tortured with a most violent head-ache, in consequence of the blows I had received.

Mrs. Ramen, with a sad and affected countenance, came to bring me word from the Queen, that I was to be examined on that day by the same personages who the day before had examined Katte. She exhorted me to be very careful of what I said, and particularly to remember the promise I had given her. This injunction was calculated to effect my ruin, since it gave Mrs. Ramen to understand that I was acquainted with circumstances of importance to the Queen. But I quickly replied : " give my dutiful respects to her majesty, and tell her, that it is the most acceptable intelligence I could have heard ; that I shall answer with sincerity to whatever I may be asked ; and that I shall so firmly establish my innocence, that no blame will attach to me."— " The Queen is however under great apprehensions concerning your examination, madam, her majesty is afraid your fortitude will forsake you."—" We need no fortitude, when we have nothing to reproach ourselves with."—" The King has dreadful deeds in contemplation," continued she, " he is determined, madam, to send you to a convent called the Holy Sepulchre ; where you are to be treated as a state-criminal, separated from your governess and domestics,

and under a discipline so severe, that I heartily pity you."—
" The King," I replied, " is my father and my sovereign ;
he may dispose of me as he pleases ; my confidence is in the
Almighty ; who will not forsake me."—" You affect so
much fortitude," rejoined she, " merely because you fancy
these to be idle menaces. But I have seen the sentence of
your banishment with my own eyes, signed with the King's
sign-manual ; and to convince you of the truth of what I
assert, poor Madam de Bülow has just been expelled from
court ; she and all her relations are banished to Lithuania ;
Lieutenant Spahn has been broken and sent to Spandau ; a
mistress of the Prince-Royal has been publicly whipped and
exiled ; Duhan, the tutor of your brother, is banished to
Memel ;[1] Jacques, the librarian of the Prince, has experienced the same fate, and Madam de Sonsfeld would be dealt
with worse than any of these, had she not been on bad
terms with the Queen last summer."

It ought to be observed, that the Queen had been vexed at
Madam de Sonsfeld, merely because she maintained that it
was wrong to attempt the dismission of Grumbkow before I
was married ; that my marriage ought to have been
realized first, and that the minister might have been removed afterwards.

I know not how I could endure the impertinent discourse
of Mrs. Ramen. However my countenance saved me, and
made the old wretch believe, that either I was innocent, or
that I should not be intimidated. At length she freed me
from her odious presence. When she was gone, I tore off
the mask of dissimulation : my heart sickened at the misfortunes of so many excellent individuals. I buried my
anguish in the bosom of Madam de Sonsfeld. Our separation, with which I had been threatened, drove me to despair.
I know not how I have been able to survive so much misery.
The day was passed in grief and tears. I expected those
who were to interrogate me ; the smallest noise heightened
my alarms. My expectation was vain, no one came.

[1] Memel is a region in the very far east of Prussia.

On the next day, the officious Mrs. Ramen repeated her visit. She again exhorted me to fortitude by order of the Queen ; and told me, that my examination had not taken place the day before, because the King had thought proper to send for the Prince-Royal to confront him with Katte and me ; that the Prince would be brought to town in the dusk of the evening, to prevent any tumult ; and that, on the following day, I was to be prepared to answer the accusations that would be preferred against me. I was not in the least disconcerted. " Give my dutiful respects to the Queen," I answered, " and tell her, that if I am examined, I shall not disguise any thing of what I know ; that I beseech her majesty to be quiet, since I am perfectly guiltless."

My answers, in the mean time, distressed the Queen ; she imagined that fear and sorrow had disordered my brain, and that I should, at the very first interrogation, disclose the secrets of which I was the depositary. To ascertain the matter, she in the afternoon dispatched to me her faithful valet Bock. I was charmed to see that domestic. I complained bitterly to him of the behaviour of the Queen, who wantonly exposed me to the greatest misfortunes by the messages she sent me by Mrs. Ramen. I told him to assure the Queen of my discretion, and to beg her majesty not to send to me so frequently, lest it might create suspicions ; and particularly not to entrust any one with any communication but himself, who alone was acquainted with the adventure of the writing-desk, concerning which I could not enter upon an explanation with Mrs. Ramen. I was obliged to have recourse to this subterfuge, that I might not offend the Queen, who would have been highly incensed against me, if she had perceived that I distrusted her favourite.

I passed the whole day at the window, in the hope of seeing my brother pass by. The mere idea of beholding this beloved brother, made me wish to have an interview with him. However I was disappointed.

The King altered his mind, and sent him on the 5th of

September to Küstrin, a fortress on the Warthe in the Neumark of Brandenburg.

The Prince-Royal had first been taken to Mittenwalde, a town in the neighbourhood of Berlin, where Grumbkow, Derschau, Mylius, and Gerbet, examined him for the first time.[1] My brother was very much frightened at Gerbet. Having seen him alight from his carriage wrapped up in a red cloak, he thought he was the executioner who was sent to put him to the rack. He was sitting on a trunk for want of a chair, and had been obliged to sleep all along on the floor. He went through his examination with great firmness : his answers corresponded with those of Katte. The contents of his writing-desk were produced to him, and he was asked whether the letters and articles it contained before were all in it yet ? My brother had the presence of mind to say that he missed none of the letters but that he saw several trinkets which he did not know.

This answer opened Grumbkow's eyes, and led him to suspect the trick which we had practised ; but there was no remedy. He rightly judged that neither menaces nor severities would make us confess the contents of the letters. He pressed my brother on several points, but obtained only haughty and harsh answers : which so exhausted his patience, that he threatened the Prince with the rack. My brother has since owned to me, that his blood was chilled at the declaration. But he dissembled his fright and replied, " that an executioner like Grumbkow could alone find pleasure in speaking of his trade ; and he did not fear his threats, having confessed every thing ; which he was however sorry to have done, because it did not behove him, the Prince to condescend to give any answer to a scoundrel like Grumbkow."

Having been removed next day to Küstrin, the Prince was deprived of his domestics and his effects ; nothing was

---

[1] A note from Frederick William to Grumbkow dated 28 August 1730 orders him, " Vous exami[nez] toute la jourre et nuit F.W."—Hinrichs, (op. cit., 65).

left him but what he had on his body. A bible and a few religious books were all he was suffered to read, and his daily allowance was fixed at four *groschen* or *6d.* sterling. The chamber in which he was confined received its light through a small grated window : he remained all the evening in the dark, and had no candle-light allowed but during his supper, which was brought to him at seven o'clock.[1] What a horrible situation for a young Prince, the idol and only hope of his country ! He was again examined a few days after. It ought to be remarked that on those examinations he was, always called *Colonel Frederick*, and I simply *Lady Wilhelmina.* Grumbkow was too shrewd not to discern that the imaginary crime of the Prince was, after all, the mere frolic of a young man, which, on considering the circumstances in which my brother had been placed, could scarcely be condemned ; he therefore persuaded the King to give the business another turn, and to treat the Prince as a deserter, according to martial law.

My brother was so exasperated at the indignity with which he was treated, that the commissaries could get nothing from him but insults and invectives. Enraged at their disappointment, they turned their fury upon Katte, whom they wished to put to the rack. Field-Marshal Wartensleben, his grandfather, who was intimate with Seckendorff, prevented it by his repeated intreaties to that minister.

My lot, in the mean time, continued unchanged. Every evening I used to take an affectionate leave of Madam de Sonsfeld and Mrs. Meermann, uncertain whether I should see them again the next day. I secretly sent my jewels and every thing valuable to the Queen ; and having thus taken every precaution, I awaited my fate with fortitude.

[1] The instructions to Major General von Lepel and to Colonel Reichman are given by Hinrichs, op. cit., 107. Frederick was to be held under lock and key the whole time. He was to be visited three times a day ; to receive a glass of water at eight o'clock, and meals at mid-day and at six. None of the visits were to last longer than four minutes, nor were questions of any sort to be answered.

At length the King left us. The Queen came to see me the very same evening : our interview was extremely affecting. She said, she though me safe against being examined or sent to a nunnery, the King not having mentioned any thing about it latterly. She also informed me, that Keith owed his safety to the Prince of Anhalt, who had sent him word of my brother's arrest though his page. Prince Anhalt had changed entirely for the better since his quarrel with Grumbkow ; he was no longer concerned in any intrigue, and endeavoured to oblige every one. I had had the good fortune to reconcile him with the Queen and the Prince Royal, to whom he was cordially devoted. As the King could not wreak his vengeance upon Keith, he had him hanged in effigy, and appointed his brother a sergeant in a marching regiment, to punish him for having brought horses to the Prince Royal. The Queen also acquainted me with a very interesting circumstance, as will be seen by the sequel. This was the marriage of my fourth sister with the hereditary Prince of Bayreuth, which the King had announced the day before. " Heaven be thanked ! " added the Queen, " I have nothing more to apprehend for you on that score : it is a good match for Sophia ; but it did not suit you." Shortly after, she told me with an air of satisfaction that this Prince of Bayreuth had died at Paris of a fever. " I am sorry for it," said I ; " it is indeed a pity : every one spoke uncommonly well of him, and my sister would have been happy with him."—" I am rather glad of his death," replied the Queen ; " I was always afraid there might be some underhand dealing ; it is one uneasiness less." The intelligence however was false ; he had been very ill : but he recovered from his fever.

On the 13th of September, the Queen set out for Wusterhausen. At parting, we both shed abundance of tears. We agreed to let our letters pass through the hands of Bock, the valet, to whose wife they were to be delivered at Berlin.

I began to be tolerably well reconciled to my confinement.

The life which I had hitherto led was not unpleasant. Now and then I had the visit of my sisters and of the ladies of the Queen's household : my time was so well regulated, that it never hung heavily upon me. I read ; I wrote ; I composed some music, and undertook some trifles in needlework to amuse myself : but all this served to divert me only for some moments ; my brother's situation, which was continually present to my mind, plunged me into a deep melancholy. My health also was very indifferent ; I had retained such a weakness in my nerves, that I could scarcely walk, and I trembled so that I could not lift up my arms.

One afternoon I was sitting in a pensive mood, when my good Mrs. Meermann broke in upon me unexpectedly. She was pale as death, and I perceived in her countenance all the symptoms of terror : " Heaven ! " said I ; " what ails you ? Is my sentence pronounced ? "—" No, madam ; but my doom perhaps will soon be signed. I am in a dreadful embarrassment. A sergeant of the Horse-Guards came this morning early to my husband to give him, by M. de Katte's command, a parcel of great consequence, he said, for your Royal Highness. My husband, who is already suspected as having been acquainted with Katte, would not accept of it, and requested the sergeant to come again to-night. Your Royal Highness is to determine what my husband is to do. You know my attachment for you : I am resolved to run any risks to convince you of it." I was very fond of my nurse who was most certainly an excellent woman ; the risk which she was incurring kept me for some time in suspense. Madam de Sonsfeld, who was present, asked whether she knew what the parcel contained.—" The sergeant," answered Mrs. Meermann, " told my husband that it was a portrait."—" Oh ! Heavens ! " exclaimed my governess, " it is the portrait of your Royal Highness, which I gave to the Prince Royal, and which he left with Katte, as he told me. You are undone, madam, if it fall into the hands of the King : he already accuses Katte of having been your lover ; should he find this portrait, he will punish you without any farther examination, and treat you cruelly.—We must absolutely get it back," continued she, addressing Mrs. Meermann ; " you hazard no more by accepting than by refusing it : the former is therefore the most eligible, since, by doing so, you have nothing to apprehend but the indiscretion of the sergeant ; whilst in the second case, your misfortune is certain : for if the Princess be ruined, we shall be ruined with her ; and her innocence and ours will be of no avail."—Mrs. Meermann hesitated no longer, and returned me my portrait in the evening. The matter remained secret, the sergeant luckily proving an honest man.

A few days after, my poor nurse had a fresh uneasiness as great as this. An unknown person had given her a letter. But what were her alarms, when, on tearing the cover, she found it contained another letter from my brother to me ! She immediately brought it to me ; it was written with a black-lead pencil. I have carefully preserved it till this moment ; it runs thus :—

"My dear Sister ;

" I am going to be declared a heretic by the court-martial which is assembling ; for not to conform in every respect to the sentiments of the master is enough to incur the guilt of heresy. You therefore may easily judge how prettily I shall be dealt with. I little care for the excommunication which will be thundered at me, provided I know that my amiable sister protests against it as unmerited. How sweet it is, that neither bars nor bolts can prevent my assuring you of my undiminished friendship ! Yes, my dear sister, in this almost entirely perverted age, there are still some honest people who procure me the means of expressing my affection for you. Yes, my dear sister, provided I know you are happy, my prison will be to me the abode of felicity and pleasure. *Chi ha tempo ha vita !* Let that comfort us. I heartily wish I may no longer need any interpreter to converse with you, and that we may see those happy days when your *principe* and my *principessa*[1] will sweetly harmonize ; or, to speak more plainly, when I shall have the pleasure to address you in person, and to assure you that nothing in the world can diminish my friendship for you. Adieu.

" THE PRISONER."

This letter pierced me to the heart : my tears bereft me for a while of the power of speech. I could not account for the sportive turn of my brother's epistles. If its style dispelled my gloom for a few moments, it was merely to plunge me again into still greater anxieties. The court-martial to which he alluded, and of which I had heard nothing, threw me into a terrible agitation. In vain I intreated Madam de Sonsfeld to allow me to answer the letter : she remained inflexible, and it was with great difficulty that she made me sensible of the justice of her denial. My situation changed a few days after.

On Sunday the 5th of November, 1730, I was quietly in my bed, when I was informed that Eversmann had a message for me from the King. I ordered him to be introduced, and concealed my confusion as well as I could. " I come from Wusterhausen," said Eversmann ; " I am commanded by his majesty to tell you, that hitherto he has treated you with lenity and indulgence. He would not have you examined, lest you might be found guilty ; particularly since the Prince Royal and Katte have confessed that you were their accomplice ; " (this was absolutely false :) " but he requires of you, in return, that you shall decide which of the two princes he has so often proposed to you you will chuse. Beware, madam, of the answer you give me ; the life of the Prince Royal, and perhaps your own, are depending upon it. The King is terribly exasperated against the

[1] My brother had given this name to his flute ; observing that he never should be truly in love with any princess but this. He frequently indulged in pretty witticisms about it, which used to make us laugh ; and it was by way of reply that I called my lute *my prince*, saying that it was his rival. (Author's note.)

Prince, and talks of having him beheaded. I dare not tell you the fatal projects he harbours in his mind against you both. I shudder when I think of them ; and you alone can avert them. Consider well. This message is only a preamble. The King will send you other persons, who will bring you to your senses, if you do not give me a favourable reply."

I sat upon thorns during the whole of this discourse, and I should have been uncertain what answer to return, had not the end of his address suggested a proper one. "The King," I replied, "is master ; he may dispose of my life, but he cannot render me guilty when I am innocent. I ardently wish to be examined : my innocence would then shine in all its splendour. With regard to the two proposed princes, they are both so hateful to me that it would be difficult to chuse betwext them : however, I shall submit to his majesty's commands whenever he agrees with the Queen." He set up a very insolent laugh. " *The Queen !* " exclaimed he, " the King has peremptorily declared that he will not suffer her to interfere in any thing."—" Yet he cannot prevent her continuing my mother, nor deprive her of the authority which that character gives her over me. How wretched is my fate ! What occasion is there to marry me ; and why do my parents not agree concerning the person whom I am to marry ? My lot is most miserable ; alternately threatened with the curses of my father and mother, I do not know what to resolve, as I cannot obey one without disobeying the other."—" Well, then ! " continued Eversmann, " prepare for death ; I must no longer conceal any thing from you. There is to be a second trial of the Prince Royal and Katte, in which you will be still more implicated ; the King's wrath demands a victim ; Katte alone will not suffice to extinguish his rage, and he will be glad to save your brother at your expence."—" You delight me ! " I exclaimed ; " I am weaned from the world ; the adversities which I have experienced have taught me the vanity of all terrestrial things : I shall receive death with joy, and without fear, since it will conduct me to a happy tranquillity of which I cannot be deprived."—" But what would then become of the Prince Royal ? " replied Eversmann.—" If I can save his life, my felicity will be complete ; and if he die, I shall not feel the misery of surviving him."—" You are inflexible, madam ; but those whom the King will send to you after me, will teach you submission. I am moreover expressly commanded by the King to forbid your communicating any part of what I have told you to the Queen." Thus ended this distressing conversation.

I remained a prey to the most piercing anguish, being impressed with the idea that I might injure my brother's cause by my obstinacy. I have been induced to believe that the court-martial had condemned him to one year's imprisonment, and that Katte had been confined in a fortress for the remainder of his life. However, I grew somewhat more easy when I considered that I was still mistress of his fate, and at liberty to return what answer I thought proper to those who were sent to me by the King ; though I did not wish to reply any thing positive to a wretch like Eversmann.

I immediately related all these circumstances to Madam de Sonsfeld. We both agreed that it was proper to acquaint the Queen with them. Convinced that I should be watched, I did not dare to risk giving my letter to Mrs. Bock, lest it might be intercepted ; I therefore had recourse to Madam de Kamecke's daughter, whom the Queen had taken again instead of Madam de Bülow. This young lady possessed uncommon merit and solidity united to an excellent understanding.

Owing to some neglect, no sentry had been placed in a small passage which formed the communication between my sisters' apartment and mine ; this had procured me the pleasure of seeing them. Madam de Kamecke came secretly to me by that passage. The difficulties which she started did not deter me. I bethought myself of cramming my letter into a cheese, which I then cut in two and joined together again as well as I could. " Send this cheese to your mother," said I, " inform her that it comes from Madam de Roucoule. No one will think of looking for a letter in a cheese." This expedient removed her fears ; she followed my plan, which proved successful. I had besought the Queen to keep the information I communicated to her majesty strictly secret, and to acquaint me with her commands in the same way. But she did not attend to my request.

Madam de Roucoule brought me the answer of the Queen the next morning. This lady was seventy years old, of great probity and merit, but her age was not calculated to inspire confidence. As she suspected some mystery, she wished to be present at the opening of the letter. I was therefore, though reluctantly, obliged to read it before her ; it contained only these few words :

" You are a faint-hearted creature, frightened at any thing. Remember that I give you my malediction if you consent to what is demanded of you. Affect to be ill, in order to gain time."

The reading of this note stunned my brain, and the last sentence, in particular, puzzled me very much. The advice was good, but it required discretion ; and I was certain that, on that point, we should be deficient.

When I found myself alone with Madam de Sonsfeld, we conferred about what was to be done. We thought it necessary to deceive Madam de Roucoule, and to impose upon her respecting my pretended illness. Madam de Sonsfeld advised me to delay the performance of the farce till the next day, for motives, she said, which she might not then explain.

Eversmann came to see her that very evening. " The King," said he, " sends me to signify to you his commands to use your best efforts to induce the Princess to marry the Duke of Weissenfels. Her obstinacy has exhausted the

King's patience. He informs you that quarters are prepared for you at Spandau, whither he is determined to send you, if the Princess does not submit to his will."—" I shall leave the court," replied Madam de Sonsfeld, " as soon as his majesty thinks proper. The King cannot have forgotten the reluctance with which I accepted the office of governess to the Princess. I objected my want of capacity for the situation ; he forced it upon me in spite of my remonstrances. I have instilled the principles of a christian into the mind of the Princess ; I love and esteem her more than life ; still I am ready to resign, if the King thinks me no longer capable of performing my office. I cannot meddle with things beyond my sphere. The Princess is old enough to know what she has to do. I wish her determination may be agreeable to the King and Queen. As for myself, I shall remain neutral, and shall not presume to advise her for or against."—" You are not, perhaps acquainted," answered Eversmann, " with the dreadful tragedy that has taken place this morning. The blood of M. de Katte has not appeased the resentment of the King : he is more exasperated than ever ; and I fear your conduct will induce him to proceed with you to fatal extremes." Thereupon he told her of the deplorable end of Katte, which I shall relate in another place, as I do not wish to break the thread of my narrative. Madam de Sonsfeld was struck with horror ; she was ignorant of this sad catastrophe, the particulars of which made her shudder : her fortitude, however, did not forsake her. " For heaven's sake, spare the Princess ! " she exclaimed : " do not mention this barbarous execution to her : her heart is kind and merciful ; the situation of the Prince Royal and the misfortunes of Katte would infallibly cause her a violent emotion, which would effectually impair her already disordered health. As for myself, I await with calmness and resignation whatever it shall please Providence to order respecting me." Being unable to obtain any other answer, Eversmann retired, rather dissatisfied.

I was a prey to the most heart-rending anguish during their conversation. Madam de Sonsfeld reported it to me, word for word, except what related to Katte. She was extremely depressed, and could not hide her tears. I mistook their source thinking they were occasioned by Eversmann's menaces.

I prepared to act the scene which we had agreed upon. I entrusted Mrs. Meermann with my secret ; I could depend upon her discretion and fidelity. I dined *tête-à-tête* with my governess in a small parlour, the door of which opened into a passage. Our ordinary was so scanty, that we were starving for the greatest part of the time. We had nothing but bare bones boiled in water with a little salt, and small beer instead of wine, which obliged us to drink pure water. When we were sitting at table, we complained that the room was too hot, and opened the door that looked into the passage, where several people were always going and coming. I gently slided from my chair, faintly screaming, " *I am dying !* " Madam de Sonsfeld immediately ran to my assistance, crying for help ; the people in the passage, seeing me in this condition, thought me dead, and spread the rumour of my decease all over the palace. The lamentations of Madam de Sonsfeld and of Mrs. Meermann confirmed them in this idea. My sisters and the ladies of the Queen's household hastened to my room. I acted my part so well for an hour, that Dr. Stahl was at length sent for. I recovered my senses before he arrived. A thousand times did I regret inwardly the necessity under which I was of performing a part so contrary to my disposition. I had been laid upon my bed ; I begged they would all retire, and leave me to take a little repose. By this means I gave Madam de Sonsfeld time to hint the truth to the physician, who was perfectly devoted to the Queen. He declared that I was extremely ill ; and thus the day passed.

The next day I had again to endure the torment of a visit from the odious Eversmann. As I had expected that he would come to examine whether my illness was true or counterfeited, I had taken my precautions beforehand, and got some turpentine cakes heated, which were concealed in my bed, and which I could make use of in case of any suspicious visitor coming. I held them in my hands, which grew burning hot, and made every one believe that I had a severe fever and a raking heat. Eversmann had been dispatched from Wusterhausen, where they had heard of the accident that had befallen me the day before. " Are you very ill ? " said Eversmann : " give me your hand, that I may feel whether you have any fever."—I held it out to him immediately. Being surprised at finding me so bad, he asked Madam de Sonsfeld " whether she had not sent for Stahl ? " —" I have ventured to do so," answered she, " for the Princess was in such a state yesterday, that there was no time to be lost : but I durst not send for him to-day again : I have, however, asked her majesty's permission."—Eversmann took Madam de Sonsfeld aside, and went out with her. " I had ordered you and the Princess," said he, " in the name of the King, not to inform the Queen of his majesty's messages to you both. However, you have had the effrontery to disobey ; the Queen is acquainted with every thing. She has treated me like the vilest of wretches ; but you may both thank my goodness, which will not suffer me to be revenged. If I should tell the King any thing of this, he would handle you both very roughly. I only hint this to you, that you may not again fall into the same error." With these words he withdrew, and saved Madam de Sonsfeld the trouble of an answer. She hastened back to my room in great consternation, to acquaint me with this fresh imprudence of the Queen : it absolutely stupified me. We doubted not but her majesty would also mention it to the King ; which would have spoiled all, and have exposed us to the greatest misfortunes.

Every day was marked by some new calamity. Nothing was heard of but imprisonments, confiscations, and executions ; which made me apprehensive that the King's menaces might at last be realized, particularly if he could find us in fault. My own fate (I repeat it) was that which gave me the least uneasiness : but that of the persons I loved absorbed all my attention. I reflected all night on my situation. Good heavens ! how dreadful it was ! I saw myself destitute of all support ; as I could not rely on the Queen, who had no power, and embroiled every thing by her imprudences and her indiscretion. My brother was continually uppermost in my mind. I suspected I was not informed of the truth respecting him : my intercession for him proved useless, and I was always told that he was confined for a twelvemonth. As I knew nothing of Katte's execution, I was afraid the proceedings might be renewed, and their termination prove fatal. My dear governess increased my alarms. I loved her sincerely, and I would rather have suffered death than have exposed her, through my obstinacy, to add to the number of illustrious victims ; I therefore firmly resolved to sacrifice myself for others, and to marry the Duke of Weissenfels, on condition, however, that the King should grant a free pardon to my brother. I delayed acquainting his majesty with my intentions until he should send me the deputation of which Eversmann had spoken. I took good care to keep my project secret from Madam de Sonsfeld, by whom it would most certainly have been opposed.

Six or seven days elapsed in the same anxieties before Eversmann renewed his visits. I affected extreme debility, which still kept me confined to my bed. He came to tell me, that the King was informed that I saw my sisters and the ladies of the Queen's household ; that his majesty was very angry, and ordered me, on pain of death, not to leave my room, nor to put my head out of the window.

Indeed, such strict orders were given, that I became a prisoner to all intents and purposes. No one was admitted into my room without an express command of the King. I resigned myself in this respect, and thought Eversmann the author of the change, in spite of his assumed generosity.

What incommoded me most was my pretended malady, which put me under the necessity of keeping my bed. I could only read by fits and starts, because the wretch came every moment to dun my ears with his Duke of Weissenfels and his threats.

The Queen came back to Berlin on the 22d in the morning. After having feigned to be ill, this constraint, combined with my troubles, actually brought on a severe illness. My sister Charlotte had obtained permission to see me. She immediately hastened to my room. I loved her much. She was very witty and lively, and of a mild disposition. But she has since ill requited me for the friendship I felt for her. She had scarcely entered the apartment when she exclaimed : " have you not very much bewailed my poor brother, and regretted Katte ? "—" Why ? " answered I, terrified.—" How ! do not you know it ? " continued she, relating the lamentable tragedy in a very confused manner. I was so shocked, that I fainted away.— But it is time to relate this mournful event.

The court-martial which was to decide the fate of the two criminals, assembled at Potsdam on the first of November. It was composed of two Generals, two Colonels, two Lieutenant-Colonels, two Majors, two Captains, and two Lieutenants. As every officer of the army wished to be excused, they were chosen by lot. The two Generals drawn, were Döhnhoff and Linger ; the two Colonels Derschau and Pannewitz. I have forgot the names of the Lieutenant-Colonels : but I remember Lieutenant von Schenck of the Gens-d'armes (horse-guards), Lieutenant von Wehyer, and Major von Einseidel of the King's regiment, being of the court. Each member gave his vote by a text of Holy Writ. I recollect that of Döhnhoff, who alluded to the grief of David, when he was informed of Absalom's death and exclaimed : *" O my son, Absalom ! my son ! my son Absalom ! "* &c. He and Linger voted for pardon : but the others, to flatter the King, condemned my brother and Katte to be beheaded : an unheard of sentence in a Christian and civilized country !¹ The King would have suffered the sentence to be executed, had not all foreign powers interceded for the Prince, and particularly the Emperor and the States-General. Seckendorff exerted himself very much. As he had caused the mischief, he wished to repair it. He told the King : " that though the Prince Royal was his son, he belonged to the Empire, and that his majesty had no right over him." It was with very great difficulty he obtained his pardon. His continual solicitations however gradually weakened the sanguinary intentions of the King. Grumbkow, who became aware of this change, sought to take to himself the merit of it with my brother. He went to Küstrin, and prevailed with the Prince to write and make his submissions to the King.

Seckendorff also attempted to save Katte : but the King remained inflexible. Sentence was passed upon the unfortunate young man on the 2d of the same month. He heard it read without changing countenance. " *I submit,*" said he, " *to the orders of the King and Providence ; I shall suffer for a noble cause, and I shall face death without fear, having nothing to reproach myself with.*" When he was alone, he called M. de Hartenfeld, who commanded the guard of his prison, and was one of his most intimate friends, and gave him the box which contained the portraits of my brother and myself. " Keep it," said he, " and remember sometimes the unfortunate Katte : but show it to no one ; it might yet harm, after my death, the illustrious

¹ The court martial, which in fact consisted of sixteen officers, took place on 31 October. Wilhelmina remembered some, but not all, of the names of those who took part. The various ranks gave judgement separately, and it is interesting to see that while all voted to pardon the Crown Prince, as well as to hang Keith in effigy, only the lower-ranking officers voted for the execution of Katte. Von Schulenberg, the president of the court, and the three major-generals voted for life imprisonment, and it was this advice which was finally submitted to the King. The King wrote back to the court martial ordering that the death sentence on Katte be confirmed. This the court refused to do, and in the end it was completely overruled by the King.—Hinrichs (op. cit., 116ff).

persons I have painted." He afterwards wrote three letters, to his grandfather, to his father, and to his brother-in-law. I have obtained copies of them and translated them literally from the German.

" Honoured Grandfather ;

" I cannot express the grief and agitation with which I am writing this. I who have been the principal object of your solicitude ; whom you destined to be the support of your family ; whom you had educated in sentiments calculated to render me useful to my sovereign and my fellow-creatures ; I who never left your house without being honoured with your kindness and your advice ; I who was to be the comfort and happiness of your old age ; wretch that I am ! I am now become the object of your grief and despair. Instead of felicitating you with gladsome tidings, I am constrained to acquaint you with the sentence of my death, which has already been pronounced. Do not take my sad fate too much to heart : we must submit to the decrees of Providence ; if it tries us by adversities, it also gives us strength to bear them with firmness, and to overcome them. Nothing is impossible to the Lord. He may help us when he chuses. I place all my confidence in that Supreme Being, who may yet incline the King's heart to clemency, and obtain for me as many favours as I have experienced severities. If it be not the will of the Omnipotent, I shall nevertheless praise and bless him, being persuaded that what he orders is for my welfare. I therefore submit my patience to what your credit and that of your friends may obtain of his majesty.[1] In the mean time, I

---

[1] This Field-Marshal von Wartensleben did, and received a very polite reply from the King, dated 3 November : " In this instance I regret that I am not in a position to grant a pardon, for at stake is the well-being of the whole country, myself, as well as my family." (Hinrichs, op. cit., 142). The king in his letter also spoke of the future, and understandably could not contemplate the idea that he might be survived by Katte, who would then be honoured by Frederick (as was to be the case with Keith).

ask you a thousand pardons for my past faults, hoping that the benevolent Creator, who forgives the greatest sinners, will have mercy upon me. I intreat you to follow his example towards me, and to believe me, &c.

" *November the 2d, 1730.*"

The following lines were found written on the window of his prison :—

" With time and patience we obtain a good conscience.— If you would know who has written this, the name of Katte will inform you : still cheared up by hope."

Beneath this was written :—

" He whom curiosity may induce to read this writing, must know that the writer was put ander arrest, by order of his majesty, on the 16th of August, 1730. He still has faint hopes of recovering his liberty, although the manner in which he is guarded seems to prognosticate something fatal.'

A clergyman having been sent to him the next day to prepare him for death, Katte said : " I am a very great sinner ; too much ambition has betrayed me into many faults, of which I sincerely repent. I relied on my good fortune ; the favour of the Prince Royal has blinded me so, as to make me forget myself. At present, I find that all is vanity. I feel a lively repentance of my sins, and I wish for death as the only road which can lead me to a lasting and eternal happiness." He passed that day and the following in similar conversations.

The evening after this, Lieutenant Schenck came to inform him that his execution was to take place at Küstrin, and that the coach, which was to convey him thither, was waiting for him. He appeared somewhat surprized at this intelligence : but soon resuming his tranquillity, he with a smiling countenance followed M. de Schenck, who got into the coach with him, besides two other officers of the Horse-guards. A large detachment of the same regiment escorted them to Küstrin. M. de Schenck, who was much affected, told him that he deeply lamented being entrusted with so mournful a commission. " I am commanded by his majesty," continued he, " to be present at your execution : I twice refused that fatal office. I must obey ; but Heaven knows what I suffer. Heaven grant that the King's mind be altered, and that I may have the satisfaction of proclaiming your pardon ! "—" You are very good," replied Katte ; " but I am resigned to my fate. I die for a Prince whom I love, and I have the consolation to give him, by my death, the strongest proof of attachment that can be required. I do not regret the world. I am going to enjoy a felicity without end." On the road he bade farewell to the two officers who were with him, and to the men who composed his escort. He arrived at Küstrin at nine o'clock in the morning, and was taken directly to the scaffold.

The day before, General Lepel, governor of the fortress, and the president Münchow, had conducted my brother to an apartment that had been purposely prepared for him on the floor above that where he had lodged. He there found a bed and some furniture. The window-curtains were let down, which at first prevented his seeing what was going on without. A plain brown coat was brought to him, in which he was obliged to dress himself. I forgot to state that a similar coat had been given to Katte. The General, having then drawn up the curtains, pointed out to the Prince a scaffold covered with black, and as high as the window, which had been widened and the bars of which had been removed. After this, both the General and Münchow retired. This sight and the downcast look of Münchow induced my brother to think that sentence of death was going to be passed upon him, and that these preparations regarded himself, which caused him a violent agitation.

General Lepel and President Münchow entered the Prince's room in the morning a little before Katte appeared, and endeavoured to prepare the Prince in the best manner they could for this horrible scene. It is said that he was in such a state of despair and grief as had never before been witnessed. In the mean time Schenck was rendering the like friendly office to Katte. On entering the fortress he said to him : " continue firm, my dear Katte ; you are going to undergo a severe trial ; you are at Küstrin, and you will see the Prince-Royal." " Rather say", answered Katte, " that I am going to have the greatest consolation that could have been granted to me." With these words he ascended the scaffold. My unfortunate brother was then forced to stand at the window. He attempted to throw himself out of it ; but was prevented. " *I intreat you, for heaven's sake*," said the Prince to those who were around him, " *delay the execution ; I shall inform the King that I am ready to renounce my right to the crown, if his majesty will pardon Katte.*" M. de Münchow stopped the Prince's mouth with a handkerchief. When the Prince saw Katte, he exclaimed : " *how wretched I am, my dear Katte ! I am the cause of your death. Would to heaven I were in your place !* "—" *Ah !* " replied Katte, " *if I had a thousand lives, I would sacrifice them all for your Royal Highness.*" At the same time he dropped on his knees. One of his servants attempted to blindfold him, but he would not suffer it, and elevating his thoughts to heaven, he ejaculated " *my God ! I commit my soul into thy hands !* " Scarcely had he pronounced these words, when his head, cut off at one blow, rolled at his feet. The trunk, in its fall, extended its arms towards the window where my brother had been : but he was there no longer : he had fainted away, and the gentlemen about him had laid him on his bed, where he remained senseless for some hours. When he recovered his senses, the first object that struck his eyes was the mangled corpse of poor Katte, which had been placed in such a manner that he could not avoid seeing it. This ghastly object threw him into a second swoon, which was succeeded by a violent fever. M. de Münchow, in spite of the orders of the King, let the curtains down and sent for physicians, who found the Prince in a very dangerous state. He

would not take any thing that was given him.   His mind
was so bewildered and his agitation so great, that he would
have destroyed himself, had he not been prevented.   Religious considerations, it was thought, would soften him ;   a
clergyman was sent for to comfort him :   but all in vain ;
the violent convulsions ceased only when his strength was
exhausted.   Tears succeeded to these dreadful agitations.
It was with extreme difficulty that he was prevailed upon to
take medicine.   Nothing could induce him to do it, but the
representation that he would also cause the Queen's death
and mine, if he persisted in his own destruction.   A profound melancholy fastened upon him for a long time, and
for three successive days his life was in imminent danger.
The body of Katte remained exposed on the scaffold until
sun-set.   It was buried in one of the bastions of the fortress.
The next day the executioner went to demand the payment
for his execution from Field-Marshal Wartensleben,[1]
which had nearly cost him his life, so greatly did it affect
him.[2]

[1] It will doubtless be recollected that Katte was a relation of the
Field-Marshal. (Author's note.)

[2] The famous story of how Frederick was made to witness the death
of Katte is fully confirmed in the various documents printed by Hinrichs
(op. cit., 146ff).   In a letter written by the Governor of Küstrin to
Frederick William, who himself had wanted to know merely about the
cost of the execution, he wrote that the Prince " . . . slept little during
the night, having eaten almost nothing the day before.   He told his
manservant of his nightmares, of how Katte was continually before his
eyes.   He is often in tears and can be heard to sigh when anyone ventures
near his room.   He spoke out against the priest and curses everyone in
sight.   He believes that his own death is being prepared for within the
next week or fortnight."   Frederick William responded by ordering a
servant to sleep in the same room as the Prince ;   also that a priest
should remain at Küstrin.

VII

THREE or four days after, Grumbkow, as I have already observed, obtained leave from the King to go to Küstrin. He entered my brother's room with a submissive and respectful countenance. " I come," said he, " to intreat your Royal-Highness's pardon for the little attention I have hitherto paid to your Royal Highness : I have been forced to obey the King's commands ; I have even punctually executed them, to be the better enabled to render you service. The pain which has been given you by the death of Katte, has caused the most heartfelt sorrow both to Seckendorff and myself. We used all our efforts to save him, but in vain. We are going to exert ourselves still more seriously to obtain your reconciliation with the King : but your Royal Highness must lend us a helping hand, and give me a letter full of submission to the King ; I will present it to his majesty and second it with all my power." My brother could scarcely be induced to take this step ; he complied however in the end.

Grumbkow drew so affecting a picture of the sad condition of the Prince, that he moved the heart of the King, who granted his pardon. The Prince left the fortress on the 12th of November ; but was kept a prisoner at large in the town. The King gave him the title of a counsellor at war, with orders regularly to assist at the deliberations of the board of finances and demesnes established at Küstrin. His place was that of the junior member of the board. The King appointed also three members of the superior court of justice to attend on the Prince. These were MM. de Wolden, de Rohwedel, and de Natzmer.[1] The latter was a son of the Field-Marshal of that name. He had a perfect knowledge of the usages of the world, having been a great traveller : but he was a mere shallow fop. I cannot refrain from relating here a trait of his inconsiderate levity.

Being one day at Vienna in the antichamber of the Emperor he saw the Duke of Lorraine, afterwards Emperor,[2] gaping in a corner of the room. Not considering the impertinence of what he was doing, he ran to thrust his finger into the Duke's mouth. The latter was a little surprised at the action : but as he knew the disposition of Charles VI to be extremely severe on the point of etiquette, he made no noise about it, and contented himself with observing that probably Natzmer had made a mistake.

The two others were men of honour, but rather dull. My brother's allowance was extremely scanty : he was not permitted to enjoy any recreation, nor suffered to read, and, above all, ordered not to converse or write in French.[3]

[1] " Instruction for Privy Councillor Wolden and Kammerjunkers Natzmer and Rohwedel on attending the Crown Prince at Küstrin, set down by His Majesty, Wusterhausen, 14 November 1730. . . .   No other language is to be spoken to the Prince but German, and especially no French. The only subjects which may be discussed with him are the Word of God, Economics, Agriculture, Industry, Police Matters, Land-usage, Leaseholdings . . . : (13) The Prince is not to be allowed to purchase, borrow or for that matter read any book other than the Bible. (14) Furthermore the Prince is not permitted to hear any music of any sort, or to play any himself. For this his three companions are answerable with their lives. Neither are they allowed to have any musical instruments or books . . . "—Hinrichs (op. cit, 169ff).

[2] Emperor Franz (1708–65), the consort of Maria Theresa, whom he married in 1736.

[3] This order, for one, was not carried out. Grumbkow certainly spoke to the Prince in French, and after his first visit to the fortress at Küstrin in November (he was in factr eleased on the nineteenth), the two began an extensive and surprisingly friendly correspondence, which lasted until Grumbkow's death in 1739. Natzmer and Frederick also corresponded, and probably also conversed, in French.

The nobility of the neighbourhood took care to provide him with a plentiful table, and the French Protestant refugees of Berlin sent him linen and refreshments.[1] Nothing for a long time could dispel his melancholy ; he would not leave off the brown coat, which had been given him in the fortress, before it was worn to rags, because it was like that of Katte. But in spite of the rigorous commands of the King, the Prince passed his time rather aggreeably, and the persons about him affected to take no notice of what he was doing.

My brother's release from confinement moderated my grief a little, and gave me sincere pleasure. My joy was yet heightened by the arrival of the Queen. She gave me an account of all the troubles she had undergone at Wusterhausen, and the painful anxieties she had felt for my brother. I alternately wept and smiled at the different situations in which he had been placed. The Queen continued her visits as long as the King was absent. She alarmed me very much about the future. " Next month I shall go to Potsdam," said she. " I am informed that you will have to undergo some dreadful trials : you are to be deprived of Madam de Sonsfeld, who will leave you very reluctantly ; and in her place you will be surrounded by suspicious persons : perhaps, you will even be sent to a fortress. Be prepared for it beforehand, and arm yourself with fortitude. Persist in refusing to be married, and leave me to manage the rest. If you follow my counsels, I still hope to establish you in England." To quiet her majesty, I promised any thing : but I was resolved to obey my father.

---

[1] Only weeks after Louis XIV had issued his famous revocation of the Edict of Nantes in 1685 the Great Elector issued his own Edict of Potsdam, encouraging the French Protestants to come to Prussia, which they did in their thousands. Their importance in building up the economy of Brandenburg-Prussia is acknowledged to have been crucial, and historians have seen their arrival in Berlin as marking the true beginning of the growth of the town—4,000 added to a town with an estimated population of 11,000. Both Frederick William and Frederick the Great continued their protection of the refugees, and encouraged their naturalization.

The latter interrupted our interviews. He came to spend his Christmas at Berlin where he stayed a fortnight. Thus ended that mournful year, so remarkable for fatal events.

The year 1731, upon which I am going to enter, proved equally afflicting to me ; it was however in the course of this year, that the foundation was laid for the happiness of my life.

The King retired to Potsdam on the 11th of January, whither the Queen followed him on the 28th. During her short residence at Berlin, M. de Sastot, her chamberlain and a near relation of Grumbkow, attempted to reconcile this minister with her majesty. Grumbkow, who surpassed him in cunning, and was resolved to make him his dupe, availed himself of this opportunity to attain his ends. He commissioned him to make all possible advances to the Queen in his name, and to assure her, that if she would con- fide in him, he would yet engage to effect my marriage with the Prince of Wales. The Queen, who loved to flatter her- self, fell headlong into the snare, and in two days they were the best friends. She acquainted me with the circumstance. Grumbkow was now the most honest man in the world ; the blame of the past was entirely thrown upon Seckendorff and upon the rash conduct of Sir Charles Hotham. I was highly surprised at this intelligence, which alarmed me very much, because I foresaw its consequences. But as I knew that the Queen could not bear to be contradicted, I dissembled my thoughts.

On the eve of her departure, the Queen looking fixedly at me, said : " I come to take my leave of you, my dear Wilhelmina : I hope Grumbkow will be as good as his word, and prevent your being disturbed during my stay at Potsdam : but as the future cannot always be distinctly foreseen, and as Grumbkow is obliged from policy to treat Seckendorff with great caution the better to impose upon him I require one thing of you which alone can quiet me during my absence ; that is, you must swear to me by your eternal salvation, you never will marry any other but the

Prince of Wales. You see, I demand nothing but what is just and reasonable ; hence I doubt not but you will yield me that satisfaction." Her demand staggered me. I thought I might elude it by reminding the Queen, that as Grumbkow was of her party, there was nothing more to be apprehended for me, and that I was persuaded he would effect my marriage, since he had promised to do so. The Queen would not suffer herself to be caught by this evasion : she insisted upon my taking the oath. Fortunately, a thought struck me, which freed me from my embarrass-ment. " I am a Calvinist," I replied, " and your majesty knows that predestination is one of the principal tenets of my religion. My fate is written in heaven. If Providence has decreed that I am to be established in England, neither the King, nor any human power, will be able to prevent it : if, on the contrary, it has ordained otherwise, all the pains and efforts of your majesty will be useless to bring it about. I therefore cannot take a rash oath which perhaps I should not be able to perform ; neither can I offend the Deity by acting contrary to the principles of my conscience and my faith. All I can promise is, not to submit to the will of the King but at the last extremity." The Queen had nothing to reply. I observed, that she was vexed at my answer : but I pretended not to notice it.[1] We were both much affec-ted on taking leave ; my heart was ready to break. I could not part with her ; I loved her to adoration ; and, indeed, she had some amiable qualities. We agreed to address indifferent letters to Mrs. Ramen, and to avail ourselves of

---

[1] The differences of opinion between the King and Frederick, and, as can be seen here, Wilhelmina also, over the question of predestination have been seen by historians as a central issue in the conflict between the two. Unlike most of the Hohenzollerns, Frederick William rejected the doctrine in favour of the more pragmatic Pietism of August Francke (see above, p. 108). Frederick, however, had come under the influence of a Calvinist priest at the Berlin court, one Andreä, who was banished from Berlin in 1725 for his beliefs. Frederick never entirely gave up his own belief in predestination, although while at Küstrin he was forced to receive instruction to that effect and to make a formal recantation of the doctrine.

the wife of her valet to transmit those which might be of consequence.

I forgot one interesting circumstance.—Madam de Bülow, before she set out for Lithuania, had had a long conversation with Boshart, a chaplain of the Queen; in which she had unveiled the character of Mrs. Ramen, and all her intrigues. This clergyman, who had many friends, had already heard something about it : he therefore resolved to inform the Queen; and had the good fortune so fully to convince her majesty of the infamous underhand dealings of this woman, that she promised she would not trust her with any thing but what she wished to reach the ears of his majesty. She communicated to us what Boshart had told her, and owned that she had perfectly well noticed the distrust which we had for that woman; but that she never could have thought her capable of so much perfidy. We advised her to be as subtle as Mrs. Ramen, to continue to treat her kindly, and to impose as much upon her as she could.

I found myself very disconsolate after the Queen's departure. Shut up in my bed-room, where I saw no one, I continued a spare diet, or rather I was actually starving. I read all the day long, and made remarks upon what I read. My health was much impaired. I grew as thin as a skeleton for want of proper food and exercise.

One day when Madam de Sonsfeld and myself were at table, looking wistfully at each other, having nothing to eat but a vile sort of soup made of water and salt, and a hash of stale bones, full of hair and filth, we heard a pretty loud knocking against the window. Surprised, we rose in haste to see what it was. We found it was a crow, with a crust of bread in her bill : as soon as she saw us, she dropped it on the outside of the window, and flew away. Tears, at this sight, started into our eyes. " Our fate is lamentable indeed," said I to my governess, " since it moves even dumb creatures ; they take more pity on us than those human beings who treat us with so much cruelty ! Let us consider it as a good omen, indicating an alteration in the aspect of our affairs. I am now reading the Roman history, and I find in it," continued I, jokingly, " that the approach of crows is a lucky presage." However, there was nothing supernatural in this incidenct. The crow was a tame one belonging to Margrave Albert. She had perhaps lost her way, and was endeavouring to find her home again. My servants, however, thought the circumstance so miraculous, that in a short time it was divulged all over the town : and it inspired so much commiseration for my sufferings among the French protestant refugees, that, at the risk of incurring the King's resentment, they sent me choice victuals in baskets placed before my door, and which Mrs. Meermann took care to empty. This action, and the concern which they expressed for my brother, have given me a high esteem for the members of the French protestant colonies ; and I have made it a rule to relieve and protect them whenever I found an opportunity.

The whole month of February passed in this way. The Queen pressed Grumbkow so much, that he at length obtained permission for me to see again my sisters and the ladies of the Queen's household. I was then enjoying a perfect tranquility, relieved from all fears for my brother, and hearing nothing more about my odious suitors. My little society was agreeable and complaisant. I insensibly accustomed myself to solitude, and grew a perfect philosopher.

Now and then the Queen wrote to me what was going on. She continued on the best terms with Grumbkow. She informed me, that he was going to make a final attempt in England, to which the King had consented, and from which she expected the happiest consequences. I differed from her. I could not conceive how she could trust a man who thought it meritorious to deceive every one, and by whom till then she had constantly been persecuted. I suspected beforehand that this great friendship would end fatally, and that the Queen would be his dupe. My conjectures proved true. Towards the latter end of March, the King again tormented the Queen concerning my marriage. She immediately informed me of it, complaining bitterly of the hardships she endured from the King's ill-humour. He publicly treated her ill at table, and appeared more exasperated than ever against my brother and me, though she could not dive into his motives. Grumbkow cast the blame upon Seckendorff, and made the Queen believe that this minister, having acquainted the King with the good intelligence that subsisted between him and her majesty, had diminished her credit with the King.

For nine months I had not taken the sacrament, having never been able to obtain the permission of the King. The Queen allowed me to write to his majesty to solicit that favour. In spite of her prohibition, I expressed my concern for the Queen's disgrace. My letter was one of the most moving, and calculated to soften a heart of stone. Instead of a direct answer, the King simply said to the Queen, that *the baggage her daughter might take the Lord's Supper*. He accordingly gave his orders to Eversmann, and named the clergyman who was to officiate. The service was performed privately in my room, where Eversmann assisted at the pious ceremony. Every one drew hence a favourable presage of my reconciliation ; the King having acted in the same way towards my brother, before he was released from the fortress.

In the mean time Grumbkow had written to England, by the order of the King.[1] He had applied to Reichenbach,

---

[1] On 16 March 1731 the second treaty of Vienna was signed, which reversed the hostility that had earlier existed between Austria and Great Britain. Thus for Prussia the main causes of disagreement between herself and Great Britain had been removed. But although the *Memoirs* are quite correct in indicating that diplomatic discussion concerning an English marriage was continuous right up to the moment when Wilhelmina (November 1731) and Frederick (June 1733) were finally espoused, there was little chance of it occurring. Frederick William was still playing with the idea, but in the margin of one diplomatic report wrote : " Death rather than marriage, single or double." At the same time Lord Chesterfield was telling a Prussian agent at the Hague that Britain was tired of Prussia's eternally insulting behaviour. —Droysen (op. cit., 131).

and commissioned him to demand a formal declaration concerning my marriage with the Prince of Wales : but he had taken care to give him secret instructions to render the attempt abortive.

Eversmann, at the same time, renewed his visits. He one day came with compliments from the Queen, and as I enquired after her health and that of the King, he answered : " His majesty is in a very cross humour, and the Queen is melancholy, without my knowing the reason. I am terribly busy myself. The King has ordered me to put the large saloon in order, and to remove thither all the new plate. There will be much noise above your head, madam : preparations are making for many entertainments. The marriage of Princess Sophia with the Prince of Bayreuth is soon to be solemnized. The King has invited several strangers ; the Duke of Württemberg, the Duke, the Duchess, and Prince Charles of Bevern ; the Prince of Hohenzollern ; and many others. I pity you," continued he, " for not being allowed to partake of these festivities ! The King has declared he will not have you to appear in his presence."—" I shall easily be reconciled to that," said I ; " but never to being in disgrace with the King : and I shall have no repose until I am restored to his majesty's favour."

This conversation made no great impression upon me, but Madam de Sonsfeld seemed uneasy about it. " There is a new storm gathering," she observed ; " Grumbkow is certainly deceiving the Queen, and I am very much afraid, madam, these preparations are intended for you. For heaven's sake ! be firm ; do not rush into misfortune. The Prince of Bayreuth is destined for you. Prepare your answer before hand ; for I fear the bomb will burst when you least think of it." As I did not wish to tell her my intentions, I merely returned an evasive answer.

As soon as the dispatches from England arrived, the Queen acquainted me with their contents. Reichenbach had extremely well executed Grumbkow's instructions. In the name of the Prussian monarch he had spoken with so much haughtiness to the English ministers, that, being already incensed at the affront given to Sir Charles Hotham, they took this declaration for a fresh insult. The King of England felt exasperated at it ; he thought proper, however, to keep his answer secret from the Prince of Wales and the nation. He answered, that " he should never give up the marriage of my brother with the Princess his daughter ; and that if this condition did not suit the Prussian monarch, he would have the Prince of Wales married before the end of the year." My father wrote by the return of post, " that he was determined to have me married in less than two months ; and that he was making the necessary preparations for that purpose." The Queen was disconsolate at this rupture, as may easily be supposed. But I do not know what hope she was yet indulging, since she still exhorted me to persist in refusing any match that might be proposed.

Eversmann came seven or eight days after. He affected a hypocritical air, and shewed himself very officious. " I have loved you," said he to me, " ever since you were born. I have a thousand times carried you in my arms : you were the darling of every one. In spite of all the harsh messages I have brought you from the King, I am yet your friend : I will give you a proof of it to-day, and tell you what is going on. Your marriage with the Prince of Wales is entirely broken off. The answer which has been returned to the King has rendered him furious ; he leads the Queen a most terrible life, who is grown as thin as a lath. He is exasperated anew against the Prince Royal ; he says that neither he nor Katte have been properly examined, and that there are many important circumstances of which he is yet uninformed and which he determines to investigate. Your marriage with the Duke of Weissenfels is firmly resolved upon. I foresee the most dreadful consequences, if you persist in your obstinacy. The King will employ the utmost violence towards the Queen, the Prince Royal, and you. In a short time you will know whether I speak truth or not. It behoves you to consider what you will do." My answer was invariably the same : it was the burden of a song which I had got by heart by dint of repeating it. Eversmann withdrew, rather dissatisfied.

I the same afternoon received a letter from the Queen, which confirmed all that Eversmann had told me. Mrs. Bock brought it me herself, and shewed me one from her husband. " It is impossible," he stated, " to describe the deplorable situation of the Queen ; the King yesterday was very near striking her with his cane. He is more exasperated than ever against the Prince Royal and the Princess. Heaven have pity on us in such dire adversities ! "

The next day, the 10th of May, 1731, proved the most memorable day of my life. Eversmann repeated his visit. I was scarcely awake, when he appeared before my bed. " I have but this instant returned from Potsdam," said he, " whither I was obliged to go yesterday, after I had left you. I could not conceive what pressing affair it was that so hastily required my presence. I found the King and Queen together : her majesty was in tears, and the King appeared in a violent passion. As soon as he saw me, he ordered me quickly to return hither, to make the necessary purchases for your wedding. The Queen made a last effort to avert the blow and appease the King, but the more she intreated him the greater was his irritation. He swore with the most bitter imprecations that he will drive Madam de Sonsfeld, with ignominy, away ; and as an example of his severity, he will have her publicly whipped in all the principal places of the town, because she alone," he says, " causes your disobedience. And as for you," continued he, " if you do not submit you are to be sent to a fortress ; and I think fit to inform you that the horses are already ordered for that purpose."—Then, addressing his discourse to Madam de Sonsfeld, he added, " I pity you with all my heart, to be condemned to such an infamous chastisement ; but it rests with the Princess to rescue you from this disgrace. It must however be confessed that it will be a fine sight, and that the blood which will run down your white back, will heighten

*Frederick,
Margrave of
Bayreuth, 1731*

*Wilhelmina, as
Margravine of
Bayreuth*

Anna Orczelska, illegitimate daughter of Augustus the Strong, and friend of Frederick

The reception of Augustus the Strong of Saxony by Sophia Dorothea in Mon-Bijou on 29 May 1728. Frederick William can be seen to the left of Augustus

its whiteness, and be delightful to look at ! " To hear such
insolent language with coolness required a heart of stone :
however I checked myself, and strove to break off the conversation without entering into any discussion.

I acquainted the ladies of the Queen's household with this
fine intelligence. They asked me what I had resolved upon
doing in such a trying emergency ? " That of obeying,"
answered I, " provided some other than Eversmann is sent
to me ; for I am resolved never to give my answer to him :
I expect all kinds of ill usage after the horrible tragedy of
Katte, and so many acts of violence that have lately taken
place. Madam de Bülow and M. Duhan were as innocent as
Madam de Sonsfeld, and yet they have not been spared ;
besides, in consideration of the Queen and of my brother I
am *determined* to put an end to these domestic dissensions."
—Madam de Sonsfeld, who had been watching me all this
while, cast herself at my feet : " For Heaven's sake," cried
she, " do not suffer yourself to be intimidated ; I know your
good heart. You are apprehensive of some misfortune
befalling me, and you, madam, are actually dragging me to
the precipice by consenting to be unhappy for the remainder of your life. I have nothing to fear : my conscience is clear, and I shall think myself the most fortunate
creature on earth, if I can procure your felicity at the
expense of my own." To soothe her, I feigned to have
altered my opinion.

In the evening, at five o'clock, Mrs. Bock brought me a
letter from the Queen ; it had been written on the same
day in the morning. It ran thus :

" All is lost, my dear Wilhelmina. The King insists upon
your being married let what will be the consequence. I
have sustained several cruel conflicts on the subject : but
neither my intreaties nor my tears have had any effect.
Eversmann is ordered to make the necessary purchases for
the wedding. You must prepare yourself to lose Madam de
Sonsfeld ; the King will overwhelm her with degrading and

infamous treatment if you do not obey. A deputation will be sent to you to persuade you. For Heaven's sake ! in no wise consent ; I shall know how to support you. A prison is better than an ill-fated marriage. Adieu, my dear child, I expect everything from your fortitude."

Madam de Sonsfeld likewise renewed her intreaties, and used her very impressive language to induce me to follow the orders of the Queen. To rid myself of these torments, I returned to my room, where I set down before my piano-forte, as if I were setting an air. I had not been there a moment, when a servant entered ; who said to me with affrighted looks : " Heavens ! madam, there are four gentlemen who would speak with you in the name of the King."—" Who are they ? " I asked hastily.—" I was so terrified," answered he, " that I did not inquire."—I hastened to the room where my companions were. As soon as I had told them what was going on, they all ran away. My governess, who had gone to receive those unlucky visitors, returned, followed by them. " For Heaven's sake," said she in passing by me, " do not suffer yourself to be intimidated." I went into another room, into which they were immediately ushered. They were MM. de Borck, Grumbkow, Powedils[1] his son-in-law, and a fourth, who was unknown to me ; but who I have since learned was M. de Thulmeier,[2] secretary of state, till then, of the Queen's party. They caused my governess to withdraw, and then they carefully shut the door. I must own, that in spite of my fortitude I felt a violent emotion at seeing myself so near to the decision of my fate, and had it not been for a chair, which I found in the middle of the room, and on which I leaned, I should have fallen on the floor.

Grumbkow spoke first.—" We come, madam," said he, " by order of the King. His majesty has hitherto yielded to

---

[1] Heinrich, Graf von Powedils (1697–1760).

[2] Heinrich Wilhelm von Thulmeier (1682–1740), Prussian minister and previously censor of Berlin newspapers.

intreaties, hoping that he should still be able to bring about
your marriage with the Prince of Wales. I myself have
been entrusted with the negotiation, and I have done all I
could to induce the court of St. James's to consent to that
marriage simply. But instead of answering, as they ought,
to the advantageous proposals of the King my master, the
English ministers have given him an insulting refusal ; and
his Britannic Majesty has declared, that his son should be
married before the end of the year. His Prussian Majesty
being highly incensed at this proceeding, replied by assuring
the King his brother-in-law, that you should be married in
less than three months. You may easily suppose, madam,
that he will not suffer himself to be disappointed ; and
though as a father and a sovereign, he need not enter upon
any such discussion with you, he yet condescends to represent to you what a disgrace it would be for him and you, to
continue to be trifled with by England : you are aware,
madam, that the obstinacy of the British court has occasioned
all the misfortunes of your house. The intrigues of the
Queen, and her perseverance in opposing the wishes of the
King, have so exasperated him against her, that nothing less
than a total separation is expected. Consider, madam, the
misfortunes of the Prince Royal and of many other individuals who have felt the weight of his wrath. The poor
Prince Royal drags on a miserable life at Küstrin. The
King is so irritated against him, that he regrets having
ordered the death of Katte, because, he says, he might have
obtained some more important information. He still sus-
pects the Prince to have been guilty of high-treason, and he
will gladly avail himself of your refusal, to bring him to a
fresh trial. But I come to the main point. To obviate any
difficulty you might throw in the way, we are ordered to
propose to you the hereditary Prince of Bayreuth only.
You can have nothing to object against him. This Prince
becomes the mediator between the King and Queen. Her
majesty has proposed him to the King ; she therefore will
approve of the choice. The Prince is of the house of Bran-

denburg, and will be sovereign of a very fine country at the death of his father. As you are not acquainted with him, madam, you cannot possibly have any aversion for him. Moreover, he is every where extremely well spoken of. It is true, that, having been brought up with ideas of grandeur, and having been flattered with the hope of wearing a crown, you must necessarily be affected at its loss : but great Princesses are born to be sacrificed for the welfare of the state. Grandeur, after all, does not constitute solid happiness. Submit, therefore, to the decrees of Providence, and give us an answer calculated to re-establish harmony and peace in your family. I have still two points to touch upon ; one of which, I hope, will be unnecessary. The King engages to give you, if you obey, advantages far exceeding those of the rest of his children, and to grant you, immediately after your nupitals, the entire liberty of the Prince Royal. For your sake, he will forget the past, and kindly use both the Queen and the Prince. But if, contrary to his expectations and contrary to arguments which I consider as insuperable, you persist in your refusal, we have the order of the King, (which he showed me at the same time) to take you instantly to Memel, a fortified town in Lithuania, and to treat Madam de Sonsfeld and the rest of your domestics with the utmost severity."

This long speech had given me time to reflect, and to recover from my first terror. " What you have been stating to me, Sir," I replied, " is so just and so reasonable, that it would be difficult to refute your arguments. Had the King known me, he would perhaps have done me more justice. Ambition is not my failing ; I easily renounce the grandeur to which you alluded. The Queen thought she was providing for my happiness by establishing me in England : but she never consulted my heart on the subject, and I never dared to communicate to her my real sentiments. How I have lost the good graces of his majesty. I know not. He always applied to the Queen about my establishment, and never let me know his own wishes on that head.

Eversmann, it is true, has frequently presumed to tell me of the King's commands on that subject : but I had so little faith in them, that I never condescended to give him any answer. I did not think proper to commit myself towards a menial servant, or to enter into any discussion with him upon matters of such importance. You promise me, in the name of the King, that he will henceforth behave better to the Queen. He grants entire liberty to my brother, and flatters me with permanent harmony in the family. These three motives are more than sufficient to induce me to submit to the King, and would exact a greater sacrifice from me, if such were his commands. I ask only one single favour, that of being allowed to obtain the consent of her majesty."

" Ah ! madam ! " said Grumbkow, " you require an impossibility. The King wants a positive and unconditional answer, and orders us not to leave you without obtaining it."
—" Can you still hesitate ? " added Field-Marshal Borck, " the tranquility of her majesty and of your whole house depends on your resolution. The Queen can but approve of it ; if she does not, she will incur general disapprobation. All is at stake," continued he with tears in his eyes, " for heaven's sake ! madam, do not reduce us to the sad necessity of causing you uneasiness by following the instructions we have received."

I was in a dreadful agitation, running to and fro through the room, searching for some expedient to satisfy the King, without disobliging the Queen. The gentlemen wished to give me time to reflect. Grumbkow, Borck, and Powedils, went to the window, and conferred in a low voice. Thulmeier availed himself of this opportunity to approach me, and seeing that I did not know him, he told me his name. " There is no time left for resistance," he whispered to me, " submit to any thing that is required of you : your marriage will not take place, I answer for it with my head. You must appease the King, whatever it may cost you ; and I engage to convince the Queen that it is the only means of obtaining a favourable declaration from the King of England." These words quickly brought me to a determination. I walked up to the gentlemen, and said : "well ! my resolution is taken ; I consent to your proposals ; I sacrifice myself for my family. I expect dreadful troubles ; but the purity of my intentions will make me bear them with firmness. As for you, gentlemen, I summon you before the tribunal of the Most High, if you do not insist upon the performance of the promises which you have given me in the name of his majesty, in behalf of the Queen and my brother." They most solemnly swore they would see them executed in every respect ; after which, they requested me to write my resolution to the King. Grumbkow, perceiving that I was in a cruel agitation, dictated the letter ; he also undertook to deliver that which I wrote to the Queen. They at length withdrew. Thulmeier again told me, that nothing was lost yet. "I care not for England," I answered, "it is the Queen alone that causes my uneasiness." —"We shall appease her, I assure you ; " he replied.

When I was thus left to myself, I dropped into an armchair, where I shed a flood of tears : Madam de Sonsfeld found me in that situation. I told her, in broken accents, what had passed. She overwhelmed me with the most bitter reproaches ; her grief was inconceivable. Every one around me was terrified, and wept. My poor heart was distracted with its own feelings ; I remained motionlesss the whole day ; and, excepting Madam de Sonsfeld, all my friends approved of my conduct, but all feared the resentment of the Queen against me. The next morning I wrote to her majesty. I have preserved a copy of that letter ; I shall transcribe it here.

"MADAM ;
"Your majesty is already acquainted with my misfortune by the letter which I had the honour to address to you yesterday under cover to the King. I have scarcely strength to trace these lines : my situation is entitled to commiseration.

It is not the King's menaces, strong as they were, that have obtained my submission to the will of his majesty ; an interest more dear has determined me to the sacrifice. Hitherto I have been the innocent cause of the pains your majesty has endured. My too feeling heart was violently affected at the moving picture your majesty lately gave me of your troubles. My mother wished to suffer for me ; is it not more natural that I should sacrifice myself for her, and put a final stop to the fatal disunion of the family ? Could I have hesitated a moment between my brother's misfortune and his pardon ? What horrible projects have been disclosed to me in his respect ! I shudder when I think of them. Whatever I could have advanced against the proposal of the King, has been reflected on before hand. You yourself have proposed the Prince of Bayreuth as a suitable match for me ; and you seemed satisfied if I married him ; I therefore cannot imagine that you will disapprove of my resolution. Necessity is a hard law ; all my intreaties for leave to obtain first the consent of your majesty, have been vain. I was forced to chuse, either to obey with a good grace, and obtain real advantages for my brother, or to expose myself to violences which in the end would still have reduced me to the measure which I have adopted. I shall have the honour to enter into a more minute account when I am allowed to embrace your majesty's feet. Full well I feel how great must be your grief ; it is that which affects me most. I humbly beseech your majesty not to be disquieted on my behalf, and to rely on Providence, which does every thing for our welfare ; particularly as I deem myself fortunate in becoming the instrument of my dear mother's and my brother's happiness. What would I not do to convince them of my affection ! I once more intreat your majesty to take care of your health, and not to impair it by immoderate sorrow. The prospect of seeing my brother soon, must alleviate your majesty's present misfortune. I hope your majesty will generously forgive the fault I have committed of entering into any engagement unknown to your majesty, in consideration of the tender regard and the dutiful respect with which I shall remain for life, &c. &c. &c."

The same evening Eversmann brought me a letter from the King, written with his own hand :

" I am very glad, my dear Wilhelmina, that you submit to the will of your father. Heaven will bless you, and never forsake you. I shall take care of you all the days of my life, and convince you on every occasion, that I am

"Your affectionate Father."

As Eversmann was going to Potsdam, I gave him my answer. It would be difficult to describe the sensations I felt. My vanity was flattered with what I had done ; I inwardly applauded myself, and enjoyed a secret satisfaction for having sheltered individuals so dear to me from all persecutions. To these considerations succeeded the idea of my own fate, which filled me with serious apprehensions. I did not know the Prince whom I was to marry ; he was generally well spoken of, but is it possible to judge of the disposition of a prince who is only seen in public, and whose prepossessing manners may hide many vices and failings ? I foresaw the rage and despair of the Queen ; and I confess that this consideration disturbed me more than the former. I was absorbed in this contemplation with a confused mixture of pleasure and pain ; when Mrs. Bock brought me the Queen's answer to the first letter I had written to her majesty. Good heavens ! what a letter ! The expressions were so harsh, that they almost killed me. I would not for the world recal the whole epistle to my mind ; I shall only give a slight sketch of it. My mother is too dear to me, notwithstanding her cruelty, that I should disgrace her by publishing a writing which would do her no honour. I did not wish to keep it on that account. Here are a few sentences :

" You break my heart by giving me the most violent pain I ever felt in my life. I had placed all my hopes in you ;

but I did not know you. You have artfully disguised the malice of your soul and the meanness of your sentiments. I repent, a thousand times over, the kindness I have had for you, the cares I have taken of your education ; and the torments I have endured for your sake. I no longer acknowledge you for my daughter, and shall henceforth consider you as my most cruel enemy, since it is you that sacrifice me to my persecutors, who triumph over me. Rely on me no longer. I vow you eternal hatred, and never shall forgive you."

The last sentence made me shudder. I perfectly knew the Queen and her vindictive disposition. It was expected that my brain would be disordered, so great was the violence of my first emotion. Mrs. Bock made a very sensible observation : she stated, that the letter was written in the heat of the first agitation. She read me a letter from her husband, who sent me word that all who were about the Queen were jointly endeavouring to appease her wrath ; that I was to continue to make her submissions, and that he doubted not but she would be herself again. Five or six days elapsed, during which I received none but killing letters.

At the end of this time, Eversmann came back from Potsdam. He brought me very gracious compliments from the King, and told me on his part, that as he intended to be at Berlin on the 23d, he had not thought proper to invite me to Potsdam ; particularly as it was better to give the Queen time to be appeased. He added that she was in a terrible passion against me, and that I ought to arm myself with fortitude for the first interview, which would be attended with great violence. Eversmann renewed his visit three days after. " The King informs you, madam," said he, " that his majesty will be here to-morrow early, and orders you to be with the Princesses your sisters in his apartment." The anxiety in which I was about the coming of the Queen, kept me all the day in a profound melancholy.

The next day I went to the King, who arrived at two o'clock in the afternoon. I expected a favourable reception : but how great was my surprise to see him enter with looks as fierce as those he had given me the last time I had seen him. He asked me in an angry tone : " *will you obey ?* " I cast myself at his feet, assuring him that I submitted to his commands, and intreated him to restore his pateral love to me. My answer brightened his countenance. He lifted me up, and holding me in his arms, he said : " *I am satisfied with you ; I will take care of you all the days of my life, and will never forsake you.*" Then turning to my sister Sophia, he added : " *congratulate your sister ; she is betrothed to the hereditary Prince of Bayreuth ; let not this give you any pain ; I shall take care to find you another establishment.*" He afterwards gave me a piece of brocade. " Here is wherewith to adorn you for the entertainments I intend to give. *I have some business to transact,*" continued he, " *go and wait for your mother.*" She arrived at seven o'clock in the evening. I went to meet her in her first anti-room, and swooned in stooping to kiss her hand. It was a long time before I could be recalled to life. I have since been told, that she did not appear affected at my situation. When I had recovered my senses, I cast myself at her feet : my heart was so oppressed and my articulation so choaked with sobs, that I could not utter a word. The Queen all this time looked at me with severity and contempt, and repeated all she had written to me. The scene would never have ended had not Mrs. Ramen taken the Queen aside and remonstrated that if the King heard of her behaviour he would highly disapprove of it, and avenge it upon my brother and her ; that my grief was so excessive, that I should not be able to restrain it before the King, which would cause her fresh troubles. This officious sermon had its effect. The Queen at bottom feared the King as much as Lucifer. She at last lifted me up, telling me, in a harsh tone, " that she would forgive me, if I restrained myself."

The Duchess of Bevern entered at that moment. She

seemed moved with my situation ; the tears I had wept had swollen my face, and rubbed the skin off. She expressed in a low voice the concern she felt for my distress. A certain sympathy created between us a friendship which subsists at this moment.

In the mean time, M. de Thulmeier performed the promise he had given me of appeasing the Queen. He secretly wrote to her the next day, that there was yet no occasion to despair ; that my marriage was a mere feint of the King to induce his Britannic majesty to come to a different resolution ; that he had enquired every where for the Prince of Bayreuth, and had been assured he was still at Paris. This letter completely quieted her majesty. I have already observed, that the Queen was apt to indulge flattering hopes. She really continued in a charming humour all the day. I was obliged to tell her all that had passed during her absence. She contented herself with making me a few more reproaches on my want of firmness, but they were delivered in a more gentle tone. But all her wrath fell upon Madam de Sonsfeld. She had used her very ill the day before, and, in spite of my solicitations, she persisted in giving her proofs of her hatred. Three days glided away in a perfect calm. The King said nothing more about my marriage : it seemed as though my consent had made him give up the idea of it.

Monday the 28th of May, 1731, was fixed for a grand review of the troops. It was to be very splendid. The King had collected all the regiments of infantry and cavalry of the neighbourhood, which, together with the garrison of Berlin, formed a corps of twenty thousand men. The Duke Eberhard Louis of Württemberg arrived in time to be present at the review. The King had passed through the dominions of that prince a short time before the unfortunate affair of my brother. Having been delighted with the eagerness which the Duke had manifested to render his stay at Stuttgart agreeable to him, the King, in his turn, had invited him to Berlin. As my father knew of no pleasure superior to that which he took in his troops, he judged of others by himself, and thought he gave great satisfaction to the foreign princes who came to his court by showing them his army. It must, however, be owned, that on this occasion he surpassed even himself by the costliness of his table, which had fourteen different dishes served up all the time that the strangers stayed at Berlin ; and this was no small effort for my father.

On Sunday the 27th, the King requested the Queen to be present at the review, and to take my sister, the Duchess, and myself, in her phaeton. As he was to rise very early, he went to bed at seven, and ordered the Queen to entertain the strangers, and detain them to supper : and we played at pharo till it was served up. When we crossed the room to sit down to table, we saw a chaise with post-horses driving into the palace-yard, and stopping at the grand entrance. The Queen appeared surprised, as princes alone had that prerogative. She immediately enquired who it was ? and heard, a moment after, that it was the hereditary Prince of Bayreuth. Medusa's head never caused a terror like that with which the Queen was struck. She was quite stupified, and her complexion underwent such various and rapid changes, that we thought she would faint away. Her situation pierced my heart ; I was motionless as well as she ; and every one appeared seized with consternation. The reflection, in the mean time, rushed upon my mind, that there was some disagreeable scene preparing for the next day ; and I besought the Queen to excuse my accompanying her to the review, as I expected all kinds of rude jokes from the King, which would give her as much pain as myself, particularly if we were exposed to them in public. She approved of what I suggested : but after having weighed the matter on both sides, her slavish fear of the King preponderated, and it was decided that I should go to the review. I could not sleep all the night. Madam de Sonsfeld sat up by my bed-side, endeavouring to comfort me, and to remove my apprehensions of the future. I rose at four o'clock in the morning, and hid my face under a triple veil, to conceal my trouble. Thus equipped, I went to meet the Queen, and we set out immediately.

The troops were already drawn up in battle array, when we arrived. The King made us ride down the line. It was, it must be owned, the finest sight that could be seen. But I shall not dwell on this subject : these troops have shown that they are as good as brilliant ; and the King my father has acquired everlasting fame for the wonderful subordination he has introduced into his army with which he has laid the foundation of the greatness of this house. The Margrave of Schwedt was at the head of his regiment ; he seemed swollen with anger, and gave us his military salute with averted eyes. Colonel Wachholtz, whom the King had appointed guide to the Queen, placed us near a battery of guns at a great distance from this small army. He approached the Queen, and told her in a whisper, that the King had ordered him to present the Prince of Bayreuth to her majesty : and he brought him a moment after. The Queen received him with a haughty air, and asked him some insignificant questions, which ended by a signal to withdraw. The weather was excessively hot ; I had had no sleep ; a thousand anxieties preyed upon my mind, and I had not broken my fast ; all this made me ill. The Queen permitted me to be removed to the carriage of her ladies, where I soon found myself better. The King and the Prince dined together, and we passed the day in our usual retirement.

On the 29th, in the morning, all the foreign princes paid their respects to the Queen. She scarcely spoke to the Prince of Bayreuth. When he was presented to me, I merely dropped a curtsey without replying to his compliment. He is tall and well made, and has a noble air : his features are neither handsome nor regular, but his open, prepossessing, and agreeable countenance supplies the want of beauty. He appeared very lively, prompt at a repartee, and was not embarrassed in the least.

Two days elapsed in this manner. The silence of the King, while it disconcerted us, revived the hopes of the Queen ; but the tables were turned on the 31st. The King having sent for the Queen and myself to his closet, " You know," said he, addressing her majesty, " that I have promised my daughter to the Prince of Bayreuth ; I have fixed the betrothing for tomorrow. I shall be infinitely obliged to you, and you will be entitled to my tenderest affection, if you behave well to the Prince and Wilhelmina : if not, you may rely on my indignation. By Lucifer !¹ I will put an end to your frivolous opposition, and take a bloody vengeance." Terrified at this address, the Queen promised whatever he required ; and the King, in return, caressed her tenderly. He requested her to dress me as sumptuously as possible, and to lend me her jewels. She was in a terrible rage, and now and then cast the most furious glances upon me. The King left us, and came soon after to the apartment of the Queen with the Prince, whom he introduced to her as his son-in-law. She gave him a tolerable reception before the King, but as soon as the latter was gone, she plied him with nothing but sarcasms. After cards, we sat down to supper. When this was over, the Queen was going to withdraw, but the Prince followed her : " I beseech you, madam," said he, " to grant me a short audience. I am acquainted with every particular concerning your majesty and the Princess. I know she had been destined to wear a crown, and that it was you majesty's fond wish to establish her in England ; it is merely the dissension between the two courts to which I am indebted for the honour the King has done me to select me for his son-in-law. I deem myself the happiest of mortals in being allowed to make suit to a Princess, for whom I already feel all the respect and esteem which she deserves. But these very sentiments inspire me with too much regard for her to plunge her into misfortunes by a marriage which perhaps does not suit her royal highness. I therefore intreat you,

¹ By Lucifer !—the French reads " *Le diable m'emporte !* "

madam, to deal with me sincerely on that point, and to be persuaded that your answer will decide the happiness or misery of my life : for if it be not favourable, I shall break off every engagement with the King, whatever may be the unhappiness I shall thus entail upon myself." The Queen remained for a moment in suspense : but suspecting the candour of the Prince, she answered, that she had nothing to object to the King's choice, and that she and I were obeying the King's commands. She could not help observing to Madam de Kamecke, that the Prince had taken a very artful step but that she had not been his dupe.

On Sunday the 3d of June, I went in the morning, in an elegant undress, to the Queen. The King was with her. He caressed me much on giving me the betrothing ring, which was a large diamond, and repeated his promise to take care of me all his life-time, if I went through the ceremony with a good grace. He even presented me with a set of gold dishes and plates ; adding that it was but a trifle, as he had still greater presents in store for me.

In the evening, at seven, we went to the state apartments. A room had been prepared for the Queen, her court, and the foreign princes, where we sat down to wait for the King. The Queen was in an agitation, which she vainly strove to conceal. She had not said a word to me all the day, and expressed her displeasure merely by her glances. The Margravine Philippa, whom the King compelled to attend at the ceremony, could scarcely restrain her vexation. Her son, the Margrave of Schwedt, bluntly refused to be present, and preferred leaving the town, that he might not hear the noise of the guns. At length the King came with the Prince. He was as much moved as the Queen ; which made him forget to betroth us in public in the hall, where the company was assembled. He came up to me, holding the Prince by the hand, and made us change rings. I trembled greatly while doing this. I would have kissed the King's hand, but he lifted me up, and held me for a while closed in his arms.

Tears trickled down his cheeks ; mine flowed abundantly : our silence was more expressive than any thing we could have said. The Queen, when I bent my knee to her, treated me very coolly. After having received the compliments of all the princely personages who were present, the King ordered the Prince to lead me to the ball-room, and to begin the dance. My marriage had been kept so secret, that every one was surprised at the intelligence. The consternation and grief were general, when it was announced. I had many friends, and was generally beloved. The King wept all the evening ; he embraced Madam de Sonsfeld, and said many obliging things to her. Grumbkow and Seckendorff were the only two contented individuals ; they had been playing a new trick. Lord Chesterfield, the English ambassador at the Hague,[1] had sent a messenger from his court, who had arrived in the morning. The English Chargé-d'Affaires, to whom he was addressed, was obliged to send his dispatches to the minister. Grumbkow engaged to lay them before the King : but he did not deliver them till after I had been betrothed. They contained a formal assent to my marriage with the Prince of Wales, without requiring that of my brother. The King who, after all, was marrying me but reluctantly, was extremely distressed by the perusal of these letters. He however dissembled his vexation before Grumbkow and Seckendorff, considering that matters were too far advanced to recede ; this last proposal having come too late, and it being impossible to recall his engagements without giving offence to a Sovereign Prince of the Empire, which might have been prejudicial to my other sisters. Besides, the King always piqued himself on a faithful adherence to his engagements, where his word stood pledged for the performance.

The Queen was acquainted with the circumstance the

---

[1] Philip Dormer Stanhope, 4th Earl Chesterfield (1694–1773) was at the Hague from 1728 to 1732. In 1736 he finally arranged the marriage of the Prince of Wales to another German Princess, Augusta of Saxe-Gotha.

next day. Though she was told of her King's refusal she yet began to flatter herself anew, that my intended marriage might be broken off : and she ordered me, on pain of her displeasure, neither to speak or behave politely to the Prince. I punctually obeyed, in the hope of appeasing her by my compliance. But, to confess the real sentiments of my heart, I wished to be married ; the ill-treatment of the Queen and the hatred which she manifested towards me at every opportunity reduced me to despair. Excepting Madam de Kamecke, I was buffeted about by all the ladies of her court, who tried my patience by the contempt and insolence, which they made me undergo. Such is the course of the world ; the favour of the great decides all : people are sought for and adored as long as they are in favour ; which when they are deprived of, they are exposed to insult and contempt. As long as I had the hope of a splendid fortune, I was the idol of all ; they courted me with the view of sharing one day in my splendour : but the instant these hope vanished, they turned their backs upon me. I was silly indeed to grieve at the loss of such friends. The magnificence of the court of Bayreuth was continually praised ; I was assured that it far surpassed in splendour the court of Berlin, and that it was the centre of pleasures :[1] but those who were amused with such discourses, had been there in the time of the late Margrave, and were unacquainted with the changes that had since taken place. These brilliant

---

[1] This was not Wilhelmina's impression when she finally arrived. She was " not much gratified by my introduction to the court of Bayreuth ; and still less so by the wretched entertainment of the evening— miserable ragouts seasoned with sour wine, large raisins and onions. I felt ill at the end of my repast, and was obliged to retire. They had not taken the least care about me ; my apartment had not even been warmed ; the windows were broken ; which occasioned the rooms to be insupportably cold. I was sick to death the whole night ; it passed away in sufferings, and in sorrowful reflections on my situation. I found myself in a new world with people more like rustics than courtiers. Poverty was discernible everywhere. It was in vain for me to look for the riches of which I had heard so much boasting. I could not discover the least vestige of their existence."

accounts gave me an extreme longing to be there. I felt no antipathy towards the Prince ; but I was perfectly indifferent about him. I knew him only by sight, and my heart had not so much levity as to be attached to him before I knew him well. But it is time to make a short digression concerning the Prince, and to make the reader acquainted with the court of Bayreuth.

Margrave Henry, the grandfather of my consort, was an apanaged Prince of the house of Bayreuth. He had married very young, and had had many children. A very small annual income was insufficient to maintain so numerous a family. He was in the greatest distress, not having wherewith to support himself, and being reduced, through want of money, to lead the life of a private citizen. He was heir of the Margraviate of Bayreuth, in case the then reigning Margrave, George-William, should die without any male issue. But his hopes in that quarter appeared rather unfounded ; George-William being young, and having a son. The King Frederick I my grandfather, knowing the distressed circumstances of Henry, failed not to turn them to his own advantage. He induced him to cede to him his claims to the Margraviate, offering him in lieu of the same a considerable pension and a regiment for the second of his sons. After long preliminaries the treaty was concluded, and the two eldest sons of the unfortunate Henry were sent to study at the University of Utrecht. On their return thence, they found their father on the point of death, and their family disconsolate, because the conditions of the stipulation had been left unperformed, and two-thirds of the pension deducted. Henry being dead, the Margrave George-Frederick-Charles, after having long solicited the Prussian ministers in vain, resolved to reside at Weverling, a small town in the dominions of his Prussian majesty. It was in this place that the Princess of Holstein, his spouse, presented him with the Prince, who was to be my husband ; and with several other children, of whom I shall speak hereafter. King Frederick I also died shortly after. The accession of my father to the crown made no alteration in the lot of those Princes. Being reduced to despair, they examined the act of renunciation, and it was pronounced invalid by all the lawyers whom they consulted on the subject. They therefore secretly removed from Weverling, and applied to all the courts of Germany to win them over to their favour. Supported by the Emperor, the Holy Roman Empire, and the justice of their cause, they succeeded in getting the treaty cancelled and being restored to all their rights. The Margrave George-William and his son having both died, the Margraviate devolved to Prince George-Frederick-Charles. He found every thing in the greatest confusion ; many debts, little money, and a currupt administration. This induced him to send his eldest son to Geneva with a tutor, a simple commoner ; a man of great probity, it is true, but not capable of imparting such an education as suited an hereditary Prince. His allowance was so scanty, that it scarcely sufficed for his maintenance. When he had finished his studies, his father sent him on his travels with M. de Voigt as his governor. The Prince was returning from his tour, when he arrived at Berlin. I do not intend to flatter any one ; I strictly adhere to truth. The portrait which I am going to give of the Prince, shall be sincere and unprejudiced.

I have already observed, that he has a great share of vivacity : his disposition is prone to anger ; but he knows so well how to overcome it that it is not perceived, and that no one ever fell a victim to it. He is extremely cheerful ; his conversation is aggreeable, though he has some difficulty of utterance as he speaks rather thick. His mind is comprehensive and penetrating. The goodness of his heart insures him the attachment of all who know him. He is generous, charitable, merciful, polite, prepossessing, of an even temper ; in short, he possesses all virtues, unallayed with any vice. The only failing I have noticed is too much levity. I must mention it, else I should be accused of prejudice : his levity is however much less than formerly. In a word, all his subjects, by whom he is adored, are ready to confirm all I have written on his subject.[1]—But I return to my own concerns.

[1] The hereditary Prince Friedrich of Brandenburg-Bayreuth (1711–63), husband of Wilhelmina, who became Margrave on the death of his father in 1735.

VIII

I feign coolness — The prince of Bayreuth is abused, and speaks with me candidly — The enchanted castle — An exchange of rings — Further threats of the Prince of Wales — My wedding — I am reunited to my brother who behaves strangely — Giants do not grow like mushrooms — The King proves ungenerous — Hopes for the future.

I have already observed, that my sister Charlotte was betrothed to Prince Charles of Bevern.[1] She was my favourite ; I had been blinded by her caressing manners, her liveliness, and her wit. I did not know her inward disposition, else I should have better placed my affection. She is one of those who only care for themselves ; deficient in solidity, satirical to an excess, false, jealous, a little inclined to coquetry, and very selfish, but of an even temper, very mild, and very obliging. I had done my best to obtain for her the favour of the Queen. As she had accompanied her majesty on her excursions to Wusterhausen and Potsdam, she had very much insinuated herself into her good graces. Madam de Montbail, daughter to Madam de Roucoule, was her governess. This woman had taken a dislike to me, because a greater establishment was destined for me than for my sister, and because I was treated with more distinction. She was continually kindling strife betwixt my sister and me ; but she now was much pleased with my marriage, hoping that my sister might fill my place in England. My sister being afraid that my presence might impair her favour rendered me every kind of ill service with the Queen. But

---

[1] Charles I, Duke of Brunswick-Lüneberg (1713–80). He married Philippine Charlotte in July 1733. Bevern was a tiny apanage of Brunswick.

she was much taken with the Prince of Bayreuth. He was handsomer, better made, and more lively, than the Prince of Bevern. He paid her great attention ; while the other was rather timid and of a phlegmatic disposition, which did not suit her. She did all she could to get him into favour with the Queen ; but her efforts proved useless.

To divert the strangers, and particularly the Duchess of Bevern, the King invited us all to a great chace in the park of Charlottenburg. The Prince of Anhalt was also invited, with his two sons Leopold and Maurice. He was much nettled at the preference which the King had given the Prince of Bayreuth to the Margrave of Schwedt, as he had always hoped I should be married to the latter. The hereditary Prince of Bayreuth was very dextrous, and so good a shot, that he never missed his aim. This chace had well nigh been fatal to him A heedless fellow of a huntsman who loaded his arms, had the imprudence to present him a gun which was cocked ; it went off the moment the Prince took it, and the ball grazed the right temple of the King. The Prince of Anhalt made much noise about the accident. His son Leopold did not fail to aggravate it ; he said loud enough for the hereditary Prince to hear him, that such a blunder deserved the instant death of him in whose hands the gun had gone off. The Prince of Bayreuth answered sharply ; and the matter would have led to serious consequences, had not the Duke of Bevern and Seckendorff interfered to effect a reconciliation. The King blamed the conduct of Prince Leopold, but took no notice of the accident.

After the chace, we all went to Charlottenburg, where we were to pass some days. The Queen continued to talk sarcastically to the Prince of Bayreuth. Her intention was to mortify me, and to sneer at the choice of the King. She once told him, that I was fond of being employed ; that I had been brought up as a Princess who aspired to a crown ; and that I was mistress of every science. (She said a great deal too much in my favour.) " Do *you*," continued she,

" know history, geography, Italian, English, painting, music, &c. ? " The Prince replied, *yes* and *no* according to circumstances. But seeing that her question had no end, and that she examined him like a child, he at length began to laugh, and said : " I also know my Catechism and the Belief." The Queen was a little disconcerted by this reply, and never teased him again with her question.

The King and all the foreign Princes, except the Prince of Bayreuth, left us soon after our return to Berlin. Vexation, anger, and the cruel constraint of the Queen, at length disordered her health. She was attacked by a certain fever, which continued three weeks. I did not quit her during the whole time, and endeavoured to regain her friendship by my attentions to wait upon and to amuse her. But I no longer found in her that tender mother who shared my pains, and whose comfort I had been. Whenever she saw me uneasy about her condition : she used to say : " it ill becomes you to be alarmed at the state of my health, when it is you that kill me." Was I melancholy, she very harshly reproached me with my uneven temper ; and when I affected to be cheerful, it was my approaching marriage that made me so. I durst not wear any dirty gowns, lest she might fancy I studied to please the Prince ; in short, I was the most discernable being on earth, and my head was almost distracted. I dined and supped in the Queen's antiroom with the Prince and the ladies of the household. The Queen sent fifty spies after me, to see whether I spoke to the Prince : but I never transgressed in that respect, for I did not say a word to him, and always turned my back to him at table. He has since told me, that he frequently was driven to despair, and on the point of setting off, had not M. de Voigt prevented him. The poor Prince was in as bad a situation as myself. Every one studied to give a malicious turn to his actions and words. He was not treated with any consideration but like an insignificant being ; which discouraged him so that he grew absent and melancholy.

When the Queen had recovered, the King came back to

Berlin, where he staid only a few days, as he was going to Prussia. He informed the Queen, that he intended to celebrate my nuptials on his return, which was to be in six weeks; that he should furnish her with the sums necessary to equip me; and that she was to amuse the Prince, during his absence, by giving balls and entertainments. The Queen, who only studied to gain time, started many difficulties; representing the impossibility of having my clothes made in so short a time, because the stocks of the tradesmen were not large enough to furnish what would be requisite. Her arguments prevailed to my sorrow; for the King was uncommonly well-disposed in my favour, and would have dealt generously with me: but his liberality vanished into smoke, like a vapour, when my marriage was put off.

After the departure of the King, the Queen altered her behaviour. She affected much friendship for the Prince, and pretended to be glad to have him for her son-in-law: but she put herself under no restraint with me; and Madam de Sonsfeld and myself continued to bear the brunt of her ill-humour. I was pining away; incessant vexations impaired my health; and at last I moved the pity even of those who were least susceptible of it. I might have said, like Alzire,

Have my sorrows softened hearts that were born to hate?[1]

Mrs. Ramen, who frequently witnessed my despair, and to whom in the violence of my grief I had often said that the Queen was driving me to extremities, and that I should cast myself at the feet of the King to beseech him to release me from my matrimonial engagement, informed Grumbkow of it, and made him apprehend that I might actually execute my resolution. The latter, knowing that the Queen was still carrying on her intrigues in England, and fearing new

[1] *Alzire*, a tragedy by Voltaire set in Peru. Wilhelmina is most unlikely to have used this line at this precise moment, as the play was not written until 1735.

proposals from that quarter, resolved to deceive her, and to put an end to her ill-humour, which she so strangely vented upon me. He sent her word by M. de Sastot, that the King was sorry he had betrothed me ; that, as he could not esteem the Prince, he intended to break off my marriage at his return from Prussia, and to marry me to the Duke of Weissenfels. Above all, he enjoined the strictest secrecy ; because he alone was acquainted with his majesty's intentions. This false confidence had the effect which Grumbkow had expected. The Queen immediately resolved upon what measures she should pursue ; she began openly to patronize the hereditary Prince. She communicated her fears to me, and ordered me to behave politely to the Prince ; declaring, that she would rather suffer death than see me Duchess of Weissenfels. Such was her disposition ; the King's approval sufficed to induce her to disapprove. I could not account for her mysterious conduct, the motives of which Grumbkow has since unravelled to me.

This happy interval was not of long duration. After the return of the King from Prussia, his actions sufficiently testified, that the Queen had been imposed upon. It is true, the polished and reserved manners of the Prince of Bayreuth by no means pleased him : he desired for a son-in-law one who delighted in soldiers and wine ; one who practised economy, and imitated German fashions. To fathom the Prince's disposition, and to train him to his liking, he every day attempted to intoxicate him. But the Prince bore wine so well, that he never varied in his behaviour, and retained his senses, while his companions were losing theirs. This exasperated the King ; he even complained of him to Grumbkow and Seckendorff, saying, that he was a mere fop destitute of talents, and whose manners he abhorred. Repeated observations of this kind made the two friends apprehensive that the aversion of the King might be attended with consequences injurious to their interests ; and to obviate these, they proposed to the hereditary Prince to obtain him a regiment in the Prussian service ; representing it as the only way of insinuating himself into the King's favour, and bringing about his marriage. The Prince felt himself greatly embarrassed on this account. The Margrave, his father, was a high-minded Prince, who never would allow his son to devote himself to the military profession ; and in order to deprive him of the means of doing so, he had actually ceded two regiments in the Austrian service, which the Margrave George-William had raised, one to his youngest son, the other to General Philippe. However, after mature deliberation, the Prince yielded to Grumb-kow's advice. The King was delighted to hear that the hereditary Prince was willing to serve in his army. A few days after, he gave him a regiment of heavy dragoons, and presented him with a golden sword, so heavy that it could scarcely be brandished.[1]

I was extremely sorry for all this. It was enough to be in the army to be treated as a slave. My brothers and the Princes of the blood had no other distinction than what they derived from their rank in the army. They were confined to their garrisons which they quitted only to be reviewed, and they associated with rude officers, men without talents or education, by whom they were made complete savages, having no other occupation than to exercise their troops. I had no doubt but the Prince would be placed on the same footing : and my conjectures proved true. Before the King returned to Potsdam, he hinted to the Prince, that it would give him pleasure if he went to take possession of his regiment : and the Prince was fain to obey.

The day before his departure, he accosted me in the garden at Mon-Bijou. He had been informed of my dissatisfaction ; Madam de Sonsfeld had mentioned it to M. de Voigt. I was walking with her, when the Prince came up to me, and said : " I have not hitherto been able to find an

---

[1] A letter from Frederick William to Anhalt-Dessau, 13 August 1731 —Krauske (op. cit., 447) : " General von Schulenberg has just died. I have handed over his regiment to the Margrave of Bayreuth, and have augmented it with twenty new officers, twenty corporals, ten drummers and one hundred dragoons."

opportunity of speaking to your Royal Highness, and of expressing my despair at beholding the aversion which your actions indicate towards me. I know what evil impressions have been instilled into your mind against me ; and I am grieved on that account. Am I the cause of the afflictions you have endured ? I never could have dared to have aspired to the hand of your Royal Highness, had not the King proposed it. Should I have refused it, and have rendered myself the most unhappy of mortals ; and can you condemn me for having accepted it ? Under such circumstances I must leave you, without knowing how long my absence may endure ; I therefore intreat you to favour me with a positive answer, and candidly to tell me, whether your Royal Highness feels an insurmountable hatred against me ? If that be the case, I shall take an eternal leave, and, by breaking my engagement, at the risk of incurring my father's and the King's displeasure, render myself unhappy for the rest of my days. But, madam, if I may flatter myself that I am mistaken, and if you really entertain some kindness for me, I hope you will have the goodness to say that you will keep the promise you have given me, by order of the King, never to accept of any other hand than mine." He had tears in his eyes when he spoke, and appeared very much affected. Being unaccustomed to such language I felt extremely embarrassed and blushed to my finger's ends. As I returned no answer, the Prince renewed his intreaties, and added, with a mournful countenance : " I see your silence forebodes nothing good, and I shall act accordingly." At length I replied : " my promise is inviolable : I gave it you by order of the King, but you may rely upon its being faithfully performed." The Queen, who then came up to us, put an end to this conversation, to my great satisfaction.

Madam de Kamecke had amused herself that afternoon with making mottoes in sweetmeats, which she distributed in the evening to every person at table. The Prince broke one of them in my hand ; he did the same to my sister :

but the Queen was irritated only against me, and immediately left the table. She bade adieu to the Prince in great haste, and took my sister and me with her in her carriage. " You are no longer," said she to me, " the same person since your confounded betrothing has taken place. You have neither shame nor modesty. I blushed for you when your foolish Prince broke a motto in your hand. These are unbecoming familiarities, and he should be more aware of the respect which he owes to you." I answered, that as he had done the same to my sister, I did not think the matter of any consequence : but that it should happen no more. This did not appease her ; she thence took an opportunity of abusing Madam de Sonsfeld the next day. Madam de Kamecke, who was present, put an end to her scolding, and spoke with so much energy in my behalf, that, having nothing to reply, she was compelled to hold her peace.

Hitherto my sufferings had been trivial, in comparison with those accumulated pangs which wrung my inmost soul about a fortnight afterwards ; being obliged to attend the Queen to Wusterhausen. The Countess de Kamecke Madam de Sonsfeld, Madam de Montbail, and my sister Charlotte, were the only persons who accompanied us to that *famous* country palace, a description of which will not be misplaced here.

By dint of labour and expence, the King had raised a hill of dry sand, which confined the prospect so much, that the enchanted castle was only seen on coming down the declivity of the hillock. The palace consisted of a very small building, the beauty of which was heightened by an ancient tower, containing a winding stair-case of wood. This building was surrounded by a terrace, along which a ditch had been dug, whose black and stagnant water resembled the waters of Styx, and emitted a suffocating smell. Three bridges, each facing a different side of the building, formed the communication with the yard, the garden, and a mill which was opposite. Two wings on both sides of the yard formed the dwelling of the gentlemen of the King's retinue. The yard itself was inclosed by a palisade, at the entrance of which were chained two white and two black eagles, and two bears by way of guards to the fortress : these animals, by the bye, were extremely savage, and attacked every one. In the middle of the yard was a well, which had with much ingenuity been converted into a fountain for the use of the kitchen. The magnificent structure was adorned with a flight of steps and an iron railing on the outside, and this was the *delightful* spot which the King had chosen for his evening's indulgence of smoking. My sister and myself, with our attendants, had only two rooms, or, to speak more correctly, two garrets. In all weathers we used to dine in a tent spread under a large linden-tree, and when it rained much we sat in water above the ankles, the place being hollow. There were constantly twenty-four persons at table, eighteen of whom were fasting, because our ordinary consisted but of six dishes, and those very sparingly filled. From nine o'clock in the morning till three or four o'clock in the afternoon, we were shut up with the Queen, without daring to breathe the fresh air, or to go into the garden, although it was close by, because she would not have us leave her. She was playing all day long at backgammon with her three ladies, whilst the King was abroad. Thus I remained alone with my sister, who treated me with contempt : I grew melancholy, through continually sitting in the house, and listening to nothing but disagreeable discourses. The King's dinner was always over by one o'clock in the afternoon. He then rested himself in an arm-chair placed on the terrace, and slept till half-past two, exposed to the most ardent rays of the sun. We shared with him this burning heat, being all stretched on the ground at his feet. Such was the *agreeable* life which we led in this *charming* abode.

The hereditary Prince arrived there some days after us. He had written to me several times : but the Queen had always dictated my answers. I also had the gratification to receive from my brother a letter, which Major Sonsfeld transmitted to me by his sister. My brother commended me much for the good resolution I had taken of putting an end to domestic dissensions by my marriage. He appeared uneasy respecting my fate, and requested me to give him a faithful account of the Prince, and to inform him whether I was satisfied with the King's choice. He assured me that he lived very contentedly ; that he amused himself much ; and that his only sorrow was not to be near me. He had been kept ignorant of what I had suffered on his account ; and he did not know that he was indebted to me for the good treatment he received, and his approaching pardon. I did not wish to inform him of it, and made answer only to those articles on which he requested information. I also acquainted him with the alteration in the Queen's behaviour towards me, and begged he would write to her, and try to persuade her to listen to reason with regard to my marriage. He did so, but without success. The Queen was only the more incensed, when she saw that she alone of the family disapproved of my conduct.

In the mean time the hereditary Prince insinuated himself every day more and more into the good graces of my sister. The fancy she took for him increased her hatred towards me ; she made me feel its effects by exasperating the Queen against me.

One day, when I had been extremely ill-used by my mother, and was shedding abundance of tears in a corner of the room, my sister accosted me, saying : " What is it that distresses you so much ? "—" I am grieved," answered I, " for having lost the affection of her majesty ; if I cannot regain it, I shall die with grief."—" You are very silly," replied my sister ; " had I as amiable a lover as yours, I should not care much for the Queen. I laugh when she chides, for it is just as well so to do."—" You, then, do not love her," I replied : " for when we love a person, we wish our affection to be returned. Besides, you cannot complain of your fate. Prince Charles has much merit and several good qualities ; and whichever way you turn, fortune smiles upon you : whilst I am forsaken by all, even by the King, who has not looked upon me of late."—" Well ! " resumed she, with a malicious air, " if you think Prince Charles so amiable, let us change lovers ; take my be-trothing-ring and give me yours." I supposed she was joking, and said, that as my heart was perfectly free, I was ready to let her have them both. " Then give me your ring ! " continued she, drawing it from my finger.—" Take it," was my reply, " it is at your service." She put it on her finger, and hid in a corner that which she had received from her admirer. I gave it no thought ; but Madam de Sonsfeld having observed that my ring was gone, and that my sister had worn it three days, she hinted to me, that if the King or the Prince noticed it, I should have some fresh trouble. I therefore demanded the ring again from my sister : but she refused, and would not yield to our most pressing intreaties. I was obliged to apply to Mrs. Ramen, who mentioned the affair to the Queen ; who severely reprimanded my sister, and compelled her to resume her own and return me my ring. But she never forgave me. I dared no longer lift up my eyes, for she instantly reported to the Queen that I was ogling at the Prince.

We left Wusterhausen for Maqueno,[1] a place fully as dis-agreeable. New scenes awaited us here. The English had long been murmuring against their King ; they had ardent-ly wished to see me settled in their country. The Prince of Wales was beginning to form a party ; he regretted that his intended marriage with me had been broken off. Seconded by the nation, he complained so loudly, that the King of England resolved to satisfy his son by making fresh over-tures to my father : but as he did not wish to expose him-self to any refusal, he employed the Hessian court to sound the intentions of the Prussian monarch. For this purpose, Colonel Donep was dispatched to Berlin by Prince William.

---

[1] Gross Machnow, near Wusterhausen. Frederick William in letters dated October 1731 calls the place " Magkeno ".

He arrived at Maqueno at the same time with us. I am not acquainted with his proposals to the King : I suppose that my brother's marriage was not forgotten. The King's first answer was so obliging, that Donep had no doubt of the success of his negociation. He had never been employed in state affairs, was an intimate friend of Grumbkow, and, not distrusting the latter, he communicated to him the object of his mission. Grumbkow, seeing the King in suspense, addressed him in firm language, and advised him to start several demands, of which I am ignorant, but which he knew beforehand would not be granted. A fortnight elapsed in discussing this affair. Colonel Donep required a positive answer. The King, owing to his own irresolution, was all the time in a terrible humour.

I just then happened to be extremely ill ; I had an abscess in the throat, attended with much fever. The Queen had the inhumanity to oblige me to walk out. For three days I was so bad, that I could neither speak nor stand upright. It may easily be supposed that I looked shockingly. But the abscess burst, and I recovered. Notwithstanding his ill-humour, the King regaled us with German plays and rope-dancing. The performances took place on a large grass plot near the house. His Majesty sat in one window with the Queen ; and my sister, the Prince of Bayreuth, and myself, occupied the other. The Prince looked very depressed, and apprised me in a low voice, so that my sister might not hear it, of Colonel Donep's mission, and his alarms on the subject. I was much alarmed at the intelligence, which was quite new to me. I earnestly besought the Prince not to mention it to the Queen, being convinced that my troubles would be increased if the news reached her ears. My precautions were however, of no avail. Colonel Donep acquainted her majesty with it the very next day. The sad and pensive air of the Prince revived the Queen's hopes : and to conceal her joy, she oppressed him with her politeness. When I had retired to my room I seriously turned over in my mind what I should do if my father were to enter into the views of

Hermann von Katte

The execution of Katte, with Frederick the Great looking from a window

Bayreuth c. 1720

The Place Royale, Berlin 1733

the British monarch. The sincerity and frankness of the Prince in acquainting me with what was going on, had won my esteem. I had nothing to object either to his person or to his character. The Prince of Wales was a perfect stranger to me ; I never had felt any inclination for him ; my ambition was limited : I had come to a final resolution : I was tired of being the sport of fortune, and firmly determined, if the choice were left to myself, to adhere to that which the King had made for me ; but if matters should take a different turn, I was resolutely fixed upon not submitting to a change without warmly expostulating on the subject.

We returned to Wusterhausen the next day, early in the morning. Immediately after our arrival the Queen closeted herself with me, and having informed me of what Colonel Donep had told her, she added : " This day your sorry match will be broken off, and I hope your silly Prince will set off to-morrow ; for I have no doubt that if the King leave you at liberty to chuse, you will give the preference to my nephew. I insist upon knowing your sentiments on this point. I do not speak to you thus without motives : do you understand me ? I hope you have too proud a heart to hesitate for a single moment." I was stupified at her discourse, and called all the saints of paradise to my assistance to inspire me with an ambiguous answer that might extricate me. Whether it was that the saints or my good genius inspired me, I know not ; but I took courage, and replied : " I have always been submissive to the commands of your majesty, and only disobeyed them when forced by a superior power. And this I did with no other view than to restore peace in the family, procure my brother's liberty, and spare your majesty a thousand troubles to which you would still have been a prey. Inclination had no share in my determination ; the Prince was not known to me. But now that I know him, now that he has gained my esteem, and I have not discovered in him any failing which could justify my aversion, I should think myself highly blameable, if I were to retract the promise I have given." Here the Queen inter-

K   289

rupted me : enraged at what I had said, she treated me with the utmost contempt. Great as was my grief, I was obliged to conceal it before the King. His Majesty had not noticed me since his return from Prussia : this circumstance increased my sorrow. He happened to be that day in excellent humour. In the evening, the Prince of Bayreuth came to sup with us as usual. Neither the Queen nor my sister were in the room when he entered. His countenance was quite changed ; it was as cheerful as it had been melancholy. He told me, in a whisper : " the King has refused, and Donep. . . ." I seemed to take no notice of it ; but the intelligence gave me great satisfaction. The Queen heard the news a few hours after. Her heart was wounded, and it was upon me that she vented her displeasure.

My wedding was fixed for the 20th of November ; the King, wishing it to be splendid, invited several foreign princes, the whole house of Bevern, the Duchess of Meiningen, the Margrave of Bayreuth my father-in-law, and the Margrave of Ansbach and my sister. The latter were the first who arrived at Wusterhausen. The King met them on horseback, and conducted my sister to the Queen. We scarcely knew her again : she had been very handsome, but her beauty had faded ; her complexion was spoiled, and her manners were extremely affected. She had succeeded me in the good graces of the King ; but she never was a favourite with the Queen : her majesty was even nettled at the caresses and distinctions which the King bestowed upon her, as she never could endure his paying more attention to any one than to herself. She was, however, obliged to assume an air of complacency towards the Margravine. The meeting betwixt my sister and myself was unaffectedly tender and mutual : she had always loved me, and I warmly returned her affection. The King, after supper, led her to her chamber, which was close to mine under the roof. As her servants were not yet arrived, the King, pointing to me, said : " your sister will supply the place of your maid ; she is good for nothing else." I was amazed on hearing these words.

The King withdrew a moment after, and I did the same. My heart was so full of grief, that I thought I should die that night. What crime had I committed that could deserve such cruel treatment in the presence of him I was destined to marry, and before a foreign court? My sister herself felt for me, and did all she could to console me. To humble me still more, the King the next day gave her the precedency over me who was the eldest. The Queen was vexed at it, but her remonstrances were of no avail. I myself felt hurt; and rather as it appeared to tally with what the King had said to me the evening before. His majesty made it his study to mortify me all the time we stayed at that confounded Wusterhausen. He himself did not know what he would be at. One while he sorely repented having betrothed me, and broken with England; then, again, he was more exasperated than ever against that court; though this latter instance of his displeasure seldom lasted long. It was, however, upon me that his ill humour was vented.

At length, on the 5th of November, we returned to Berlin. The Duchess of Saxe-Meiningen, my great-aunt, a daughter of the Elector Frederick William, arrived two days after us. This Princess was then a widow after her third husband, having been married first to the Duke of Courland, and after his death to the Margrave Christian Ernest of Bayreuth. She had wholly ruined the dominions of those two princes. It was said that in her youth she had made it her study to win admiration, which was still apparent from her affected manners. She would have been an excellent actress to have performed the parts of antiquated lovers on the stage. Her ruddy face, and her figure of a size so monstrous that she could scarcely walk, gave her the appearance of a female Bacchus. She delighted in exhibiting her large, flat, and shrivelled breasts, which she was continually patting with her hands to attract attention. Though she was above sixty, she tricked herself off like a young person. She wore her hair in large curls, with pink ribbands, of a shade somewhat lighter than her face; and the stones of her jewels were of as many colours as the rainbow. His majesty obliged the Queen to pay her the first visit. "When I come back," said she to me, " you may go to the Duchess." I punctually obeyed her orders. As it was late, and the Queen held a drawing-room in the evening, my visit was not a long one. But I found the drawing-room had already commenced when I returned to the Queen, who was engaged in receiving the court. As soon as the Queen saw me, she asked in an angry tone, why I came so late ? " I have been with the Duchess, as your majesty ordered."—" How ! " replied she ; " by my order ! I never ordered you to be guilty of a mean action, or to forget your rank and your character : but latterly you have been so much in the habit of demeaning yourself, that I am not surprized at this." So severe a reprimand, in the face of every one, greatly irritated my feelings. I cast down my eyes, and in spite of all my efforts I could not help changing countenance. Every one secretly blamed the Queen, and pitied me. Madam de Grumbkow, though married to a very malicious man, was a woman of great merit. She came up to me, and inquired what could induce the Queen to treat me with so much severity ? I only shrugged my shoulders, but gave her no answer.

The King, the Margrave of Bayreuth, and the family of Bevern, arrived the next day. The Queen introduced me to the Margrave, who loaded me with endless assurances of his esteem. As my nuptials were to be solemnized in six days, the King ordered the Queen to permit the Margrave and his son to visit me freely. They did not profit much by this permission ; I was the whole day with the Queen, and saw them only for a moment in the evening in the presence of company.

On the 19th, I was surprised to find the Queen's behaviour towards me completely changed. She lavished her endearments upon me, affirming that I was the dearest of her children. I could not account for this change ; but she herself explained it in the evening, when, taking me into her closet, she said : " to-morrow you are to be sacrificed ; my exertions have not been able to delay your marriage. I expect a message from England, and I am certain before hand, that the King my brother will no longer insist upon my son's marriage ; his majesty will not then farther object against breaking your engagements with the hereditary Prince. However, as I do not know how long it may be yet before the messenger arrives, and can hit upon no pretence to put off your wedding to-morrow, a thought has occurred to me, which may quiet my mind ; and to you I look for its execution. Promise me you will have no familiarity with the Prince, and live with him as a sister with her brother, since this is the only way to dissolve your marriage, which may be annulled, if it be not consummated." The King came up to us when I was going to answer, and the Queen was so beset, that she could not find any opportunity of speaking to me all the evening.

The next morning I went to the Queen in an elegant undress. She led me to the King to pronounce the customary renunciation to the allodial estates. The Margrave and his son, Grumbkow, Powedils, Thulmeier, and Voigt, minister of Bayreuth, were with his majesty. The oath was read to me. Its purport was, that I renounced all my claims to the allodial estates as long as my brothers and their male posterity lived ; but that, in case of their demise, I should re-enter upon all my right of presumptive heir. After I had taken this oath, a second was required, which extremely surprized me, as I had not been apprised of it before hand. I was also to renounce the inheritance of the Queen, if she should die intestate. I stood motionless. The King perceiving my perplexity, said with tears in his eyes, and encircling me in his arms : " you must, my dear daughter, submit to this hard law. Your sister of Ansbach has gone through the same ordeal. It is, in fact, nothing but a formality. Your mother is always at liberty to make a will, whenever she chuses." I kissed his hands, reminding him that he had given me an authentic promise to take care of me ; and adding that I could not have believed he would have treated me so harshly. " This is no time for starting difficulties," answered he in an angry tone : " sign with a good grace, or I will make you sign by force." These last words he spoke in a low voice. I was reluctantly obliged to obey. As soon as this confounded ceremony was over, the King caressed me much, praised my submissiveness, and was profusely liberal of promises, which he had no intention of performing.

We afterwards sat down to table ; where the King made me sit near himself : the company consisted only of the Prince of Bayreuth, my brothers and sisters, and the Duchess of Bevern. I was in a sad pensive mood. Reflections naturally crowd upon the mind when we are on the point of forming ties which determine the happiness or misfortune of our lives.

When we had dined, the King ordered the Queen to begin to dress me ; it was then four o'clock, and I was to be ready at seven. The Queen wished to arrange my head dress : as she was not clever at acting the waiting-maid, she could not succeed at all : her ladies took her place ; but as soon as my hair was ready on one side, she spoiled it ; and all this was a mere feint to gain time, in hopes that the messenger might arrive : she did not know that he was already in town, and that Grumbkow had the dispatches. It may easily be supposed, that he did not deliver them to the King till the marriage solemnity was over. All this made my head-dress appear so uncouth as to give me the appearance of a mad creature. It had been so much handled, that it was quite out of curls : I resembled a little boy : for my hair was falling flat in my face. The royal crown was placed on my head with four-and-twenty hair locks as thick as my arm : such were the orders of the Queen. I could not hold my head up ; it was too weak to sustain such a weight. My robe was of a very rich silver brocade, with a Brussels gold lace ; and my train was twelve yards long. I had wellnigh died under this attire. Two ladies of the Queens' household and two of my own carried my train ; the two latter were Madam de Sonsfeld, and a sister to my governess, with Madam de Grumbkow, and a niece to my persecutor ; the King having insisted upon my accepting of the latter. Madam de Sonsfeld was proclaimed Abbess of Wolmirstedt ; and the King himself invested her with the insignia of the chapter. We repaired to the state-rooms ; of which I shall subjoin a short description.

They form a suite of six large rooms which lead to a hall magnificently adorned and equally remarkable for its paintings and its architecture. At the end of this hall are two richly decorated chambers, forming the passage to a gallery of very fine paintings. All these apartments communicate in a straight line. The gallery, which is ninety feet long, leads to a second suite of fourteen rooms, as spacious and as well decorated as the first ; at the extremity of which there is a very extensive hall, destined for the grand ceremonies. There is nothing extraordinary in what I have described : but now comes the marvellous. The first room contains a silver chandelier which weights ten-thousand Prussian dollars ; the whole assortment is equally heavy in proportion. The second room is still more superb ; the pier-glasses are of massy silver and the mirrors twelve feet in height ; twelve persons may conveniently sit at the tables placed under these glasses. The chandelier is much larger than in the first room, and the furniture of each apartment increases proportionally in size : the last hall contains the largest pieces. Here are the portraits of the King and Queen, and those of the Emperor and Empress, as large as life, in massy, silver frames. The chandelier weight fifty thousand dollars : the globe is so large that a child of eight years old might conveniently sit in it : the plates are six feet high, and the stands twelve. The gallery for the musicians is also of silver : in short, this hall contains more than two millions of plate in weight. It is all wrought with much taste : but, after all, it is a magnificence which does not please the sight, and is attended with many inconveniences : for, instead of wax candles, tapers are burnt, which cause a suffocating vapour, and blacken the faces and clothes. The King my father got all this plate after his first journey to Dresden. He had seen in that town the treasure of the King of Poland ; he wished to surpass that monarch, and being unable to excel him in precious and rare stones, he bethought himself of getting what I have described, that he might possess a novelty of which no sovereign of Europe had yet been possessed.

It was in the last hall that my marriage was solemnized. A triple discharge of guns took place when the service was finished. All the foreign ministers, except the English, were present. The Margrave of Schwedt was obliged to attend, by the express command of the King. After having received the compliments of the company, I was seated in an arm-chair under the canopy near the Queen. The hereditary Prince opened the ball with my sister the Margravine of Ansbach. It only lasted one hour ; after which, we sat down to supper. The King had ordered lots to be drawn for the seats, to avoid all disputes about precedency among so many foreign Princes. I was placed at the top with the Prince, each of us in an arm-chair. The Margrave my father-in-law sat next to me, and the King next to the Prince. There were thirty Princes at the table. The King would gladly have intoxicated the Prince ; he made him drink so much, that he was actually a little flushed. Twc ladies stood all the time behind me, and the gentlemen ot my household, who were Colonel Vreiche and Major Stechow, waited upon me, as well as M. de Voigt, who had been appointed my grandmaster of ceremonies, and M. Bindemann my groom of the chamber. After supper, we returned to the first hall, where every thing had been prepared for the dance by torch light. The dance is an ancient German custom ; it is performed with great ceremony. The Marshals of the Court with their staves begin the march ; then follow all the Lieutenant-Generals of the army, bearing each a lighted taper. The new-married couple

296

gravely march twice round the room ; the lady, with all the Princes present, one after the other ; and when she has finished her round, the gentleman takes her place, and does the same with the Princesses. All this is performed to the sound of cymbals and trumpets. When the dance was over, I was conducted to the first apartment, where was a state-bed of crimson velvet embroidered with pearls. According to the etiquette, the Queen was to undress me ; but she thought me unworthy of the honor, and only handed me my shift : my sisters and the Princesses undressed me. When this was done, they all took leave of me and retired, except my sister the Margravine of Ansbach and the Duchess of Bevern. I was then removed to my real bed-room, where the King made me kneel, and ordered me to recite aloud the *Belief* and the *Lord's Prayer*. The Queen was in a dreadful humour, ill-treating every one : she had learnt that the messenger had arrived : this completed her despair. She said a thousand cruel things to me before she withdrew.

It must be owned that my marriage was attended with very extraordinary circumstances. The King my father had reluctantly solemnized it, and repented of it every day ; he might have broken it off, and had it performed against his wishes. I need not mention the sentiments of the Queen ; what I have stated of her, is a sufficient proof how greatly she was set against the match. The Margrave of Bayreuth was as dissatisfied as either my father or mother. He had given his consent in the hope of obtaining great advantages, of which he saw himself frustrated by the avarice of the King. He was jealous of the good fortune of his son, and his suspicious disposition made him a prey to heavy alarms, on which subject I shall have occasion to speak hereafter. I thus found myself married contrary to the inclination of the three principal persons who had a right to dispose of my fate and that of the Prince, and yet it was with their consent. When at times I reflect upon all this, I cannot help be-lieving in predestination, and my philosophy yields to con-siderations suggested by experience : but I must not stop to moralize : these memoirs would never have an end, if I attempted to state the thoughts that occurred to my mind in the different situations in which I have been placed.

The next morning, the King, attended by Princes and Generals, came and complimented me with a silver set of plates and dishes. The Queen, according to usage, ought to have done me the same honour : but she refused to do it. In spite of my vexation, I did not forget my brother. I sent M. de Voigt to Grumbkow, to remind him of his promise. He answered, that he would most certainly prevail with the King, but that I must have a little patience, because it was absolutely necessary to watch a favourable opportunity to obtain a chance of success.

On the 23d, there was a grand ball in the state-rooms. We drew lots, to avoid disputes about precedency. My lot was number one. Together with the Prince, there were, in the whole, seven hundred couples, all of noble extraction. We had four quadrilles. I led off the first, the Margravine Philippa the second, the Margravine Albert the third, and her daughter the fourth. My party danced in the gallery of paintings. The Queen and all the princely visitors were there.

I was fond of dancing, and availed myself of the opportunity. Grumbkow came to interrupt me in the midst of a minuet. " Really, madam ! " said he, " it seems as if your Royal Highness had been bit by a tarantula ! Do you not see those strangers who are just arrived ? " I stopped short, and looking on all sides, I actually beheld a young man in a grey coat whim I did not know. " Will you not embrace the Prince-Royal ? " said Grumbkow, " he is before you." All my blood was in a paroxysm of joy. " O Heavens ! my brother ! " I exclaimed, " but I cannot find him ! where is he ! let me see him for Heaven's sake ! "—Grumbkow conducted me to him. When I drew near, I knew him again but with difficulty. He had grown very lusty and short-necked ; his face was also very much altered, and not so handsome as formerly. I leaped into his arms. I was so agitated, and I uttered nothing but broken sentences : I wept, I laughed, like a person beside herself. Never in my life have I felt a joy so lively. When my first emotion had subsided, I threw myself at the feet of the King, who said aloud in my brother's hearing : " are you satisfied ? You see that I have kept my word ! " I took my brother by the hand and besought the King to admit him again to his favour. The scene was so affecting, that it drew tears from the whole company. I afterwards went to the Queen. She was forced to embrace me, the King being opposite : but I observed that her joy was only affected. I returned to my brother, and tendered him a thousand endearments, using the most affectionate language : but he remained cold as ice, and answered only by monosyllables. I introduced my husband to him ; but he did not utter a word. I was thunderstruck at his behaviour ; I however ascribed it to the presence of the King, who had his eye upon us and intimidated my brother. His countenance even surprized me. He appeared proud, and looked at every one with contempt. At length we sat down to table. The King was not with us ; he supped alone with his son. The Queen seemed uneasy, and sent emissaries to know how they were going on. She was informed that the King was in excellent humour, and conversing in a very friendly way with my brother. I thought this would afford pleasure to the Queen ; but in spite of her efforts, she could not hide her secret vexation. Indeed she loved her children only as far as they served her ambitious views. My brother's obligation to me for his reconciliation with the King gave her more pain than satisfaction, because she was not the author of it. On leaving the table, Grumbkow told me that the Prince-Royal would again spoil all : " the cold reception he gave you," continued Grumbkow, " displeased the King. He says, that if it was owing to his presence, it must of course offend him, as it shows a distrust which does not augur well for the future ; and if his coolness, on the contrary, proceeded from indifference and ingratitude towards your

Royal Highness, it betrays an evil disposition. But the King is highly satisfied with you, Madam : you have acted with sincerity. Do so always, and for Heaven's sake ! persuade your brother to behave with frankness and without guile." I thanked him for his advice, which I thought good. The ball recommenced. I went up to my brother, and told him what Grumbkow has said : I even reproached him slightly respecting his change. He answered, that he was still the same ; and that he had his reasons for acting as he did.

The next morning, he paid me a visit by order of the King. My husband had the civility to withdraw, and left me alone with him and Madam de Sonsfeld. My brother then related his misfortunes, such as I have stated them. I acquainted him with mine. He appeared much disconcerted at the end of my narrative ; he thanked me for the service I had rendered him, and made me a few caresses, which however did not seem to proceed from the heart. He entered upon some indifferent subjects, in order to break off the conversation, and under pretence of viewing my apartment, he passed into the adjoining room, where my husband was. He surveyed him for some time, and, after having used a few cold expressions of common civility, he retired.

I was, I own, perplexed at his behaviour. My governess shrugged her shoulders, and could not recover from her surprise. I no longer found in him that beloved brother who had cost me so many tears, and for whom I had sacrificed myself. My husband perceiving my confusion, and dissatisfaction, expressed his astonishment at the unfriendly behaviour of my brother ; and added, that he was sorry he had not the good fortune of pleasing him. I endeavoured to dispel these notions, and continued to behave as formerly to my brother.—I shall here allow myself a short digression. These Memoirs are filled with tragical events which must tire the reader in the end ; it is but just that I should enliven them with more diverting adventures, though they do not concern myself.

The Queen had about her person a young lady of the name of Pannewitz, who was her first maid of honour. She was beautiful as an angel, and as virtuous as handsome. The King, whose heart had hitherto been unmoved, could not resist her charms : he began at this time to pay her much attention. His majesty was not a man of gallantry. Sensible of his deficiency in this respect, he foresaw that he never should be able successfully to imitate the manners of a coxcomb, or the style of a melting lover ; and, unwilling to disguise his natural disposition, he commenced the intrigue by bluntly proposing that in which it generally ends. He gave Miss Pannewitz a very slippery description of his love, and asked whether she would be his mistress ? The fair maid being highly offended at the proposal, treated the King with great disdain. He however, nothing dis-heartened, continued to speak love to her for a twelvemonth. The termination of this adventure was rather singular. Miss Pannewitz having attended her majesty to Brunswick, where my brother's nuptials were to be celebrated,[1] met the King on a back stair-case which led to the Queen's rooms. He caught her in his arms, and attempted to salute her. But the enraged maid of honour gave him such a vigorous slap in his face, that the blood gushed from his mouth and nose. He was not angry with her, and contented himself with calling her ever after the savage witch.—I return to myself.[2]

All the tenants of hell seemed let loose against me. The

[1] Frederick was finally married on 12 June 1733 to Elizabeth Christina of Brunswick-Bevern.

[2] Johanna Maria von Pannewitz (1702–71), whose daughter, Sophie Marie, Countess of Voss, also wrote some memoirs of the Prussian court. She noted of Frederick William that he " was not very tall, but looked pleasant and quite like what he was—that is, like a King. He had not a bad disposition, but he was passionate, and sometimes treated the poor Queen and the royal children very ill. In spite of his great thriftiness, he could on occasions be very generous, and I remember well how he once, when Kleist and Einseidel were, without any fault of their own, in great pecuniary embarrassment, sent them unasked a considerable sum of money. He took it to them himself in his carriage, in a great sack, full of gold dollars ". (*Sixty-Nine Years at the Court of Prussia*, London, 1876 i, 6–7.)

Margrave of Ansbach also attempted to augment the list of my persecutors. He was a young Prince who had been very badly educated. He continually ill-treated my sister ; they led the life of dog and cat. My sister, it is true, was sometimes in fault. The courtiers of the Margrave were malicious and intriguing individuals, who prejudiced him against the court of Bayreuth. The dominions of the two Margraves border upon each other ; and though it be their interest to live on friendly terms and to act in concert, the mutual jealousy of the two sovereigns causes their disunion. The Margrave of Ansbach and his court could not become reconciled to my marriage with the Prince of Bayreuth A thousand false reports were carried from one to the other. The Margrave of Ansbach being exasperated against us, strove to set us at variance with the Queen by giving a wrong interpretation to our words and actions. He was seconded by my sister Charlotte who added as much fuel to the flame as she could. My younger sisters informed me of it, but I pretended to be ignorant of the fact.

Several more balls were given in honour of my nuptials : the rest of the time was passed at cards with the Queen. The Princes were obliged to spend the evening with the King at his smoking club, where they remained till supper-time.

The Margrave of Ansbach had the impudence to ridicule the hereditary Prince, and to banter him on a very serious subject. I have already stated, that the mother of the latter was a Princess of Holstein. She had behaved so ill, and had been guilty of so many outrages, that her husband, who was then but an apanaged Prince, had found himself under the necessity of having her confined in a fortress belonging to the Margrave of Ansbach. She was made the object of his sarcastical remarks to my husband, who expressed his displeasure, and very sensibly said : " I respect the presence of the King too much to answer immediately and in the manner I ought to such remarks : but I shall find an opportunity to obtain satisfaction." My brother and the foreign

Princes were present : they did all they could to effect a reconciliation : but all they could obtain of the hereditary Prince was, that he would let the matter rest till the day after the morrow. In the evening, I observed a great alteration in the countenance of my husband : but my intreaties to be informed of the cause, remained of no avail. I heard it the following day from the Margrave my father-in-law, who learned it from the Duke of Bevern. We both spoke to the Prince. I suggested that this quarrel might be attended with very injurious consequences : first, it was reviving an old calamity, very disagreeable to both his father and himself ; and, secondly, his adversary was his brother-in-law, a Prince without any heirs, whose dominions were to devolve to him after his death, which circumstance, in case of any misfortune happening, might give rise to erroneous judgments prejudicial to his glory. His passion would not allow him to listen to our arguments. The Duke of Bevern, who now joined us, read him such a lecture on the subject, that he pledged his word he would remain quiet, provided the Margrave of Ansbach sent him an apology. All advised me to speak to the latter, and to endeavour to reconcile the parties. The day passed quietly over. In the evening I concerted my measures with the Duke and Duchess. I was extremely sad and uneasy, under the apprehension that the business might terminate fatally.

My sister, who had been informed of it and was watching us, suddenly threw herself into my arms ; saying : " I am excessively grieved at what happened yesterday. My husband was wrong. I ask your pardon for his rudeness ; I shall seriously chide him for it."—" I am sorry," answered I, " that you have overheard our conversation. Be assured, that the quarrel of our husbands will not diminish my affection for you. I ask you one single favour ; that is not to interfere in the business. You would only bring yourself into trouble, and increase the irritation of the parties." After many more remonstrances, she promised me to be quiet. The Margrave of Ansbach always used to sit near me at table. When we arose, and the Queen had left us, I very civilly addressed him, and was going to speak to him on the business ; but my sister interfered, and began abusing her husband. He flew into a passion, raised his voice and gave her some hard words. The hereditary Prince, who heard some of them, thought they were addressed to him : he immediately came up, and insisted upon satisfaction for his behaviour.—" Come, come," said he, " let us settle our quarrel ; actions, not words, will do it."—The poor Margrave was stupified. " Well then ! " continued the Prince of Bayreuth, " come, let us fight it out, or else I will throw you into the fire, where you may roast at your ease." This menace frightened his adversary so much, that he wept bitterly ; which produced a tragi-comical scene. My brother, and all who were present, began to laugh aloud. The Margrave, in his fright, fled into the audience-hall of the Queen, who was gravely pacing the room without noticing any thing. He there hid himself behind a curtain. The Duchess, who had followed him, performed the office of a nurse, and quieted the babe by assuring him that the hereditary Prince would not kill him. But all this did not remove the fears of the poor child : he durst not leave his hiding-place till his antagonist was gone. My brother, the Margrave my father-in-law, and Prince Charles, led my husband away. I yet found them together when I returned to my room. The scene which we had witnessed, caused us a great deal of mirth, and the poor Margrave of Ansbach was not spared. The Duke of Bevern attended him home, where he exhaled his irritation by vomits and a diarrhœa, which had well nigh sent him out of the world. After this copious evacuation had purged his bile, and composed his mind, he seriously reflected on the danger to which he had been exposed. The menaces of the hereditary Prince induced him to offer terms through the Duke of Bevern. My husband accepted of the Margrave's apology ; harmony was restored ; and they never since had any personal quarrel.

Some days after, the King gave my brother a regiment of

foot and restored him his uniform and his sword. His
residence was fixed at Ruppin, where his regiment was
quartered. His allowance was increased, and though not
very liberal, it yet would enable him to live in the style of a
rich private gentleman. He was obliged to set out for his
garrison. Although his behaviour towards me was much
altered, I yet felt excessively grieved at his leaving us. I
had no hope of seeing him again before his departure ; the
thought affected me much. He too seemed moved, and our
parting proved more affectionate than our first interview.
His presence had made me forget all my sorrows ; his
departure made me feel them more keenly. My situation
with regard to the Queen was still the same. She constrained herself in public, and treated me so much the
worse in private.

The King looked no more at me since my wedding, and all
the great advantages which he had promised me vanished
into air. There were but two ways of getting into his
favour : one, to send him men of an uncommon tall size ;
the other, to invite him to dinner with his favourites, and to
give him plenty of wine. The first was not in my power.
Giants do not grow like mushrooms ; they were so rare,
that any country scarcely afforded three that would suit him.
I was therefore obliged to resort to the second expedient. I
gave him a grand dinner, to which I invited all the princely
visitors. The cloth was laid for forty ; we had every thing
that was most rare and exquisite. My husband performed
the honours of the bottle. He was the only male that stood
the contest ; the King and the rest of the guests were in a
high state of intoxication. I never saw my father so
cheerful ; he loaded the Prince and myself with caresses.
My arrangements pleased him so much, that he staid all the
evening. He sent for his musicians, and for several ladies of
the nobility in town. He opened the ball with me, and
danced with all the ladies ; which he had never done before.
The entertainment lasted till three o'clock in the morning.

On the 17th of December, the King set out for Nauen,

where he had prepared a fine chace of the wild boar. All the Princes followed him. This excursion lasted four days ; during which I experienced fresh troubles.

The Margrave of Ansbach had only dissembled his resentment against the Prince of Bayreuth since their last quarrel. He ardently sought for an opportunity to be revenged. But, to do justice where it is due, the Margrave of Ansbach has some talents and a good disposition, though prone to anger ; those by whom he is surrounded, are true imps of Satan, who have plunged him into vice, and still endeavour to stifle his good qualities. He was but seventeen, destitute of experience, and badly advised. I have already stated, that, to make his court, to the Queen, he acted as her spy. She did not fail to address herself to him for news on his return from Nauen. He answered, that he had none but bad news ; that she had every reason to be dissatisfied with my marriage ; that I should become the most unfortunate female on earth, as my husband was a monster, plunged in the most dreadful debauchery, who spent his nights at public-houses, drinking with footmen and girls of ill-fame ; that he was extremely familiar with such strumpets, and that, according to the *scandalous chronicle*, he had been in a fray in which he had been roughly handled. This insinuation, far from afflicting the Queen, gave her great pleasure. She resolved to make it a matter of triumph over me. When the company was assembled in her room, she made us sit down in a circle, and skilfully turned the conversation upon the excursion to Nauen. Without particularizing any one by name, she began to banter the Prince of Bayreuth in a cruel manner. I immediately perceived that she was alluding to him : but I could not make any thing of her inuendoes. She spoke of a battle and wounds, and cast malicious looks upon my sister Charlotte, who answered her by nodding, and looking at me. The Margrave of Bayreuth was grave and in an ill-humour, and the whole company sat with downcast eyes. Cards put an end to this conversation. My sister, the Margravine of Ansbach, who had much friendship for me, seeing my uneasiness, made me acquainted with the secret. I had not been married about five weeks. I had studied the character of the Prince, and had found him to be a man of too much feeling and too proud a heart to be guilty of the vile things of which he was accused. The Duke of Bevern himself assured me, that there was no truth in the report ; that the hereditary Prince had not left him for a moment, and had slept in a room next to his. We both concluded that the story must be a contrivance of the Margrave of Ansbach. The Duke undertook to undeceive the King, who had been imposed upon by the same report, and he intreated me not to heed the railleries of the Queen, which would only render me miserable. The Margrave of Ansbach, or rather his courtiers, had also reported the same story to the Margrave of Bayreuth. The latter, without making any enquiry, was terribly enraged against his son ; he attended me in the evening to my room, where he abused him very much. The Prince had no difficulty in exculpating himself : and had we not prevented him, he would have shown his resentment to the author of the story.

The circumstance was known the next day all over the town ; it disgraced the Margrave of Ansbach, and rendered him odious. The King was exasperated at it, but he concealed his anger, that he might not add to the general irritation. The Queen was quite ashamed, and sorry at being unable to fasten any blame upon a son-in-law whom she cordially hated.

She asked me, a few days after, with a malicious smile, whether I had enquired into the stipulations of my marriage settlement ? " I long to hear," said she, " wherein those great advantages consist, which the King has given you, and what your incomes will be. I do not know how Mr. Gidikins[1] (the English resident) learned it, but I know he has said that a waiting woman of the Princess of Wales had

---

[1] Mr Gidikins was Guy Dickens, secretary to Sir Charles Hotham, now the English ambassador.

higher wages that what your annual income amounts to. I advise you to take your measures accordingly ; for if you make a poor figure, it will not be my fault ; at least you have nothing more to expect from me. I did not contrive your marriage ; it belongs to the King, in whom you have had so much confidence, to take care of you."

This speech prognosticated nothing favourable. I enquired that very evening of M. de Voigt about the matter. What was my surprise when he gave me the following account ! The King, for all in all, had lent the Margrave a capital of two hundred and sixty thousand dollars without interest. Every year, beginning in 1733, he was to repay five and twenty thousand. My portion consisted, as usual, of forty thousand dollars. To this were added sixty thousand dollars by way of indemnity for having renounced the inheritance of the Queen. They were the same stipulations as had been made for my sister. The annual allowance of the Prince and myself, including our court, was fixed by the Margrave at fourteen thousand dollars, of which two thousand were for me. From this sum were to be deducted Christmas-boxes and extraordinary presents : therefore I had just eight hundred dollars left for my clothes and pocket money. The King considered as advantages the regiment which he had given to the Prince, and the plate with which he had complimented me. My astonishment will easily be credited. M. de Voigt told me, the King had settled everything ; that he thought it had been with my consent, or else he would have sooner informed me of it, and that the evil was not to be remedied, the stipulations having been sealed and signed.

After having reflected upon my situation for a while, I resolved to apply to Grumbkow. I sent for him the next morning. M. de Voigt explained the matter to him in a few words. He protested he had never been consulted on the business. " I am surprised I was not acquainted with it," added he. " There is no remedy left : we must resort to other expedients, and endeavour to extort a pension from

the King ; but we must wait till the Margrave your father
is gone. I know the King : he is as hard as a flint when he
has to part with money ; if I mention any thing now, he
will pick a foolish quarrel with the Margrave, to induce him
to increase your revenue, which will create disagreements
of which you will be the victim. But when he is gone, his
majesty will be obliged to redress the wrong which he has
done you. I promise you my assistance, madam ; and I shall
let you know when it will be time for you to speak to his
majesty yourself." I returned him many thanks, and promised to follow his advice.

The Queen had been diverting herself at my expence.
She knew how the matter stood, and only wished me to
enquire into it for the sake of mortifying me. She continually kept emissaries near my rooms ; she was immediately informed of Grumbkow's visit, and instantly guessed
its object. But she wished to be sure of it, and to learn it
from me. After having conversed in a very friendly
manner for some time, she spoke of my approaching
departure, and said : " I am sorry to lose you. I have
exerted myself to the utmost to procrastinate your departure. What grieves me most is to see you so badly provided for ; I know it all. The King has cruelly forsaken
you. I had foreseen it, but you would not believe me.
However, I am glad you have spoken to Grumbkow. I
am convinced that, if it be in his power, he will render you
service. What has he advised ? " I confess my stupidity. I
related my whole conversation with Grumbkow, and intreated the Queen to keep it secret. " That I will," answered she, " I know the importance of what you have told me
too well ever to mention it." Unfortunately for me, she
was left alone with the King in the afternoon. Not knowing
how to entertain him, she disclosed all I had told her. The
King affected to pity me, and to be moved with my situation
but he felt angry that I should have applied to the Queen
and to Grumbkow. He was naturally suspicious ; he
fancied that I was intriguing, and resolved to punish me for

it. Scarcely had he left the Queen, when he asked for my marriage settlements, and struck off four thousand dollars of the sum destined for the Prince and me.

The Queen, triumphing at the the good turn which she had done me, sent for me in great haste. " You need not apply any more to Grumbkow for your affairs : I have spoken to the King," said she, embracing me ; " I have related to him our conversation of this morning. He appeared affected, and promised to give you satisfaction." I was nearly being petrified like Lot's wife. My first emotion vented itself in lamentations and respectful reproaches to the Queen for her indiscretion. She grew angry, and harshly bade me be silent. I cursed my imprudence a thousand times over : I was rewarded for it. I could not complain. Grumbkow loaded me with bitter reproaches, of which he made M. de Voigt the messenger, and acquainted me with the fine thing his majesty had done. He justly complained of my having exposed him to the anger of the King, and protested he would never more trouble himself about my concerns. This last misfortune exhausted my patience, and caused me the most poignant grief.

The Margrave my father-in-law, and the families of Ansbach, of Meiningen, and of Bevern, left Berlin in the mean time. I regretted the latter very much, particularly the Duchess, for whom I had conceived an affectionate friendship. She had been the confidant of my troubles, and had done me many good offices.

The King returned to Potsdam, whither the Queen was ordered to follow him with me, as I was to set out thence for Bayreuth. My impatience to be settled in my new residence, made me count hours and minutes. Berlin had become as odious as it had formerly been dear to me. I hoped, though poor, to lead a quiet and comfortable life, and to enter upon a more propitious year than that which had just ended.

INDEX

INDEX

For the principal characters, main references only have been indexed. A note in italics following a person's name defines that person's relation to Wilhelmina.